D0742341

Also by Dirk Bogarde

Autobiography
A Postillion Struck by Lightning
Snakes and Ladders
An Orderly Man

Novels
A Gentle Occupation
Voices in the Garden

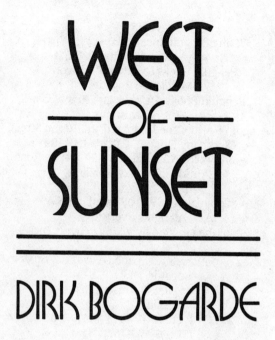

WEST
— OF —
SUNSET

DIRK BOGARDE

THE VIKING PRESS NEW YORK

VIKING
Viking Penguin Inc., 40 West 23rd Street,
New York, New York 10010, U.S.A.
Penguin Books Ltd, Harmondsworth,
Middlesex, England
Penguin Books Australia Ltd, Ringwood,
Victoria, Australia
Penguin Books Canada Limited, 2801 John Street,
Markham, Ontario, Canada L3R 1B4
Penguin Books (N.Z.) Ltd, 182–190 Wairau Road,
Auckland 10, New Zealand

Published in 1984 by Viking Penguin Inc.

LIBRARY OF CONGRESS CATALOGING IN PUBLICATION DATA
Bogarde, Dirk, 1921–
West of sunset.
I. Title.
PR6052.O3W4   1984   823'.914   83-40254
ISBN 0-670-75784-5

Printed in the United States of America

For Rosalind and Nicholas Bowlby.
With my love.

Author's Note

Los Angeles is the only thing in this book which is not fictitious, and I have tried to evoke it with as much accuracy as possible.

On the eve of my first visit there in the late fifties I was strongly advised that, as a European, I must accept the fact that it was an Oriental city: should I attempt to equate it with anything else I would, without question, not survive the experience which lay ahead.

The advice was accurate. I accepted it, ultimately, surviving the visits which I made there in the years which were to follow, observing the rapidly changing city if not with love then at least with wry affection.

Anything, they say, can happen in Los Angeles.

Anything, and everything, does.

However, all the characters in this book are entirely my own invention and bear no resemblance whatsoever to anyone alive or dead; and none of the events, apart from the obvious historical ones, ever took place, to the best of my knowledge.

I am grateful to Messrs Duckworth and to Alfred A. Knopf Inc. for giving me permission to quote from *Cautionary Tales for Children* by Hilaire Belloc, to Miss Boaty Boatwright for reminding me of some important 'local details' which I had forgotten and, as always, to Mrs Sally Betts for making something legible from my original typescript.

D.v.d.B.

All spirits are enslaved which serve things evil.

– P. B. Shelley,
from *Prometheus Unbound*

1

Supper with Alice

The telephone in his bedroom purred discreetly; it was that kind of an hotel. Do not alarm the guests: alert them gently.

He hurried through from the bathroom doing up his flies.

'Jon? It's the Widow Arlington. Are you all right?'

'Very all right. Now. I just got in from a long, long in-depth meeting on the script.'

'This a bad time to call?'

'A good time. I just had a pee. Perfectly comfortable.'

She laughed lightly, some miles away. 'Tonight still all right?'

'Perfect. The thought of it kept me going through the whole soggy afternoon.'

'And don't change, remember? Jeans, sweater, whatever. Informal anyway. It's just candles, cracked crab, white wine and a few oddies.'

'Oddies?'

'Oh, you know. People.'

'Anything I can bring you?'

'Ah ha ... well, if you are passing, and if they are still open, grab a couple of French loaves from Jurgensen's, would you? I assume that they have given you a car and a driver?'

'You assume correctly. I have a brand new orange Ford, and a white rat to drive it.'

'White rat?'

'He's called Wayne and he plays in a combo all night, drives me all day, never sleeps. He looks like a potato shoot.'

'Attractive. Everyone in this town has two jobs.'

11

'So I have gathered in my twenty-four hours here.'

'Are you feeling very jet-lagged? I mean, if you are, don't ...'

He cut in quickly. 'I'm supposed to be, but I'm not yet. If I slump suddenly under your table you'll know it's caught me up. Right?'

'Right. The address? You have it?'

He reached out for his personal telephone book on the night-table, rustled pages.

Her voice, in his hand, was accusatory. 'You've lost it.'

'No. Front page almost. Arlington. 1265 Gretna Green Drive. Which I just don't believe ...'

'You'd better, it's where I live. We've got a Balmoral, a Ben Nevis, a Lomond and a Glasgow around us. Must have been a homesick builder at work.'

'Brentwood. Los Angeles.'

'That's it. Tell the White Rat to go down Wilshire to the San Diego Freeway, under it onto San Vicente, turn right opposite the Country Club. He can't miss that, it's got trees. Gretna Green Drive climbs up, but tell him not to go as far as Sunset, I'm sort of west of Sunset ...'

'Alice dear. You can't be west of Sunset. Sunset *is* west.'

'I know what *I* mean. Bring the telephone number with you, call from a drugstore if you get lost.'

'The number is engraved on my heart.'

'Silly idiot. Really. And the bread. If you can?'

'I will. I really do rather long to see you.'

'I do too. And so do Clemency and Hope.'

He laughed suddenly. 'Point taken. Warning me with your off-spring.'

'I wouldn't dream of using my children to warn you.'

'Good.'

'And Dubrovnik is cooking.' She had pitched her voice a little higher for someone else to hear. 'Poor darling's in the kitchen at this very moment, preparing his gazpacho ...'

'I get it,' he said.

'And the bread, remember?'

'Entendu. Ciao,' he said, and heard her laugh gently as he re-placed the receiver.

*

12

She hadn't changed at all. Slender, small hands and feet, the cascade of ash blond hair tumbling round her shoulders, the same wide smile, the troubled eyes in a smiling face.

She took the two loaves and a package which he had brought from the hotel, kissed him warmly, but lightly.

'This is Wayne who drives me. He didn't make a single error ...'

'Howdy,' said Wayne. 'This thing is heavy.' He was holding a large basket covered in clear yellow plastic. 'Can I set it down someplace ...?'

'In here,' she said and moved back into a small, cramped hallway. 'Just put it anywhere.'

Wayne was wearing an orange suit which matched the car and white sneakers which matched his face. He put the basket down on a chest covered with coats and books. A book fell, others scattered.

'Sorry ...'

'Don't worry. The house is a mess. That's just fine.'

'What time you want me back?' he asked Jon, loosening the knot of his tie.

'Not too late. I have an early morning. Say about elevenish, okay?'

'Okay. You got my number if you want me sooner? I'm at my sister's.'

'Yes, I have it. Eleven will be fine.'

'Shall do. Pleased to meet you,' he nodded at Alice. 'Have a nice time now.'

She closed the door. 'Eleven is a bit early.'

'Breakfast with a producer, *the* producer. Breakfast! God, America!'

'Breakfast is usual. Don't waste a moment of the day. Thanks for the bread.'

'It's in poor shape. Limp.'

'Five minutes in the oven. What's all this in the goodie-basket?'

'Present from Cristal Productions. I don't know. A pineapple, I see ... a bottle ...'

'Come and meet Dubrovnik. He's sweating away in there, my tame Slav.'

A tall, burly man with shaggy hair, in a striped butcher's apron in a too small kitchen.

13

'This is Jonathan Pool, Boris ... you didn't meet in London, did you?'

'Not London, no.' The tall man wiped his hands on the apron and shook hands. 'Hi! Alice don't cook. You know this? I cook. All she do is coffee.'

'Stop complaining,' said Alice, turning on the oven. 'It's a cold supper and the main course has all been prepared for you. I just hope to God it thaws out in time. Alaska crab. Ripped from the heart of a glacier by the look of it.'

Dubrovnik turned back to his chopping board, took up a half glass of wine and drained it. 'Too soon for the oven. I do. You leave me sweat, okay? Please darling, huh?'

'Come into the sitting room. The only room,' said Alice and led him out through the cluttered hallway. 'Bring the basket of goodies. We can open it in there.'

A long, dauntingly rectangular room. A bow window at the far end with bottle-end panes of glass here and there. Walls lined with planking, whitewashed; board floor and scattered rugs, an open fireplace built of river-washed boulders in which an ox could have been roasted but in which a single log steamed with a sigh. The whole effect strove to suggest a fisherman's cottage on some bleak East Coast shore: California style.

Woven Indian blankets on the long settee, a poster for some forgotten Paris exhibition of Dali; crushed-looking armchairs in mattress ticking, a table at the hall end vaguely laid for supper, candles in Mexican pottery holders, a glass bowl of dried flowers.

Alice snapped a switch somewhere; Gershwin came up very low. There was a lost scent of joss-sticks.

'Calm,' he said. 'Nice.'

'Cheap,' she said. 'Rented monthly. A drink? Scotch, vodka ... or there's wine?'

'Scotch, no ice.'

'*No* ice? Golly. Water?'

'A tear.'

She handed him the glass, poured herself a glass of wine, carried it to the far end of the blanket-draped settee.

'Sit down. Relax. No one's arriving until eight thirty ... we can have a chat.'

14

He raised his glass to her. 'Like old times.'

'Very old times.'

'Yah ... they were a while ago, I suppose.'

'Amazing to find you here. You, of all people who hate moving ... Who bought your book? I forget. Head like a sieve.'

He indicated the yellow plastic-covered basket. 'Cristal Productions. One Andy Shapiro thinks it has "great, great potential".'

'Big deal. Big-time stuff. Hope they paid you.' She stirred the ice cubes in her wine. 'I'm managing,' she said, as if he had asked her.

'Well, or medium well?'

She shrugged. 'Sometimes it's well. Sometimes just medium.'

'And you'll stay here? In California?'

'They say there are worse places. I'm in trade. Did I tell you?'

'No. Buying and selling?'

'Selling. I'm a "booteek". Very chic. Called County. Updated English classics. Tweed, cashmere, flannel. Not a sequin, a rhinestone or a feather in sight.'

'Clever.'

'I thought so. Hugo's American publisher set me up. Interest on the loan, naturally.'

'Naturally. High?'

'Moderately. But he's waived the advance for the book he commissioned from him. It was quite a fat one.'

'Generous fellow.'

'Shrewd. There's a catch. He's claimed all the material Hugo had done before the accident – a third of the book plus all his notes, research stuff, tapes and so on.'

'Ah.'

'And now he wants his journals for '79 and '80. Covering the period he was working here. I'm frankly not so keen about that.' She ran fingers through her hair, absently pulled an ear lobe. 'However, beggars can't be ... y'know.'

'And he's got someone standing by ready to whip it all into shape. Am I right?'

'Of course. There's a third of a book completed, he likes it ... he's no fool. Things don't come for free in this place ... sympathy stops at the graveside.'

'But it's working? The shop?'

15

She laughed suddenly. 'Shop! You are marvellous, so English. Yes, the shop, as you call it, is working. Early days, but the Rich Bitches are catching on. Very important. I make a few pennies.'

'All your own work? Your designs?'

'Mine. All mine. I had to do something. Hugo left nothing. I mean you should have seen the will. God! As muddled and hopeless as he became in the end. Fortunately I've still got Daddy's wedding present. A wealth of old oak beams in a ten-acre paddock outside Horsham, called, appropriately enough, Farthing Hall.'

'You got my letter? After the accident . . . I mean.'

'Didn't I write back? Oh God . . . I'm impossible . . .'

'You weren't meant to. But you did?'

'I did, and you were angelic. No one else thought of money. They all assumed I was stinking rich. Only you thought. Thank you.'

'I knew Hugo too . . .'

'Not a bloody sou. All I have is the rent from Farthing Hall in Sussex, let, thank God, to a very important Lebanese something-or-other. All that was left was a raft of bills and a mass of debts. I mean a mass.'

'The good life costs. Maseratis, Laurent Perrier, handmade shirts.'

'Not to mention various little peccadilloes.'

She got up and kicked the sighing log, placed another across it, blew with a pair of bellows, sending up a spiral of ash and tired smoke.

'Clemency lit this. Said she had. Children, God!' She returned to her corner of the long settee, curled up like a cat.

'At least he gave you those. Clemency and Hope.'

'At least those. I'm very, very grateful. But his peccadilloes came dear. Very dear. I had no idea that they could cost so much.'

'His kind perhaps? You pay for rarity.'

'They were rare all right. I don't know all of it, but it was rare. That's what I'm really dreading, The Life and Times of Hugo Arlington. Apart from the debts, he left a library of journals. Very secret. Now they belong to me and I am about to read them and perhaps discover who my husband was. Odd?'

'Odd. But then most of us have a secret life, don't we?'

She smiled a neat, cat smile, wagged a foot. 'You? I don't believe that you have, you're too open. Honest.'

16

'Oh God. That's cruel.'

'Not meant to be. A blazing compliment – coming from me anyway.'

'I sound like something out of Warwick Deeping.'

'Don't look like it.'

'*Sorrell and Son?*'

She laughed, bending her head towards her knee, the heavy fair hair falling; she shook it back behind her ears, with a gesture which had once been so familiar to him and now sparked memory.

In Avignon.

A high wooden bed, a beamed ceiling with faded heraldic signs painted on the sagging plaster, her hair, as she lay beneath him, spread wide, like the rays of a symbolic sun across the sheet.

'You should shave before doing this to a girl,' she said.

'You have such delicate flesh. I didn't know I was going to do this – you tempted me from the narrow path of Just Friends.'

'You lie.'

'You have your own room.'

She moved beneath him, stretching, arms reaching up to curl round his shoulders and pull his head to hers. As her lips touched his, her tongue flicked across them.

'It was too small, hot, over a garden full of bourgeois eating ice creams.'

He took her again, easily, slowly, gently. Then she rolled away from him, her hands pulling her hair over her face, hiding.

'Alice Arlington. I love you,' he said.

She shook her hidden head, hands flat about her ears. 'No.' Her voice was muffled. 'You don't, please don't. Just *like*. Not love. I love Hugo.'

'I like you, then. All right? I like you like ... like ... what could I possibly like you like, after this?'

She rolled backwards, hands to head, dragging the heavy hair upwards, lips wide in a grin, eyes clear.

'A sister perhaps?' she said.

'Incest in the family?'

She pulled herself up on to her elbows, sat upright against the

17

heavy carved bedhead, swung the hair back. 'No. A moment of mutual attraction. I'm a happily married woman.'

'Happily married whore.'

'Perhaps. But all good happily married women should be whores, no? Part of the job, like cooking the breakfast, washing his jockey-pants . . . I love Hugo. I enjoy you. Okay?'

'You really do that? Wash his underwear? Wifely touches . . .'

She swung herself suddenly off the high bed, crossed to the shuttered windows and pushed them open. Her body was lean, small. Bones high-points at shoulders and pelvis, the heavy hair swinging. For a moment she leaned against the window frame looking down into the street below, arms crossed over breasts as small and modest as impudent buds. 'There's a man with a little dog, *France-Soir* and a beret. It must be France.' She picked up a dressing gown from the floor, started towards the doorway. 'No. Of course I don't wash his underwear. I'm not *that* wife. He didn't marry me for that, thank God. I'm going to the bathroom. The lavatory is there, if you need it, and then you'd better dress, don't you think?'

'If you do?'

'Yes I do. I'm calling Nanny in Sussex – and no cracks please – in half an hour. The wifely touches . . .' She laughed suddenly, shook the hair behind her ears. The spark of memory died.

'Open and honest,' she said. 'I would have thought you'd be pleased. Where have you been?'

'Been?'

'You left for a moment. I saw. Jet lag?'

'Avignon.'

'Oh. Oh that. Yes. *Mousseline de brochet aux morilles* at Heily's. Goodness yes . . . how one remembers delights like that! You won't get that tonight. Dubrovnik has two main dishes, his gazpacho and something like a moussaka . . . but not tonight. Alaska crab. I'll take him a refill.'

She got up and took a bottle of wine from the table. 'It wasn't an accident, you know. With Hugo. It was deliberate. He drove into that truck quite deliberately in his white Maserati. They all think it was an accident, but I know it wasn't.'

'How do you know?'

18

'I must take this to Dubrovnik. The whisky is here, help yourself.'
She went to the door and turned just as a young girl arrived. 'He
told me. "It'll be quick," he said. "No second thoughts." This is
Clemency. Remember Jonathan Pool? Freshen his glass like an
angel.' And she left them.

Clemency was almost as tall as her mother, trim corduroy slacks,
a Fair Isle pullover, white silk shirt, her mother's heavy hair
tumbling, a small string of pearls round her neck.

'We did meet,' he said, getting to his feet. 'Years and years ago,
when you were five, I think.'

She made a slight movement of a hand to indicate that he should
sit again, and said, 'Eight years ago. I almost remember. It was most
frightfully hot and I was car-sick, and was it you who bought me
some lemons? With real leaves on them?'

'It was I who did that.'

'Then we have met, and I do remember. It's a scotch, isn't it.'

When she had refilled his glass she sat upright on the arm of the
settee, slightly above him. He felt squashed among the Indian
blankets. 'So you know that I am Clemency? They call me Clemmy
at school. Sickening. The Americans are quite nice, I suppose, but
they have to abbreviate everything, every name. It's their way of
trying to make you feel integrated, or something. Cosy, they call it.
I loathe it, personally, but there isn't much I can do. One can't, can
one? Be too rude.'

She crossed her legs thoughtfully, pulling neatly at the crease of
her cords. 'My sister, whom I don't think you will have met – she's
nine – has completely swapped sides. I mean she has become an
American, literally. Become one. I find it so dreadfully disloyal.'

'To whom?'

She looked at him with her mother's eyes, as yet untroubled: cool,
clear, unafraid, now mildly surprised. 'To England, of course. We
are English, you know. I keep telling her, but she doesn't give a fig.
It's something I simply couldn't bring myself to do. Swap sides.'

'I don't suppose, do you, that ... what is her name, Hope ...?'

Clemency laughed politely. '*They* call her Hoppy.' She sighed, ran
the pearls round her neck once. 'I mean, really! But yes, it should
be Hope.'

'Well, I don't suppose that Hope has really swapped sides, do you, honestly? Don't you think that perhaps she's just trying to fit in, so to speak, with her schoolmates ...'

'It's possible. I didn't have to become a Yankee to do that. But, of course, she is quite young. Only nine.' Suddenly her face broke into a wide and delighted smile. 'As a matter of fact, Mr Pool ...'

'Jon will do, if you don't think it's too familiar.'

'Not a scrap. Jon. As a matter of fact the boys rather like my accent. I really do pretty well, frankly. Mind you, I'm choosy ... you have to be here.'

I bet you bloody well are, he thought. You are the spitting image of your mother; you won't come amiss.

'What I will say, Jon, if you don't think I am being too personal now, is that you have the most super voice. It's just glorious to listen to you, really.'

'How very kind of you. Thanks.'

'It's super. So English. I mean none of those dreadfully flattened vowels, that awful thing they do through their noses, you know? Nasal. I believe that they do speak quite beautifully on the East Coast. Almost like we do. ... But your voice is like April air.'

'I think that you really are going a little too far now ...'

'Oh! I'm sorry. But what I mean is that after being cooped up in school all day, with that nasal noise, and then coming home and hearing old Dubrovnik droning on in that awful way he does, you really sound ... well ...' suddenly she leant down and shyly touched his sleeve, her eyes smiling, lips slightly parted, 'like April air.'

Dear God! he thought, Alice has competition. Serious competition.

'Do you think that one can "sound" like April air?' He was well aware that he was starting to flirt a little. Jet lag.

She removed her hand slowly. 'Well, to me, April air does *sound*. Do you know what I mean? Wind in spring grass, lambs, the cuckoo, birds singing ... I mean that's April air, isn't it?'

'I'll give you that, right.'

'I just didn't say what I would have said until we were, ummm, better acquainted ... you know?'

'And what would you have said then?'

'Well I actually said it.' She got up and walked over to the dying

20

fire, picked up the bellows. 'Mother simply can't come to terms with this fire. All she has to do is turn on the gas underneath, but she won't – or forgets. What I said was that your voice is like April air. It makes one breathe again, fresh, clean, lovely.' She turned suddenly, the bellows in her hand, head to one side. 'That's all.' Smiling.

'Thank you,' he said. There wasn't much else he could say.

Hope appeared at the door, a froth of broderie anglaise. White socks and black patent leather pumps on her feet, her hair tied in two bows on either side, a pink and a blue.

'Hi! We have company. I'm Hoppy. Who are you?'

'I'm Jonathan Pool. Or Jon. Use which you like.'

'I'll use Jon, that okay? ... Hey, Clemmy, you killed the fire!'

'I have not killed, as you call it, the fire. It's gone out.'

'Well light the gas for Pete's sake, I mean this room is spooky ... don't we have any music?'

'We did have Gershwin. It's just stopped,' said Jonathan.

'Oh, jimminy-jim-john, Gershwin! Everything is so square in this house I could die.'

'Well die,' said Clemency coldly. 'But before you do, bring me a lighter, or some matches and I'll light the fire.'

'You like my dress?' asked Hope cheerfully. 'I put it on especially because Mother said we were having English people, and this is kinda, well I don't know, it's kinda frilly, you know what I mean? Like the Queen wears ...'

'I am ravished.'

'Great,' said Hope. 'I hoped you would be. Here's the lighter, and don't go and blow us all up, we got cracked crab for dinner.'

The gas bar under the sighing logs lit with a gentle plop! and ten small fingers of wavering yellow flame flickered uselessly beneath them.

'They'll never catch. Never,' said Clemency. 'Wrong wood. It should be eucalyptus.'

Hope was clattering through a pile of cassettes. 'How's about the Rolling Stones? At least it's alive. You like the Rolling Stones?'

Before he could reply Clemency said, 'She'll kill you if you play that, it's what she calls Destructive Music. There's von Karajan. Put that on.'

21

'I mean *that* is just the pits!' said Hope disgustedly. 'It's just doom, doom, doom. We're supposed to be having a party!'

Mahler drifted into the whitewashed-plank room, the fire plopped; flames wavered.

'Say, are you a very old friend of ours?' said Hope, sitting carefully in one of the crushed mattress ticking chairs. 'I mean, I don't know. Did you know my father?'

'Our father,' said Clemency.

'Well, did you?'

'Yes I did. For a long time, years and years. Well, really quite a long time.'

'I'm nine. How come I don't remember you?'

'I've known Jon for ages, haven't I?' said Clemency, leaning against the fake beam above the fireplace.

'Ages,' said Jonathan. 'Since you were five.'

'I was just a baby then,' said Hope. 'I guess that's why I don't remember you.'

'I expect that's why,' said Jonathan.

'He bought me lemons once.'

'Lemons!' said Hope in disgust.

'I was quite ill, wasn't I? And they had real leaves on them.'

'Big deal,' said Hope.

'We were in France. You live there, don't you?'

'I do.'

'In Paris?' said Hope, with some degree of interest. It was the only place she knew in France.

'No. In the south. A long way south. It's almost like here. But not quite.'

'Is it near, what is it, Yugoslavia? That's where Dubrovnik comes from. He says it's quite like this. I mean they have lemons and oranges.'

'No. It's quite far from there.'

'Did you know Dubrovnik before this evening?' said Clemency. 'He's really Boris Something-or-other; I mean, an impossible name, you'd never be able to say it or even remember it. So we just call him Dubrovnik.'

'No. I never met him before. He seems very nice.'

Hope found something of intense interest on the toe of a shoe and

22

stooped to examine it. 'He's all right, I guess,' she said. 'He's a friend of our mother, and he cooks.'

Clemency came across the room and sat beside him, her fingers toying with the pearls at her neck. 'He's got a wife already. And children, I understand. But we don't speak of them. He makes movies. Are you in movies too?'

'No. I just write.'

'What, write movies?'

'Books.'

'Oh! How civilized!' said Clemency. 'Almost everyone in this place makes movies. It's so *boring*.'

Hope had done whatever she had decided to do with her left shoe and looked up sharply. 'Clemency Arlington! Who went to see *Star Wars* three times? *You* did! Who has a crush on Clint Eastwood? You do! Boring! You are *so* awful. Just so awful.'

'How long,' said Jonathan carefully, 'have you known Dubrovnik? I'm a bit out of touch, you see, since you all came to live in California.'

Clemency reached for his almost empty glass. 'Would you care to finish that? I'll give you a refill.'

He finished the drink, handed her the glass. 'No ice and just a titchy amount of water.'

'Titchy!' said Hope. 'What's titchy, for heaven's sake?'

'It's an English word,' said Clemency grandly. 'You wouldn't know – it means very small. Doesn't it Jon?' The smile with which she turned to him could have blinded him, he looked away.

'Slang word I suppose, Hope . . . not everyone knows it,' he said.

'Except that I did,' said Clemency going over to the drink table.

'She's just scoring off me,' said Hope comfortably. 'I don't care. We've known Dubrovnik for simply years and years, well two anyway. Our father,' she emphasized the 'our' heavily, 'brought him to stay one Christmas. He liked him. He said he was a Pinko. You know what that means? It means a Commie. But I don't think he is really, he just had to be because he lives wherever it is, and they are all Commie people. If you don't join them they just shoot you. I mean, you know . . . they're real mean, real nasty. But not him. He was very kind to Mother, after the – you know . . .' She got up suddenly and went over to the tape deck, snapped a switch.

23

Mahler died. 'That is the most miserable music in the whole world.'

Clemency came back with the drink. 'Just a titchy amount of water. Try it for size.'

'After our father got killed,' said Hope and came back to sit in the chair she had left, fixing her hair ribbons.

'Put your arms around me, honey, hold me tight, Huddle up and cuddle up with all your might, um um, dum dee dum dee dum ...' Clemency's voice was clear, soft, true.

'What in the name of goodness is that supposed to be?' said Hope.

'A song. Do you know, Jon, that tomorrow is Inauguration Day! We, or rather I should say, they, are going to inaugurate their new President. He used to be a movie actor.' She tucked her hair expertly behind each ear, pursed her lips. 'Imagine!'

'Isn't that part of the American Constitution? I mean that any-one can grow up to become the President of the United States, Clemency?'

'Sure is,' said Hope cheerfully. 'Wowie! Here I come kids! Offa my runway!'

'I just think that this time they're carrying things a bit too far,' said Clemency.

Alice reappeared in the doorway and came towards him with a packet. 'Jon. This is yours, I think. You brought it with you – left it in the hall. Have my babies been looking after your needs? Liquid?'

'Oh jimminy! Babies. Mommy, come on now ...'

'Mother or Alice, if you like. I will *not* be Mommy, Hope, get that into your addled head.' She poured herself some wine. 'Poor Dubrovnik's up to the elbows in cucumber and tomato. It's a hell of a mess to make.'

Jonathan held the packet towards her. 'I brought this for you as a matter of fact. From London.'

'Oh Jon! You've brought enough. Bread, and that gigantic basket ... why don't you two open it up, see what we have in the treasure-basket?' She was tearing the wrapping from a box of Bendicks Bittermints.

'I imagine you can get them anywhere on Rodeo Drive now,' he said ruefully.

'You can't,' said Alice. 'Anyway these are more precious, they are hand-made and hand-delivered.' She bent down and kissed his head. 'Thank you.'

24

'Candy,' said Hope flatly.

'Not candy. Look.' Alice held the box towards her.

'Hey!' said Hope, suddenly reviving interest. 'Is that the royal sign, you know ... By Appointment to Her Majesty the Queen! Oh Gawd! The Queen eats these too?'

'I imagine so, it says so, doesn't it?'

Hope went on reading under her breath in a monotony of sound. 'Manufacturers-of-chocolate-Bendicks-Mayfair-Ltd-Winchester. Wow! Get that ... it's just *steeped* in royalty.'

'I didn't know,' said Clemency coldly, 'that Mayfair was actually in Winchester.'

'I think you'll find that Mayfair is in brackets, in fact,' said Jon.

'Meaning what?'

'Meaning that the shop is in Mayfair and the factory is in Winchester, okay?'

'A bit cheaty. But okay.'

'Can I have the box, when it's empty?' said Hope. 'I mean can you imagine Esther Winckler's face when I show her a box the Queen of England owned ... I mean, it's too much!'

'She didn't own it,' said Alice. 'I own it.'

'Esther Winckler is such a schmuck she won't know the difference.'

'And don't use schmuck. I've told you before.'

'Daddy didn't mind. He laughed.'

A sudden intense silence spread across the room. In the kitchen a tap ran, and china clinked.

'Poor Dubrovnik,' said Alice, too quickly. 'Tomato pips and cucumber peel everywhere – he's very fussy about his old gazpacho.' Her face was suddenly tight, sharp; she took a good sip of her wine. 'Which reminds me, Clemency, I haven't laid out the little bowls we have to use with it ... for the croûtons and so on. Get them darling, in the pantry-place.'

'I don't remember them,' said Clemency.

'Don't be dense, child. Top shelf on the right, little china bowls, they'll need a bit of a wash. Do that for me, will you? And lay them out, we're six.' And as Clemency left the room, straight-backed, elegant, assured of herself, Alice took the box-lid from Hope. 'And you could undo that yellow basket, see what's inside.'

Hope ripped the crackly plastic wrapping off the flat-bottomed,

25

high-handled basket and stuffed it in among the dead logs: the yellow flames caught; it curled, writhed and melted.

'There's a pineapple, two bottles of white wine, there are some crackers, English crackers, Jacob's . . . apples and cheese!' She held up a rectangular block. 'Processed cheese! And there's another bottle!'

'A bottle,' said Jonathan, taking his eyes, for the first time, from Alice's drawn face. 'What does the other bottle contain? Champagne or Lake Arrowhead water?'

Hope squinted at the label as if she was near-sighted. 'It says, it says: Hine V.S.O.P. Cognac.'

'Terrific!' said Jonathan. 'Or are you awash with brandy in this house, Alice?'

'Not here, by God! No. Napa Valley Chablis is my limit. Hope, take the bottles and put them on the table, take the rest of the stuff into the kitchen, find a bowl for the fruit, then lay up your own suppers, if Dubrovnik is halfway through clear, will you?'

'Will do.' Hope sighed and started putting the stuff back in the basket. 'That's our sign for dismissal. We don't get to eat with you-all, we eat in the kitchen among all the gook and stuff. Like slaves.'

'And hurry up about it,' said Alice. 'It's almost eight thirty and I don't want you hanging about when the others arrive.'

'Not even in my best Saks broderie anglaise?'

'Not even in that. Get on now.'

'I'll get – dismissal, see?' said Hope.

'Little girls should be seen and not heard,' said Alice, springing Mahler from the player and sliding in another cassette.

'Yeah, but we don't even get to be *seen*,' said Hope, going through the door with the ugly basket, trailing ribbon and shredded paper-packing as she went.

'Go on, out,' said Alice. She pressed a switch, a soft hissing, the music came in. 'Cole Porter Selections. Do you awfully mind? I mean it's just background stuff, no one listens.' She sat in her far corner of the settee.

'You are damned lucky, you know. With those two.'

'I know. I know. I really do know. Sometimes it's a hell of a problem, but as I know that it's going to be a problem for some years to come, I manage to handle things. You have to, or go under.'

26

'I can tell you one thing for sure, you're going to have problems with Mata Hari. I can tell you that right off.'

She laughed. 'Clemency? Right. A problem now. And only thirteen, well . . . nearly fourteen. The competition is amazing – jealousy showing its little horns already, at that age. Precocious? God help me when she hits sixteen. She'll have me out of the ring in ten seconds flat.' She held her glass up to the light, squinted through it. 'Of course she was Hugo's girl. Not mine. Adored him from the start. I somehow got stranded with my happy idiot Hope.'

'Hope,' said Jonathan, 'isn't such a bad thing to be stranded with.'

'Are we talking academically? Or about my daughter?'

'Both really.'

'Yes. Yes, she makes me laugh, she's a good child, Hope. But I mean, what about those names? Absolutely typical Hugo. Nothing to do with me. I had no choice. Nothing as simple as Rose or Grace. He chose names which were, I think, symbols for him. Not for me, or the children, just for himself. I often thought so in the past; today I am convinced. Hope: a desire for something and the feeling that it could, quite possibly, be fulfilled, and Clemency: leniency or mercy.' She shrugged her shoulders under the man's shirt she was wearing. 'All hopelessly involved, of course, my poor out-of-true Hugo.'

'And you loved him. I know that. Remember it all too clearly.'

She looked at him directly, her eyes steady, one finger tapping the rim of her glass. 'Goodness I loved him. There was no one else. For loving. No one.'

'I know.'

'Poor Jonathan. I'm not patronizing. Really. I mean poor. Truthfully. Women are quite batty sometimes. I was. Hugo was a superb lover, number one; a rotten husband, number two; an amusing father, when he remembered; a quite brilliant poet, when he took the trouble; but above all, and this you must remember yourself, he was the most staggering, glorious, amazing fun. Sheer fun. For that I think that people forgave him just about everything, at least in our early days, and there was a hell of a lot of forgiving to do. Perhaps there'll be more . . . sweet God I hope not . . . and if there is, then we'll see. But none of that mattered to me. I was utterly bewitched by his joy, his fun, his beauty, his madness, the insane ideas he could

27

construct, and I use the word advisedly, even his restlessness and his terrifying moods. But, God! He was the most fun, the most fun anyone was ... as a young man.'

'I remember.'

'I know that you do. There was something ... did I ever tell you? Or perhaps you were one of the evil planners even? Something he did, a triumph!'

'No. I was in on some, not many, nothing I think to do with you ...'

'This was to do with me all right. Once, when we were a-courting, as they say, the most enormous hearse arrived outside my parents' house in Chester Square. I mean it really was enormous. Smothered in wreaths, this huge Daimler hearse with a coffin, and mourners with top hats on their knees! Can you imagine the consternation of my papa! The Major-General who hated larkin' about ... it was stupefying. One of the men in black gave him a card, or an envelope, which was addressed to me. I remember opening it with terror, I'd no idea what was happening. Mother was whimpering about all the fuss, and the card said, "With love from Hugo Arlington. Please Open As Soon As Possible." And I said to the man, almost unable to breathe, "Open what?" and he said, with a polite cough, "The coffin, miss, otherwise you'll have a real corpse on your hands, I fear." And of course it was Hugo. Inside a *white* coffin, mark you, with a dozen bottles of champagne round him, covered in camellias or gardenias or some damn flower, plastic of course ... the final touch.'

Jonathan was laughing with her. 'No, not that one. I never knew about that one from him, I heard the stories, mind you. What did you do? Why all the theatricals?'

'Oh. Well. You knew Hugo. I'd said No to him time and time again. He made me laugh all right, but I didn't think that was quite enough reason to marry him, even though the bed side of things was really pretty terrific. But I just said No. I mean *No*. And of course he wasn't used to that. Hugo didn't like the word No. Ever. Hence the theatricals, as you call them. He arrived in his coffin, in the most glorious tail suit, and said that if I would marry him he'd leap out immediately and we could drink all the champagne, or else, and this was very typical I was to discover, he'd cut his wrists.'

'Christ!'

'And my dear, he had a very neat cut-throat razor stuffed up the cuff of his coat. I mean it was completely dotty. Crazy. It was the most momentous proposal a girl ever received.'

'And you accepted.'

'What else.' She picked a piece of red wool off her knee, a long thin strand, and rolled it into a ball between her fingers.

'But a razor,' said Jonathan. 'Why a razor . . . why would he think of such a thing?'

'It was all perfectly worked out, and he said it was very convenient because, if I said no, they just had to put the lid on again and he'd be all ready for Putney Vale . . . I mean it was utter lunacy. And of course he jumped out and scattered his bloody plastic gardenias all over Chester Square and we humped the bottles into the house and even my bewildered, unsmiling father had to laugh.'

She lay back in the corner of the settee, one leg curled underneath her, head resting on the high back among the rumpled Indian blankets. She was weeping. 'Of course,' she said, 'it was a small fortune. I mean it cost him that. I don't know how he planned it, or conned people, or who they were even . . . they were all in the act, that was certain. Madness.'

'Do you want a handkerchief?' said Jonathan.

'Oh Lord. Am I snivelling . . .?'

'Without sound,' he said.

She wiped her eyes on the sleeve of her shirt. 'A silly thing to do. They just come. I don't make a noise, no boo-hoo stuff . . . it is just the remembering. Odd.'

'And anyway, you got married?'

'No. Not right away. I accepted, and like the well brought up young woman I was I made him wait. I promised, but he didn't get a wild runaway canter for his pains. I was designing for a nice little Japanese fag at the far end of the King's Road. We were highly successful. I had exceptionally bright prospects personally . . . it was the start of the sixties . . . just into them, the swinging London bit, the never-had-it-so-good time. And we hadn't.'

She poked a finger under the strap of her sandals. 'No, I didn't capitulate right away. I was still a little bit scared of him in a way, and my parents didn't really approve. I mean as far as they were

concerned there was no "family" behind him. He was out of nowhere. Then we went away for a month together ... he had a rather
super old Bentley. We drove down to Italy, ate in all the best
restaurants, stayed in the best hotels – Rome, Naples, Siena, Perugia
– we even went through the hell of Capri for a few days, and then
one evening, on our way home to England, we were eating in a tacky
little bar on the harbour at Portofino and he suddenly said, "Will
you marry me, Alice, please?" and I said, "Yes". And that was it.'

'And Alice was hooked.'

'Alice was hooked. And happy. I still am. Not happy I don't mean,
just "hooked".'

'But all the money, did it never occur to you that he hadn't got
any?'

'No. Because he always seemed to have a mass. I don't know how,
or where, he got it, I didn't even ask. Too in love, as the song goes,
was I.'

'All I know is that he did get paid a hell of a bit for some of his
early work: the best, frankly, in my humble opinion. He didn't brag
about it, just made bloody certain that one knew. I do remember
him telling me that he had met this simply amazing girl who was
wildly grand.'

Alice laughed, balanced her glass on her knee. 'Oh come off it,
Jon! He thought that anyone was grand if they had a house in town
and another in Sussex, and that I could have been presented at
Court with a bunch of feathers stuck in my hair ... I suppose, in
those days, I *was* grand. But I didn't get the ostrich-feathers, the
Sussex house was a ruin, and we were about as grand as any retired
Major-General with dry rot in the roof and a whacking great over-
draft could be ... still I knew he was impressed.'

'It was so funny how he kept you under wraps, so to speak. Never
let any of his old friends meet you, if you remember, until the
wedding.'

'Well, I suppose he was a bit suspicious – of you anyway, far too
attractive.'

'But it was a bit dotty.'

'He was frightfully busy cultivating my friends. Moving up and
onward, taking every invitation that might better him socially. He
admitted it freely. He just dropped his old crowd, although I do
confess that he spoke often of you, and with affection.'

30

'That was kind of him, at least.'

'But he said that you lived in Kenya. I mean, why would he do that when he knew absolutely for a fact that you lived at the other end of the Fulham Road? We could have run into each other a thousand times. It was madness.'

'Not to him. And if we had met by chance, because I was not in your sort of world, weeviling away with my books and so on, he'd have cut me, pretended he didn't know me, or just crossed the road. I've been cut by Hugo in my time. It was always an extraordinary experience. The absolute deadpan face, the positive dislike. Odd.'

'It was the kind of danger which he enjoyed. I suppose you can call it that?'

'Suppose so. I remember that he told me he had started negotiations to do a book on Modigliani, I think, and that his publishers had given him a terrific advance to go off to France and Italy ... that was also the time that I first heard of the "amazing" girl. You.'

'And *that's* where the money came from for the proposal trip! Modigliani never got a look in.' She got up and wandered across to the black fireplace and the ten little pale yellow flames wandering in the draught, leant her head against the fake beam, prodded the dead logs with a foot. 'How long did you know Hugo, Jon? He never really said. I never asked. And you were always rather clam-like.'

'After he came down from Cambridge. Not longer.'

'My word. Quite a long time. I suppose I shouldn't say this, but did you know that his real name was Arthur Sean Sproule, that his father was an Irish God-knows-what and his mother a trainee nurse at St Thomas's, and that they lived, and he was born, in a semi-detached house in Herne Hill. Did you?'

'No,' said Jon quietly. 'No. I didn't know that. I only knew him as Arlington.'

'He picked that name when he was taken to tea at the Ritz by a rather unscrupulous gentleman who ran a now defunct literary magazine and who thought that Arthur Sean Sproule, on the strength of the stuff with which he had been bombarded, might well be the new James Joyce. He went in for the boyish looks too, I gathered, but lost out heavily on both accounts. However, Hugo Arlington was born that afternoon.'

'I had no idea.'

'You weren't supposed to. No one was. He dropped Mum and

31

Dad and Herne Hill like hot bricks, never to be mentioned again.'
'When did you find out? I mean, not that it really matters . . .'
'No, it didn't matter a bit to me. I found out at marriage. It is a
very inconvenient business sometimes. All sorts of little things
which were swept under various carpets emerge again. Oh! You
needn't worry! I'm not Mrs Sproule. He changed his name by deed-
poll almost as soon as he had finished his tea that day!' She turned
away from the fake beam. 'Poor Hugo. He trod such a dangerous,
delicate line in life.'

From the hall the sound of muffled door chimes.

Hope's voice yelled out. 'I'll get it! It's the company! Trillions of
them, at least two cars.'

'Ding dong dell,' said Alice. 'Pussy's down the bloody well. I wish
they weren't here, I wish I wasn't such a bore. They are sweet and
I like them, but I was just getting under way, wasn't I? Thank you
for bearing with me. I suppose that I still miss him dreadfully. I'm
terribly lost. I pretend that I am not, try not to let it show, but I know
I want him back again, even though I know that he went out of my
life, as far as loving goes, a long time past; but I never went out of
his, and I know more than anyone what an utter, utter bastard he
was.' She started towards the door. 'Makes no difference.' She
smiled at him, a neat, bleak movement of her lips, straightened her
shirt, put the empty glass down on the table and went into the hall.

He sat perfectly still: I never had a chance. Not a hope in hell. Why
did I ever think that I might? So now you know: the years are fled
and all hope too. Cole Porter ended, rattled, whispered to a stop in
the machine.

Outside doors were slamming, cars revving up, reversed, swung
about, driven away, people were talking and laughing, Hope's voice
high with pleasure rising far above them all: 'It's too much! It's just
the most! I'm *amazed* . . . how did you know I wanted one? I lost mine
somehow. Thank you . . .'

He rose to his feet as the hall filled with voices and figures and
a slight, freckle-faced woman in her late thirties hurled into the
room as if she had been thrown to him from a runaway truck.

'Oh! God!' she said. 'I am a wreck, a total wreck! I mean just look
at me, all loose ends. I'm falling apart, exhausted, but exhausted.
Ballet class, hence the costume.' She wore a swaddle of woollen

clothing. A long, knitted scarf wound round her neck, knee-warmers, sagging, black woollen tights, a short coat that had seen better days on the back of some sailor, a handkerchief knotted on her head, mittens. In one hand she held a large glass jar, in the other a blue canvas tote-bag with 'San Francisco' printed on the side.

'Who are you? I'm Sybil Witt. I dance and I sing, in a desultory way ... "Let me entertain you ..." I can't shake your hand, I'm loaded like a pack-mule.'

'I'm Jonathan Pool,' he said. 'I write.'

'Scripts?' Her eyes narrowed.

'Books.'

'Jesus! Intellect! I adore intellect because I have so little myself. Jonathan dear, be sweet, give me a hand with this crap. Just hold out your arms and Auntie will peel it all off for you.' Suddenly she·turned back towards the hall and yelled, 'Alice Arlington! I *know* you didn't invite me, but don't worry: I brought my own food and I only drink Perrier water.' She started to unwind the long scarf, handed it to him, then the coat.

'Do you call this a "coatee" in England? It's a bit short. Navy surplus. I believe it's kinda cute, and now my clutch-bag. Would you believe my whole face is in there? I just never get the time to stick it on, and this ...' she held up the glass jar, '... is my dinner, see? Nuts? I mean nuts. I am the one and only original Squirrel Woman ... I got Brazils here, I got pistachio, hazel, walnuts; all kinds. Protein ... do you know about protein? It's revolutionized my life.' She shook the jar. 'This is just so simple. Anything you think is a nut – apart, that is, from myself – is in this jar, I even got pignolias here. I'll go and show Boris. He gets so uptight when he's cooking the meal, which he most often is – Alice couldn't bake a fortune cookie.' She left him, colliding instantly with Alice on the way out. 'Don't let that intellectual out of your sight,' she said. 'He's holding everything I own, even my face. Look, my dinner!'

'Syb,' said Alice. 'You're completely nutty.'

'I loathe puns!' said Sybil from the hall.

'Unintentional. Sorry.'

'Anyway, it is the only way to be to get you through life in this goddamned town.'

'Where is Boris? In his kitchen ...'

33

'Yes. With the kids and Irina.'

Jonathan dumped the wardrobe carefully on the settee, put the tote-bag beside it.

'I'm terribly bad at formal introductions in a crowd,' said Alice. 'I even forgot my own sister's name in the middle of Harrods once.'

He turned as she moved beside him. Behind her two hesitant people: a tall, elegant man with a pale, amused face and tightly curled grey hair beginning to recede from a noble brow; beside him, smiling uncertainly, a dark-haired young woman in a white cotton dress.

'But I'll try,' said Alice. 'This is . . .' she paused, flushed, laughed. 'Pole?'

'Pool,' said Jonathan.

She buried her face in her hands. 'God! I've done it again! I told you I would. What on *earth* is it with me? I've known Jonathan . . . Pool . . . for a hundred years!'

'One loves you, Alice,' said the elegant man. 'But one does find you incredibly disconcerting. You manage to engender an atmosphere of doubt and unease about you. I have known, for at least sixty-seven years, who I am. But dare I be sure? Can I be certain? Am I not who I have thought I was and shall you relegate me with one brisk dismissal to the hideous anonymity of this dreadful city of Los Angeles? My name *was* Geoffrey Nettles,' he said, 'but can I be certain? And this was Lea, my daughter.'

Jonathan took the hand she offered him, which felt, in his, as warm and as fragile as the folded wings of a bat. He was frankly overwhelmed by the vivid smile, the dark eyes sparking with laughter, the lips parted in pleasure.

'My father is also quite disconcerting, I might add. It is not poor Alice's prerogative. I think that, at this very early stage Mr . . . Pool, I should perhaps explain that although his name is indeed Nettles, mine is Rooke,' she said. 'With an "e".'

'No blood ties,' said Nettles.

'Not even father,' said Lea. 'Guardian covers it, I think.'

'Bequeathed to me,' said Nettles sadly. 'At a very early age by her parents. A thoughtless gesture which absolutely ruined my life. However, one does one's duty.'

'Really frightfully well. Speaking for myself,' said Lea. 'And if that sounds at all conceited, it is not meant to be. I only wished to imply that I was fed and watered and schooled most correctly. And sometimes allowed to go to concerts or even the theatre. It wasn't such a hideous experience. I survived.'

She was smiling and it was only when she gently disengaged her hand from his that Jonathan let it go. Jet lag has hit me, he thought. Music was playing again, and Hope and Clemency were coming towards him dragging a large woman in a grey dress, fluttering with yellow ribbons. He thought that perhaps it might be wiser to pass out; but the clear, cool voice of Clemency stilled panic.

'Jon. This is Irina Miratova. She's Russian, and quite possibly my very best friend, aren't you, Irina?'

Irina Miratova was stuffing ribbons into a large black bag which hung from her arm. 'I cannot tell. How can I tell?' she said.

'She's a countess too!' said Hope.

Irina hit her hard with the black bag. 'Hush! Child ... such vulgarity before a stranger!'

'He's not a stranger. He's a very old friend,' said Clemency.

'We have not been introduced, yet. So he is a stranger to me,' said Irina.

'Jonathan Pool, and he writes.'

'I am most happy to make your acquaintance,' said Irina. 'You know what all these ribbons are for?'

'No ...'

'The release of the Iranian hostages. It must be soon, don't you think? Perhaps even tomorrow? We inaugurate a new President, Mr Pool ... don't you think that it would be fitting if, when he takes his oath, they release those poor creatures at the same time? In the circus of American politics it is not enough to have just a *clown*: one must have a big act to follow him. Reasonable?'

'I suppose so. Why yellow ribbons?'

'Oh! come on, Jon ... there's a song, don't you know it?' said Hope and sang: 'I'll tie a yellow ribbon to the old oak tree ...'

'I appreciate neither the song nor your voice, Hope. Both are sentimental,' said Irina pleasantly. 'But then I suppose that I also am sentimental? To tie yellow ribbons on my poinsettias.' She turned to Jonathan with a shrewd smile. 'I have no oak tree, and I *cannot* celebrate the first act in the circus. But I will do for the

35

second, if they have arranged it for tomorrow, as I am sure they have. We'll see.' With a polite inclination of her white head, improbably crowned with an untidy brown plaited chignon, she left him and moved away murmuring, 'A little vodka, my darlings. Who has a little vodka for Irina?'

'She lives in a fantastic house,' said Clemency. 'It's falling into the sea day by day but she won't budge. Each time we have a torrential rainstorm a bit more of the cliff slides down into the ocean. I think where she lives is called the slide area, and it's doing just that. They keep on trying to move her out, but she won't. She's been there for hundreds of years. She's in constant pain. Arthritis. But she won't let it show ever.'

'She's very splendid.'

'You remember that I told you that your voice sounded like, ummm, well, like April?'

'I do indeed,' he said gravely.

'Well, Irina's voice sounds to me like December. You know? Sleighs skimming over the snow, the horse's bells jingling, ice crackling, birch trees furred with frost.'

'Clemency. Is that yours? Or is it paraphrased Pushkin?'

She looked at him flatly. 'I don't know what you mean.'

'It's very romantic anyway.'

'I *am* romantic. I am desperately romantic. It is quite the hardest thing to be in this ghastly city, and no one is going to take it away from me.'

'I honestly don't think that anyone would dare!'

She laughed, touched his arm, turned with a frown of anger as Alice called her. 'Clemency? The little bowls for the croûtons? You know I *did* ask you ...'

'They're all ready. Coming,' said Clemency. 'I'd better get them, excuse me.'

She left him as Sybil started rummaging about among her piled effects on the settee.

'Gimme, gimme. My clutch-bag. Your dinner is about to be announced. You know, the moment Boris takes off that damned apron and slicks his hair he really does look terrifically ballsy. No wonder Alice is hooked on him.' She found the bag, pulled the knotted handkerchief from her head. Her hair was the colour of pink brass, spiked as a hedgehog. 'Hair's a mess, right? Wigs. I get to wear wigs in my act and having this hair is a great help – you just pull 'em on like hats. No problem. Here's Boris with his gazpacho. It's all so damned reverend you'd really think that he had every cucumber personally blessed and made the stock from holy water.'

'It's all vegetable, isn't it? You could eat that?'

'Uhuh. I'm not into vegetarianism, honey. Just hitting the proteins. And I was not asked to dine. I know the rules. So I'll sit and watch you all eat and chew my nuts.'

Boris had set the big bowl in the middle of the table and had begun to ladle the soup into smaller ones for Clemency and Hope, with care and obvious affection.

Irina, her large black bag hanging from the crook of her elbow, was trying to fix a yellow ribbon bow to her hair. Nettles stood attentively beside her holding a glass of vodka.

'You need, I think, a longer hairpin,' said Lea. 'A longer hairpin. Look, let me try ...' She took the bow in slender fingers, twisted it, bent it, fixed it with precision in the untidy brown chignon on Irina's head, then stood back, arms clasped before her. 'There!' she said. 'Perfect. Secure as you like. It will stay as it is even in a force-nine gale.'

'I am unlikely to encounter such a phenomenon,' said Irina. 'Is it *becoming?*' She took her glass from Nettles and drained it in one long swallow.

'Most,' said Nettles. 'Like a tiara. A perfect symbol of freedom.'

'Hah!' said Irina, looking vaguely about for replenishments. 'It is supposed to be a symbol of welcome, I am told. If it falls, it will not be welcome in Boris's soup. Like all his countrymen, his humour is heavy – there is no gaiety in those Slavs unless they are drunk. Or they have assassinated a king.'

Lea turned suddenly and looked at Jonathan, and laughed. He discovered, to his consternation, that although he laughed himself, he was quite unable to hold her look, and began to examine the bottom of his glass with close attention. He looked up just as Hope and Clemency were leaving the room.

'And cracked crab to follow. Yum yum yummy!' said Hope, and then, setting down her bowl, she thrust her arm towards Alice. 'Hey, I forgot. Remember the bracelet I lost? My lady-bug one? Well,

Irina bought me another. She found it in some drugstore in Pacific Palisades. Isn't it great?'

'Great,' said Alice sharply. 'Now take your bowl and let us get on with dinner.'

'Alice, my dearest child, shall we sit anywhere?' said Nettles.

Alice looked up from placing a brimming bowl. 'Not quite so full, Dubrovnik darling. Geoffrey, you sit here. Irina dear here, Lea and Jonathan on that side.' She looked across to Sybil who was sprawled in a chair by the dead fire reading a newspaper. 'Syb? Syb, there's a mass of room, come on over.'

'Happy as a clam,' said Sybil. 'I'm reading Misty Layne's review, she opened last night.'

'Good?' said Alice, setting a bowl before Nettles.

'Well, with a review like this, honey, she doesn't need legionnaire's disease.'

Alice suddenly took Boris's head between her two hands and kissed him firmly on the lips. 'My beloved Slavic cook. What would I do without you?'

Dubrovnik wiped his mouth on the back of his hand, grinned, lifted a big pepper-mill. 'Pepper,' he said. 'Lotsa pepper is good for this. You like?'

Jonathan was curious to discover that this overt display of affection caused him no pull of regret, no muted thrust of jealousy, as such actions had in the past. After so many years, more than he cared to admit to, these things had suddenly disappeared. He took his place beside Lea.

'Have you won something wonderful?' she said.

'Won something?'

'You look very smug and happy.'

'Smug? Oh Lord! Probably jet lag is catching up on me; it makes one look pretty silly.'

'I didn't mean smug to sound rude. I should have said happy. Not silly. Not *smug*.'

'Well, I'll tell you what I think has happened. I think that a ghost has been laid, right this very moment. Or that very moment rather.'

'A ghost? I know about ghosts. Was it a very bad one?'

'Pretty bloody sometimes.'

'But you think that it's gone now?' She reached for her spoon.

'I think that it's gone.'

'That's marvellous. What a relief! So, in fact, you *have* won something?'

'I'm not absolutely certain, but I think so, yes.'

She looked at him with a sudden, swift, turn of her head, the spoon halfway to her lips, looked down again, prodding the vegetables in her bowl, and when she looked back at him he was overwhelmed with happiness to see that she was smiling.

2

Alice

Apart from the weary plop! plop! of the wavering gas jets, the room was as still and silent as an empty church. She stood dead centre, legs apart, arms at her sides, hands clenched into fists, nails pressing into her palms, head bowed.

The moment I dread. The loneliness.

Somewhere on San Vicente, or Sunset, a fire siren wailed; grew louder, came closer, veered, faded, was gone.

She turned, put off the gas, drew the steel spark-curtain across the dead fire, snapped off the tape deck and the lamps in the sitting area, leaving only the fake oil-lamp hanging over the dining-table to cast a cold, shadowy glitter across the debris of the evening. Crumpled napkins, a scatter of dirty glasses, the bottle of brandy two thirds empty, Irina's bow.

'I think that it is uncomfortable. I don't feel that it is *becoming*. I will remove it. It is perhaps more a Star of David than a yellow bow?' She bowed her handsome head towards Nettles. 'Will you assist me?'

He had little opportunity to refuse, with her head almost in his lap, and so he did.

'I was considering how splendid you looked, Irina. Like a lighthouse.'

'Hah!' she said. 'God! I've been called some things in my time, but never, as far as I am aware, a lighthouse.' They had laughed as she wrestled with pins and tumbling chignon.

*

40

There was no echo now in the ugly room. She picked up the brandy bottle, switched off the lamp, went into the kitchen. Wreckage. Beloved Boris. Too big for so small a space, too volatile a cook for so confined an area. She wondered who had designed the thing. Narrow as a coffin: obviously someone who only made coffee, or opened a tin.

Wooden spoons, plates, dirty bowls, an apron and oven-cloths dropped anywhere, a packet of salt, hastily opened, spilled, left to lie in a puddle of milk. Mechanically, without thought, she took a pinch and threw it over her shoulder: for luck. Put the brandy in a cupboard from which three recipe books instantly fell; she kicked them under the table.

Jupiter could deal with all this tomorrow: if Jupiter arrived, that was to say. There was no knowing these days. She was a law unto herself, and had been ever since the cataclysmic day that her beloved Julie-Mae had been taken by the Lord. Or so it was supposed. Hoped. For no one really knew. She had just gone away. 'Why He punish me? I ain't done the least little thing wrong,' she said. 'What I do He punish me like this? I worship! Yea Lord I worship You! And You gone take my child. Where she go? Where she went? That's the bad part. Not to know. That's the punishment of Hell, oh Lord! No one can find her; no cops, no Chapel people; we all look, and no sign. Why He punish so cruel? Why she go so silent?'

Why indeed. Poor Jupiter. Poor all of us. Poor me.

Beyond the kitchen in this ill-designed house, the long passage which led down to her bedroom at the back of the place; the children's rooms on either side, dark, emphasizing, curiously, her bleakness, even though unlike Jupiter she knew that they were there, asleep, breathing, part of her. Her life.

She moved quietly past the half-open doors. Clemency called. 'I'm awake!'

'Oh darling! At this time? It's long after midnight. Was there too much noise?'

'No. I'm just awake. Wait, I'll put on my lamp.' Clemency rustled in the darkness; a soft pink glow on a hideous Minnie Mouse lamp.

'I don't think you could hear much at this end of the house. There are two doors between you and the sitting room.'

Clemency was sitting up, one arm across her forehead, shielding

41

her eyes from the sudden light, the other across her chest. 'It wasn't the party noise. I didn't hear that. Just, well, I've got a lot of whirling going on in my head. You know what I mean? Thinking.'

'Bad thinking?'

'Some of it. I'm not tired.'

'*I'm* dead,' said Alice.

'Could you sit down for a moment, please, Mother?' Clemency patted the edge of her bed. 'For a moment.'

The request was so unusual that Alice sat immediately, took her daughter's hand in her own. 'What bad things were you thinking of?'

'Well, not so much bad as difficult.'

'Can I help?'

'I don't know.' Clemency withdrew her hand and looked at the Minnie Mouse lamp. 'Perhaps.'

'Try me.'

'I expect you'll laugh.'

'I don't see why I should.'

'Neither do I. But people do.'

'I'm not people, am I? I hope, anyway.'

'Well, there are two things.' Clemency folded her arms behind her head, resting against the wooden headboard of the bed.

'First one?'

'Will you promise me, faithfully, that when I die you'll have me buried at Farthing Hall?'

'Clemency darling! For God's sake ...'

'I knew that you'd laugh.'

'Darling girl, I'm *not* laughing. I'm just absolutely shattered that you mind so much. Do you really hate it here so terribly? Do you?'

'Will you promise me faithfully?'

'I promise. All right. Of course I do. But, darling, we won't have to face such a dreadful thing for years, you're still very young ...'

'How can you tell? Like Julie-Mae? She was much younger than me. How can you tell?'

Alice shook her head, ran her fingers through her hair, brushed them over her face, digging into her cheeks. 'Okay. I promise. But remember, we don't know about Julie-Mae ...'

'It makes it easier if I know that, one day, I'll go back to England. For ever.'

42

'I really didn't know you hated it here so. I am very ashamed.'

'You needn't be. I didn't want to make a fuss, but I'm glad you promised.'

'Well I do. And what else? You said there were two things?'

'Oh yes.' Clemency stared up at the ceiling. 'The second thing is that I am in love.'

'Why did you think I'd laugh about that? I've been in love too, remember. I know what it's like. It's not a funny thing. Why would I laugh?'

'Because,' said Clemency, 'he's very old. Terribly old.'

'Old?'

'As old as you are. Probably older.'

'That's a problem,' said Alice evenly. 'I do see. Would I know him?'

'Very well.'

'Then who?'

'Jonathan Pool is who.'

'Jonathan? Here tonight?'

'Here tonight. I'm in love.'

It occurred to Alice that perhaps if she leant her back against the bedhead it would ease her aching body, and possibly afford a feeling of mutual comfort to her daughter. She wasn't absolutely certain. But at least she would then no longer be looking at the tense, pale face, and the anxious eyes pretending that they weren't. So she tried. Clemency shifted slightly, but said nothing. So far so good. They lay together in the glow from the Minnie Mouse lamp looking at the ceiling.

'My back is absolutely breaking. You don't mind, do you? Sharing your bedhead?'

'Not in the least. I'm glad you didn't laugh.'

'Well how could I possibly laugh about something which is so very serious for you? Falling in love, being in love, is nothing to joke about. I can understand how you feel. He *is* very attractive.'

'Terrifically. It's his voice, of course; that really is amazing.'

'Yes. He has a very pleasant voice.'

'That's what I thought. Pleasant. How old is he? He said he's known you for simply years and years.'

'Well, old. I have to admit that. In comparison to you.'

'That's the main trouble.'

43

'It is a point worth considering.'

'Is he married?'

'He was. Divorced.'

'Children?' A hint of unease in the question.

'No children.'

'*That's* a relief. Two obstacles out of the way at least.'

'From that point of view,' said Alice, 'he's perfectly eligible.'

'By being unencumbered, you mean?'

'Well, yes. I suppose that's what I mean.' She looked at her hands. 'My fingernails! God! Broke this one wrestling with that damned cracked crab. I'll have to get a file. You're fourteen, aren't you?'

'Almost. As good as. People get married at fifteen, of course. It's not so long.'

'No, a year I suppose.'

'In India,' said Clemency, stretching her arms towards the ceiling, 'they get married at ten, sometimes. Did you know?'

'Yes. Yes, I knew. Arranged marriages. But I don't think that the rule applies in America. Yet.'

'God!' said Clemency. 'I *hate* America.'

'Well you really shouldn't, Clem. It's been wonderfully kind to you and to me, and Hope. It's the most generous country in the world.'

'It's his voice really,' said Clemency, folding her arms and ignoring any possible plea on behalf of America. 'It's so gentle, very ... seductive, I think.'

'Are you any good at mental arithmetic? I'm hopeless ...'

'Not terribly. Why?'

'Well, I was trying to work out that when you are, say, well ... twenty-one or two ...'

'Yeuch!' said Clemency. 'Twenty-one or two! That's *years* away. Twenty-two! I mean that's almost at death's door.'

'But if you avoided death's door and *got* to be twenty-two, I think, but I can't quite be certain because I'm a bit silly tonight, but I think that Jonathan would be, oh I don't know ... knocking his middle fifties. He was younger than Daddy, you know?'

There was a profound silence from the slight figure beside her. Alice made a move, sat up, looked at her hands again. 'I must get a file; this nail catches in everything ... awful in wool. Don't you

44

hate a broken nail catching in things? Shivers down my spine.'

'Knocking his *fifties*?' said Clemency. 'You mean that?'

'Who? Oh, Jonathan. Something like that. I think he's about my age, forty-something.'

'It's a bit boring.'

'Well. As I said. You do have a problem.' She eased herself away. 'I'm off to my bed now. I am really bushed. Try not to let things go on whirling in your head. I promise you about England – that was one of the main worries, I think?'

'I would be grateful.'

'I don't know what we can do about Jonathan Pool. Talk about it in the morning, if you like?'

'It's Inauguration Day.'

'So it is.'

Clemency slid down into her bed. She was not a child that one tucked up for the night: at least not a child that Alice could. Hugo, yes, Hugo always did that.

She went over to the door. 'You put out your lamp? It's terribly late.'

'Yes. I'll do it. I heard Dubrovnik leave. The soup wasn't much, was it? Not after all the fuss he made.'

'Dubrovnik always leaves, darling. He doesn't live here.'

'I know. I heard his car. Vroom, vroom, vroom.'

An oblique reminder that I have to stay away from anyone who might stand in Hugo's golden light? Possibly a form of thank you, for the mother-and-daughter chat? One could never be absolutely certain.

She said: 'I'm off. I'll just look in on Hope, see that *she* hasn't been having any whirling thoughts.'

'Goodnight,' said Clemency. The room was suddenly dark. 'Hope won't be having any whirling thoughts. She hasn't the sensitivity. Anyway, she looks like a pig when she's asleep. Nose in the air, mouth open. I expect she's got adenoids.'

She was lying with one arm thrown wide across the counterpane, the other close to her side, thumb in mouth. A little like a pig, thought Alice. Nose in the air, a sweet pig. God, I'm lucky: at least I have these two. Growing people. Part of what was once, and what was sweet, and funny: perhaps not always good. But life doesn't

45

come in comfortable segments like a piece of fruit cake, with the cherries scattered all the way through. Sometimes there aren't any cherries in the bit you get at all. Make do, then, with the currants. She leant down and took Hope's wide-flung arm, the ladybird bracelet round her wrist, put it under the sheets. Hope groaned, stirred, mumbled. Was asleep again.

Her own room, in comparison with the spartan order of Clemency's, was a wreck. Cupboard doors half open, powder spilt on the too small dressing-table, bed unmade, roughly drawn up, a pair of shoes tumbled at the side.

At her desk, jammed into the shallow bay window which looked out onto the dark, forlorn backyard, papers and letters held down by assorted paper-weights, her drawing board angled beside a glass jar of drooping marguerites in water that was low, and scummy.

Standards falling, she thought. I never really lived in a mess like this before. It was not, shall we say, my habit. I liked it all nice, all tidy. All proper. This is my office, my bedroom, the place where I weep, the only place: my cell.

Jupiter can have a clear-up. If Jupiter comes. Probably won't. Inauguration Day, so she'll be glued to her television set all morning.

She ran water in the wash-basin, cleaned her teeth carelessly. The toothpaste tube squashed in the middle, cap missing. Something which Hugo would have killed me for.

No Hugo. So who cares now?

I think I managed the mother–daughter thing all right? Oh God! Poor Clemency. It's all just beginning for her, and I hadn't an idea that she loathed it here: that wild Gray's Elegy bit. Lying in her coffin, smooth in white, beneath towering elms and cawing rooks at Farthing Hall. What brought that to a head? English voices perhaps. Nettles. Lea. Jon.

Poor Jon. The next time she'll have him under a microscope. Every line and wrinkle will be searched for, and found. Not that he has many, in truth. He's worn well.

She took a towel and rubbed her face with a wet corner, looked at the smear of stale make-up which betrayed her slovenliness. Decided to wash. Washed, rinsed, rubbed hard with the towel.

She's right, of course, about his voice. It's good, comforting,

46

caring, warm. I wish that I had been able to care for him, as they say, more. God knows that he hoped so too, but I met him too late, or rather he met me too late. I'd already been caught. Spoken-for, thankfully. And he would never have been fun. Not as much fun as Hugo was, never have been as ... she reached for a hairbrush, started to brush her hair harshly, head forward and down ... dangerous. Sexually he was all right, pleasant. Nothing remarkable, all right. Why did he remember bloody Avignon tonight. I suppose because it was the first time? She shook her head, hair flying about her face, dragged the brush backwards through it, hard, her neck straining.

I suppose that the trouble with me is that I find sex distinctly agreeable. I always did. Learned a lot too. So I am therefore an easy lay. With the right man. And bloody little future.

Who will take on the Widow Arlington and two growing children, female?

Clemency. Sharp little bitch. 'I heard his car. Vroom, vroom, vroom.' She knows perfectly well what's going on, and she equally knows that I have never defaulted under this hideous roof. And never would.

She threw the brush onto the dressing-table, unzipped her jeans, undressed.

If I'd married Jon and not Hugo. Play games. What would I be like now? Tweeds and amber? Hardly fair. Anyway not suitable for the south of France. Probably a white shift, espadrilles, a straw hat, painting earnestly in a cool whitewashed room.

She pulled back the untidy bedclothes, smoothed the bottom sheet roughly, got in. I forgot the breakfast things. I could have cleared the table, put out the bowls, the cornflakes, the coffee things. She reached out and took up her travelling clock, set the alarm for six thirty a.m. I told Jon far too much: talked up a storm. That warm, caring voice, I suppose. It's good to have someone to listen. No harm done, except to bore him witless. Poor Jon. One of life's eternal victims. Why did he think that I liked peppermint creams?

Oh, Clemency! I hope you'll never know rejection. That staggering moment of shock when you suddenly realize that you no longer appeal sexually to the man you adore. That you are suddenly 'a wife'. To be served. Occasionally, casually, as in some veterinary

47

gesture. No tenderness. Like a cow. Loving someone is no laughing matter, my darling. It's a matter, too often, for tears.

Jonathan

The Pigalle Suite, on the sixth floor, looked north across the ugly city towards the Santa Monica mountains: a ridge of scabby pumice-stone swelling up from a sea of two- and three-storey buildings and a mass of telegraph poles. It looks, he thought, from here anyway, like one of those shanty towns they built for a gold rush. Beyond them, and only really visible on a smogless day, the high barrier of the San Gabriel mountains, a protecting arm holding back the ugly flood on the plain, bounded on the west by the Pacific.

Immediately below him on the wide street, a car salesroom built, for some unknown reason, with a Tudor façade. Leaded lights, little gables, beams and bricks. All the rest, stretching far behind, a flat concrete block. Beside it the multi-floors of a Bank of America's giant car park, the bank building itself a monolithic black glass box, up-ended. There was very little traffic, no one walking on the streets.

'Mugging,' the White Rat had said, driving him back from Brentwood up Wilshire Boulevard. 'Shit scared of being mugged. We got more violence in this town than Chicago, you believe that?'

'If you tell me.'

'I do.'

'It seems pretty quiet tonight.'

'It's early yet. Eleven thirty around ... they come out later.'

'Who do?'

'The niggers. Pardon me. Blacks.' He slowed down at a crossing; the lights were red. 'There's two things is wrong with this city.' The amber flashed, went to green. They moved forward, slowly so that he could concentrate. 'You know what they are?'

'No. Stranger here. I only got in a day ago ...'

'Stranger myself. From Oregon. Up north. It's blacks and Jews.'

'I had no idea.'

'Yes sir. The main problems. Take them away and we wouldn't

48

have none. Take the Jews, they got everything. Every fancy store on Rodeo Drive they got. You know that? Every movie got a Jew behind it somewheres; every TV show got its Jews. This city is all about movies and TV and music, you won't dispute that?'

'No I won't.'

'And all of the Jews are right in there behind it all. Even my own fuckin' agent, he's a Jew. All the fancy itty-bitty palaces in Bel Air, all Jews! Some places are restricted, mind you. But not so many. And medicine! *Sheet* man, all medicine is fuckin' Jews. I mean, take Frood, eh?'

'And where, then, do the blacks come in. Doesn't seem much for them left to take over?'

'They's about. The blacks are about. Creeping around every-wheres. Ever since Watts. You know about Watts in Europe?'

'Yes. We read about it.'

'Readin's different. They burned it down and then started goin' wild. Crazy wild. And the Jews up here! *Sheet* man! They scrammed outa here. They went off to New York or Palm Springs ... they was so scared they just cleared. Scared they'd be lynched.'

'I'm learning something every hour.'

'Plenty to learn, yes sir. You˙know Saks? The big store? Right. Broad daylight, see? Two blacks hit a woman with a wrench, she falls, they kick her, take her bag and run. Know what happins? *Nothing* happins. In broad daylight, the sidewalk covered in people, they just leave her, and she was screamin' ...'

'Why did they leave her?'

'Didn't want to get involved is why. That's this city. You've arrived in the Inferno. You better be warned.'

'I'm grateful. Aren't you playing tonight, Wayne?'

'When I get you off-loaded. We're right near. I had a real nice evening at my sister's, we had some chili and watched a movie. It was real nice. Relaxed. I go to work anytime I like. Just join the combo, mosey in, start fooling about for a little, get the feeling, start to play. It's good. There's your hotel ... we make a turn here ...'

The suite itself was predictable expense-account luxury. A long, low settee against one wall, customary twin tables at either end supporting twin lamps of no particular design, except that it was bad.

A circular coffee-table in the centre; a bowl of red apples, a knife and plate. 'With the Compliments of the Management.' Two bergère armchairs in fake stressed fruitwood, a desk under the windows, a blotter, telephone, jar of disposable pens. Walls covered in taut stretched fabric of no particular colour or pattern. Hot bran-mash, would you say? Hot bran-mash with little white daisies.

Three pictures, hung too high: the Moulin Rouge, the Arc de Triomphe, the eggshell domes of the Sacré Coeur. Lending a Gallic atmosphere to the room? Amazing. 'These are genuine hand-painted pictures. Copies may be purchased from the drugstore in the lobby ...'

Dominating everything, bran-mash and daisies, an immense television set. In the bedroom, twin American colonial beds. Blue hessian walls, another giant television.

The telephone beside his bed blinked urgently. A cyclopian eye. Scarlet, angry. He dialled 'O'.

'This is your Night Operator. May I help you?' A low, long-defeated, woman's voice.

'Room 701. Mr Pool. Jonathan Pool. The message light is flashing. Is there a message for me?'

'When the red message light is flashing, that is an indication that there is a message for you.'

'Could I have it then?'

'What room number is this?'

'Room 701.'

'Room 701. What name might that be?'

'Er ... the Pigalle Suite ...'

The woman cut in sharply. '*Your* name?'

'Pool. Jonathan Pool.'

'One moment please.' A pause. 'You are Mr Jonathan Pool in Room 701?'

'I am.'

'Right. I have it. At ten forty-six you had a message from Mr Andrew Shapiro ...'

'Ah. Yes. Ummm. Just hold on a moment, will you, I think I have that message.' He scrabbled through a small sheaf of yellow message-sheets in his hand. 'Yes I have.'

'You already have it? I only just came on duty. We have to verify

all messages. Our motto here is "Service and Our Clients' Welfare".'
She rang off. The red eye went out.

I'm in the Inferno all right. Christ. He looked at the messages
which he had spread across the made-down bed. All from Mr
Shapiro who, it would appear, had telephoned him every half hour
since six thirty. The final one read, 'Expect you breakfast tomorrow
seven thirty a.m. Cordially.'

It was already after midnight. He knew that he wouldn't be able
to sleep: jet lag had finally slammed him with a face like a Francis
Bacon portrait. If I try to sleep I'll wake in an hour, starving.

He got up and went to the bathroom. White tiles, stacks of towels,
a paper strip across the lavatory seat. 'This has been made hygienic-
ally clean for you ...'

They must all be barking mad! I've got indigestion from that
bloody awful soup whatsisname made. No wonder he finished the
brandy. Two Alka-Seltzers in a glass of cloudy tap-water. He
watched them fizz, rise, fall. Stirred them irritably with the handle
of his toothbrush, winced at the taste of recycled chlorinated water.

At the sitting room window, looking down across the night city;
the outline of buildings, a scattering of lights. He pressed his forehead to the glass. Below, a car screamed past, lights flashing, sirens
howling. He removed his jacket, slung it over a chair, lay flat on the
long settee. Beyond the net curtains, somewhere across the city, a
pink sign winked HARRY'S EATS! On. Off. On. Off. He started to
doze. The air-conditioning throbbed. The way she shakes her head,
the hair falling about her shoulders, tossed behind her ears. That's
the same. It was always that gesture which grabbed me. A form of
subliminal sexuality? I don't know. That hasn't changed; only my
attitude to it. And the eyes, those incredible eyes; now dull. They
never smile while the whole faces smiles. Not dull: that's hardly fair.
Dulled. Dulled with fading pain, as if hurt and secret distress had
washed them clean of joy. I wonder why? Arthur Sean Sproule.
Christ! *That* was a strange moment. Hugo Arlington the so highly
cultured; the writer of the most elegant prose of this century. Some
idiot critic said that. A number of them did. The Irish blood and a
touch of the blarney? And Arthur Sean Sproule killed himself?
Crashed deliberately? Why? The golden poet, writer of fine prose,
fleeing something which he was unable to face?

51

And Alice now: the sharp lines in the exquisite face, the tension in her throat and neck muscles. The coldness which has come with the onset of her personal winter. The dismissal of Avignon, and that night, by the remembrance of the meal. That was deliberate, of course. The determined refusal to accept guilt. Not a bad feat of memory, nonetheless, indicating that the dish was far more memorable than the event which had preceded it: a perfect put-down. Clever girl. I got it.

This was all Hugo's training, of course. He pulled her into shape, moulded, formed her in his likeness. More like twins, really, than man and wife. She accepted and absorbed his coldness, his arrogance, the points of view which were most particularly his own, his opinions: took them all in a strange chameleon-love. She literally, and obviously willingly, sublimated whatever her original mind had been to the one which suited him: taking all her colours from his. It was not altogether attractive to observe.

The first time we met, after the marriage, she seemed to be a radiantly ordinary, joyous creature. Gay, excited, ravishingly beautiful. The heavy golden hair, the open generous smile, the eyes which literally sparkled with delight at the thought that she had escaped from the mundanities of a Major-General's daughter who had suffered, as her family due, all the restraints on overt emotionalism and deeply restricted affections.

With Hugo she knew that she could let all that rip; and she did. What was so strange is that beneath the correct behaviour of her early life there must have always been a strong streak of amorality. Perhaps the word 'streak' is not quite right? A seed. A seed buried far inside, lying dormant, which began to shoot and to grow in the warmth of Hugo's demands: and knowledge. And the flower of carnality flourished. Making her more glorious, more exciting and, because she was his wife, more desirable as she was, apparently, unattainable. Anyway at first.

Hugo's bride. Hugo's wife. Perfect wife for an ambitious man, she helped him on his steady climb towards the Gods on whose right and left hands he was determined to sit. And in time it really was remarkable how one watched the transformation begin to take shape, how she managed, with that glowing and radiant smile, to step carefully, and ruthlessly, with elegant heel, on the fingers or even, in time, the faces of any of those who might pose any form of threat to her God. Unattractive, of course; but amusing to watch just as long as you yourself were fingerless and faceless. That was an asset.

Very possibly why I survived out of the hundreds who did not. I sat and watched with wonder from a distance; a faceless admirer. Safe, apparently posing no threat. And was despised by Hugo for those qualities. I know that. It amused me. The despising: his dislike was manifest, but overlaid with a casual acceptance that his wife liked me. I don't know why really. He never, for one moment, thought that I might like his wife. I never let it show.

On purpose.

The Safe Neuter, he once remarked. He never knew how deeply I disliked him. Never a single hint of that. Hated the pretentious prick from the first instant I met him, ages before, being lionized by his aficionados ... he was instantly aware of my lack of threat to him: I was the plebeian writer with no intellectual gifts, no pretentions to them either, smug apparently, comfortable, not worth the trouble of consideration. The Eunuch Scribbler was another of his name-tags neatly wired to my stem. I was perfectly safe to be left in the company of his wife. A kind nanny. He was certain that he had nothing to fear in any direction from me, whatsoever. Silly bastard.

I detested most of what he wrote. Admired grudgingly, because I really grew to loathe him, some. Never the bloody *Treblinka Trilogy*: that pretentious bit of sanctimonious twaddle which was simply an excuse to use every sexual expression known to man, every ugly word and deed, and collect them under the guise of Literature.

God!

Someone called it 'a Byronic exercise in its majesty'. Who the hell was that? Can't remember; but there were a lot who thought so. I mean, honestly, the rubbish they wrote, and write still. Byronic balls. Byronic in its turgid length, I give you that, and bulk. A kind of hard porn *Don Juan* if you can put *that* together. I know what I mean. Absolute obscenity in the most elegant, graceful poetry. Like antichrist sexual graffiti sprayed about Canterbury Cathedral. Something like that.

But from that cheating piece of bulk-nonsense the myth of Hugo

53

Arlington really began. The Greatest Lyric Poet. No matter what he wrote in future. That was the solid foundation stone. And it supported a rotten man; unsuspected. Woodworm in a slowly crumbling piece of self-construction. Arthur Sean Sproule! Stand up and be counted! There is no one else to do it, because Hugo Arlington didn't really exist.

He half rolled, half crawled, off the long, low settee; wandered in a wavering line to the netted windows, hands in rumpled hair. Blurring pinkly through the folds of draped nylon, HARRY'S EATS! On. Off. On. Off. In England it's breakfast time. About. Bacon curling in the pan; eggs with trembling yolks in fans of white, frilling at the edges. Fried bread sputtering. Fried bread! With mushrooms and bacon! God, I'd settle for just the eggs even so. Anything, anything. The time is all wrong, out of kilter. My gut knows the time better than my watch.

My watch lies.

'I'm simply starving,' she had said as they sat down. 'I warn you. No lunch. No time. Coffee for breakfast. Tell me, I must know, are you immensely rich tonight?'

'Tonight yes. Immensely. Anything you want.'

'You must be. Dining here.' She took an offered menu. 'It could be a whole horse. It's all so tempting. I don't think that they should put the price beside the course, do you? I mean for lady guests anyway. Terribly intimidating. Is that what I am? Your lady guest?'

'That's what you are. Mine. For the evening. That's why I'm immensely rich, you see.'

'Oh! Stuff . . . you really *are* idiotic.' She looked carefully down the menu, then back to him, tapping the large white card lightly against her chin. 'Really immensely rich, you said?'

'Really.'

'Then *longe de veau matignon en crôute* with artichoke hearts. I mean why not? When the cat's away the mice will play. Mouse, rather. Me. A starving mouse.'

The look of her, the scent of her, the laughter in her eyes, lightly mocking.

'Where is your cat, I ask myself.'

'You ask yourself, or you ask me?' Head tilted, lips in a Madonna smile, eyes narrowed now.

'You. But you needn't tell.'

'He's in Provence. Having a look at Mary Magdalen's pad. Did you know that she lived for thirty-three years in a cave in the South of France? Madly chic.'

'I didn't.'

'Somewhere called St Baume, near Aix. Well, not far. Angels led her to the cave and she sat there all that time, for years and years. A desperately boring thing to do, I'd say.'

'What did she do there?'

'Shouldn't we order? Please? I'm really famished. Altogether famished. Do catch a waiter's eye.'

He did, and ordered.

'You learn the oddest things, I suppose, from your Lyric Cat? But tell. Come on. What did she do in her cave?'

'Prayed and meditated. Poor bitch.'

'All the time?'

'That's what it says in the books. It does seem a bit excessive, but after all she had quite a deal to meditate on, hadn't she? All that grisly past of hers, then joining the Leader and casting aside her gaudy raiments, or whatever. Her wickedness, sins I suppose? Would *you* call them sins? Then the Crucifixion and all, and then, my dear, the Resurrection! I mean that must have been quite a moment, mustn't it? Enough to make you think a bit, wouldn't you say? I suppose, you know, she was the first groupie ...'

He was laughing, his hands clapped over his ears. 'You are disgraceful! Alice, you say appalling things. It's blasphemy!'

'I know. But look here, work it out in today's currency. What else was she? She trailed about all over the place with Him while He was doing his miracles and washing feet and so on. She had a brother called Lazarus, don't forget, and he'd had a bit of a surprise, let's face it, and then when it was all over, and Pilate had done his elegant bit of hand-washing, she went off and shacked up with the Virgin. I mean, I ask you!'

'You are an extraordinary creature. You are as wicked as hell ...'

'I have never denied that. But, Jon, she *did*! I mean, you laugh at me but it's the truth. It's history. Gospel, you might say.' She laughed suddenly, a low, caught sound, reached across the table and took his hand in both of hers. 'How funny it is. How strange. I *do* laugh with you. I wonder why? You bring out all the worst in me I suppose.'

'I wish that I could believe that. Wish that I could see it. Where is St Baume? Near Aix, you said?'

'Somewhere near. I'm to call Hugo there on Sunday. He'll be through by then. He's presently following in the footsteps of the lady with a little notebook and a camera. Likes to do his Wander Research by himself now. Absolute commitment, he says. Writes up his notes by candlelight of an evening. Or something.'

'Deadly serious.'

'Deadly. About work.'

'I'm going down on Thursday.'

She looked up sharply. She had been spooning salt into little hillocks across the tablecloth, brushed them aside with the flat of her hand, took up a pinch and threw it over her shoulder. 'To Provence? To your house?'

'Driving down.'

'Where is it, I forget. Near Aix?'

'No. But I have to go through Aix. I could drop you off . . .'

'Thursday? No, it's madness . . .'

'Spur of the moment stuff. Better than a boring old telephone call isn't it?'

'I do rather love your car. It's terribly tempting . . .'

'We wouldn't need to hurry. Stop off somewhere pleasant, calm. Good food, good wine.'

She was smiling her agreement. 'Where? You know somewhere simply splendid?'

'Well. Look here. What would you say to the Ritz? Paris. Thursday evening?'

She had bent her head over another little hillock, brushed it flat, looked up at him. 'Say? I'd say, well, "Good evening, Ritz." And . . . Friday?' She carefully spooned out more salt, swept it away, took a pinch, threw it over her shoulder, brushed the cloth clean, folded her hands, one on top of the other, wedding-ring glinting.

He balanced a fork carefully across his index finger, watched it swing gently.

'*Avignon?*'   *

56

HARRY'S EATS! On. Off. On. Off. He turned away from the draped windows abruptly. All gone. All gone. The past. And not a thread of it remains. Now. A ghost laid. To hell with the yearning, passionless years. The Best Friend, the Standby, the Extra Pair of Trousers when she needed her table completed, the patronage from Hugo; all gone. As if it had never existed.

Those slender fingers fixing an idiot yellow ribbon. That simple gesture, those dark eyes, doused the guttering candle of my waiting years.

'You *have* won something!' she said. It was not a question: a statement.

I'm pretty certain about that. And I have fallen deeply, irrevocably, in love. How curious!

He dialled Room Service and ordered a full breakfast.

Nettles and Lea

'Everyone seems to light fires in this extraordinary place. I can't imagine why,' said Nettles, switching on lamps in the high-ceilinged white room.

'Because, my darling, this is a desert coast. Clammy. Sea fogs. Desert nights. It's not the tropical haven they all pretend it to be. Anyway not in January.'

'It's certainly not that,' he said. 'And you have lit a very attractive fire. Better than poor Alice's effort. That black cavern full of scorched logs. Too unattractive.'

Lea knelt back, hands on her thighs. 'You must admit I make a good fire? Do say so? Lovely birch logs and an extremely helpful gas burner. The whole thing is a fake of course, like the city.'

'A very pretty fire,' said Nettles, settling into the fat plumed cushions on the metal campaign bed which served as a settee in this pleasing house. 'I'm seeing, and feeling, the point of the business now. Birch logs. Imported, I imagine? They so remind me of poor Irina, all that Russian stuff. Very *Cherry Orchard* and all the rest of it.'

Lea got up, brushed her skirt, put the matches on a table. 'A whisky nightcap? Or brandy?'

'Nightcap? God. Are you about to stay up all night? It's after twelve already.'

'Not all. No. Just a part of it. You'd better have a brandy after that odd soup, and all the brandy you drank after dinner.'

'Self-defence. That strange fellow was pouring it out like milk. Yes, a brandy.'

He heard her clinking about among bottles and glasses, singing softly to herself. A sound which he was instantly aware that he would miss dreadfully, should he not be able to hear it. The soft, involved, preoccupied singing of Lea. But she was here. Close. With him.

He lay back comfortably in the flickering light. An odd place. Odd people in Los Angeles. Wonderfully kind. Needing kindness too. The rag-tag-and-bobtail –whatever did that really mean?– of the human race packed together in an area of two hundred square miles facing the grey Pacific, why did I always think it would be blue? With their backs to a desert.

The only things that were indigenous to the place were the rattlesnakes and the coyotes. Everything else was imported. From the gin to the palm trees. Even the smog. What can it have been like when the first Spanish invaders saw it and called it the city of the angels? God knew.

He had rented the house, at the start of his term of office at the Beekmann University, lecturing on Early Roman culture and litera-ture (on the strength of two academically important books: one on Pliny the Elder, the other on Catullus), from a charming and highly civilized woman writer who had, with great acumen, he thought, decided to let her house and move East to Connecticut for the winter. 'I just can not deal with Santa Claus *and* Florida palms,' she had said, and charged him a modest rent.

Perhaps, he thought, looking about from his plumed depth, it was a trifle feminine? Rather a lot of frills to the pillows, patchwork quilts, stump-work pictures on the walls, glazed-eyed French dolls lying about here and there, and a sight too much gingham at the windows. Nevertheless it was welcoming, and he was comfortable, and it suited him perfectly, and with the added charm of the contained courtyard outside, which he shared with five or six other householders whom he hardly ever saw, he considered himself more than fortunate.

He might, although he was eternally grateful that he was not, have been living in a college, instead of behind a high brick wall on Twentieth Street, Santa Monica, California. A don.

All it lacked, really, were the reminding bells from countless steeples at dawn and at sunset, and at moments throughout the day. On the other hand, at the age which he had managed to reach in comparative comfort, he was perfectly happy not to be reminded that time, his time, was passing. Uncomfortably quickly.

Lea came back, gave him his drink, took her own and sat on a cushion beside the elegant small mantelpiece of French marble.

'I was just thinking how ineffably pleasant it is here,' he said. 'Especially in your company.'

She bowed her head with grace. 'Thank you.'

'I was also thinking that I felt a little like a don. Do I look like one? Oh dear God! These grey hairs add *such* distinction to one. But there is an atmosphere here of, I don't know ... in this little courtyard, college bells, matins, evensong, chalk and ink, mortar boards. Does that sound complete rubbish? Or merely like shorthand?'

'Shorthand. Your sort. But I understand that. I should do after twenty-odd years. I see what you mean. It's Rupert Brookish ... Grantchester and so on ...'

'Dreadfully overrated, Grantchester.'

'You mean the poem or the place?'

'Well both, sadly. It is always very regrettable to lose one's illusions, even at my age.'

'I lost mine, about all that I mean, the day I went there. Filled with flowery thoughts and longing to tread hallowed earth. All I can remember now is that there was no sign of tea, let alone honey, a sullen woman pushing a pram in the rain and a telephone box. My Grantchester. Dreadfully, sadly, crushing.'

'Oh, crushing indeed.'

'But I know what you mean about this place. Secret, shut away. Little brick paths, snapdragons and roses. Do you feel donnish or really monkish?'

'Neither. Thank God. I feel me. Nettlish.'

59

'I'm very glad indeed to hear it. Beyond the wall is so incredibly strange. I haven't come to terms with this place, even after a month. All those flabby young men jogging along Santa Monica Boulevard. Do you remember that first time I saw them? With Alsatian dogs on leashes! I was staggered.'

'To defend themselves from muggers.'

'I thought they were being kind, of course. Tender-hearted nitwit. Those silly little shorts, the pot bellies, sweaty tee-shirts, puffing along with a huge dog on a leash! The whole place is, shall we say, bewildering?'

'I beg you to forgive me, Mr Nettles, if I say that the whole situation is, well, shall we say, bewildering?' Miss Brace had said, twenty years ago.

A tall, comfortable, big-boned woman; good ankles, good shoes, a well-cut flannel suit, small amethyst clip on the left lapel, pleasant smile. A good person. Behind her at the desk in her study, a flock of distant schoolgirls playing lacrosse, a wind whipping the last yellowing leaves from a trail of wisteria swinging and twisting against the leaded lights of the study window.

'Madness, I would venture, Miss Brace. But what does one do otherwise?'

'She's only ten, you know.'

'I am well aware of her age, I assure you.'

Miss Brace poked a sharpened pencil into her blotter. 'I mean, Mr Nettles, do you know anything at all *about* ten-year-old girls?'

'Nothing,' he said. 'But I will learn.'

She looked at him with a vague suggestion of helplessness. Miss Brace was not a helpless woman, but here, for once, she felt she was fast approaching that state. 'Of course,' she said, hurrying a little in her speech, 'I do see that it is a cataclysmic experience for her, poor child. I mean to lose *both* parents in one go!'

She spoke, Nettles thought, as if she were talking about a coconut shy at a fair. In one go.

Rooke swerving, as he would of course, to avoid a dog on a wet road, and he and Emmie crushed to pulp, and burned, under a too fast petrol tanker.

Cataclysmic all right.

60

In one go.

'Well,' he said, crossing his legs and leaning back in the hard chair opposite her, 'I made a very strict promise, as her godfather, to follow all the rules at the time of her christening. It was not my first attempt. Or theirs. There was an earlier child who died when he was four months. I believe they call that form of death a cot death, am I right? Anyway it doesn't matter now. But I am not a religious man, never have been, and I never pay much attention to all that mumbo-jumbo vicars use as their stock-in-trade.'

'Really?' said Miss Brace.

'Yes. Really. But I listened to the man and I promised to do all that I could, should the time, or need, arise, to care for her, bring her up in the Faith, and all that sort of thing. I made a personal vow, Miss Brace, to myself that I'd stick to the rules and do everything to protect, love and guide Lea Emily Rooke. That's what I am here to do today.'

'I think it is splendid of you,' said Miss Brace and meant it. 'But you know, a child, at this tender age especially, needs a mother's love.'

'Well, she hasn't got one, has she? And I'm not about to alter my sexual status to accommodate that need. She'll have to put up with me as I am.'

Miss Brace smiled politely. 'Normally, you know, a married couple is preferred to a single parent. I mean you *must* see that?'

'I *mustn't* see it at all. She is mine. Left to me in both wills. Now look here, Miss Brace, there is nothing that you and I can do about it. I was willed the child. I am expressly charged with taking her and bringing her up as my own. I loved both her parents keenly, I miss them quite appallingly. I shall do everything that I conceivably can to help repair this most grievous loss which she has had to suffer. We know each other, and we like each other ...'

'A difference, I think, Mr Nettles, surely between liking and loving?'

'Of course there is! Do you think that I am unaware of that fact? The loving comes a little later, that's all.'

'And there are no other relations? No, well, aunts ... uncles? Married couples with families?'

'There are none. Two doodly uncles of Rooke's somewhere in

Suffolk, and an aunt who is at present climbing in the Upper Himalayas. She has a Swedish lady friend. They live together, in extreme discomfort, in Simla.'

'I see,' said Miss Brace, and snapped her pencil in two.

'Mr and Mrs Rooke were both orphans. There is no family, as such, on either side. Mrs Rooke's were massacred, as far as I know, to a man, by the Japanese in 1943.'

Miss Brace, who had by now more or less collected her wits, collected her broken bits of pencil, and put them in the wastepaper basket, threaded her fingers, laid them calmly on the top of her desk. 'Now look here,' she said briskly. 'We really aren't here to discuss all this. Lawyers and judges and so on have done all that, as you are, I am sure, only too well aware. There is no question, Mr Nettles, that Lea Rooke is your responsibility. For as long as you, and she, may live. I do, most sincerely, wish you luck. It is a tremendous responsibility, and naturally I will do anything that I possibly can to help. She is, I assume, staying on here at Branstoke Park?'

'So long as she is happy here.'

'That she is, and most popular.'

'And I can afford the fees.'

Miss Brace allowed herself to look about her desk, rearrange a pottery jar of asters with some attention. 'I think that would be very wise,' she said after a moment. 'She is an industrious child. Very, shall I say, precocious, in its pleasantest sense. Precocious. Yes.' And then she decided to look him straight in the eye. 'Young girls of her kind mature rather more quickly than our children.'

'I don't follow you?'

'She is, I think, of mixed blood?'

'Her mother was Eurasian. Dutch and Indonesian.'

'Exactly. That is what I mean. I imagine that, like all men, you are really not fully acquainted with the ... er ... complex development of the female body? Am I right? I speak of nature's little tricks, you understand?'

'If we are speaking of menstruation, then I can't say that I have been privy to the phenomenon every day of my life: no. But I do know that it happens, and why. I had two sisters, Miss Brace, one of whom was so distressed by the awareness of her breasts that she bound them tightly down with a damp towel and hid in a wardrobe,

62

defying anyone to come to her aid. I know what happens, I assure you. I am very well aware of life in general, I am also an historian. Ancient Rome, Miss Brace, was not sparing in its detail, nor was it Branstoke Park.'

'I beg your pardon. I simply wanted you to be aware that Lea is, well, precocious. But we'll jump that hurdle when we get to it.'

'We have quite a number of those, I fear.'

'Yes, indeed,' she said lightly. 'But I am certain that if we all pull together we'll get safely under sail.'

Goodness! thought Nettles, how she mixes her metaphors. I suppose one really can't blame her. It must be the first time she's ever had to deal with a situation exactly like this. Most irregular, poor woman. He started to rise from his chair. 'I really think that I must be on my way. I want to catch the four twenty-five if I possibly can.'

'No tea? Ginger snaps . . .'

'No, thank you so much. No tea. But I'd like to have a quick word with Lea again, if I might. I have something to tell her.'

'She's next door, with Miss Anstruther. I'll get her, and leave you in peace. Just give me a tap when you are leaving, and . . .' she suddenly put her hand on his sleeve, 'I really do mean good luck. It's a splendid thing that you are doing, and though it won't be easy, I don't think you'll regret it, in the end.'

'I'm certain I won't,' said Nettles, and watched her cross the pleasant panelled room, with well-concealed doubt.

Lea was tall for ten. She stood before him, hands clasped, long dark hair gleaming brilliantly in the autumn light, her eyes, Emmie's eyes, clear, perfectly set in a small oval face.

'My dear. You know the wallpaper you said you wanted? Cow parsley, that stuff?'

'Queen Anne's lace.'

'Queen Anne's lace, I can't tell a dandelion from a daisy, well, it's up! Your room is a bower of summer flowers, green and white.'

'And the curtains?'

'And the curtains. And all the pieces you wanted from home are there too. We've arranged them, Mrs Curtis and I, but of course you must change things about when you arrive.'

'Half-term is quite near.'

'That's when we'll do it. But I just wanted to tell you that, in spite of the quite amazing sloth of the English working man, the paper, *and* the curtains, are done.'

'Thank you. Super. Have you been talking to Miss Brace?'

'A long talk. She's worried, of course, that we'll have difficulties ... it's a very unusual thing for her to understand. You aren't an ordinary orphan, you see. Most orphans have some kind of relations, family. You only have me.'

'Do *you* think we'll have difficulties?'

'Well, impossible to say. We might, mightn't we? I mean, suppose you clobbered Mrs Curtis with a rolling pin? Or set the house afire?'

'Like Matilda?'

'Like Matilda! Matilda told such dreadful lies, it made one start and stretch one's eyes ...'

Lea laughed suddenly: 'And every time she shouted "Fire!" they only answered "Little liar!"'

'Absolutely correct,' said Nettles. 'And therefore when her aunt returned, Matilda and the house were burned.' He touched her hand.

'Well, you wouldn't do that, would you, after such a dire warning? And if we do have what you call difficulties, we'll talk them over, sort them out. That's the best way, isn't it? You must promise me that.'

She nodded, turned, looked out the window at the lacrosse game. 'Do you go away a lot? Travel to places?'

'I? Go away? Well not a lot. Sometimes of course I have to. Research, you know ...'

'I mean, actually what I mean, is that when you do, and I'm not here at school, would I be left alone? Except for Mrs Curtis, of course. By myself, in the flat?'

First dangerous corner, thought Nettles, and to his amazed delight he heard himself reply with a firmness which astonished him. 'If I go away, and it's out of term time, you'll come too, understand? You won't be left alone ever, unless you want to be.'

She turned quickly from the window. 'I don't.'

'It's just that some people do. They like to be alone, have their moment of privacy, you know?'

'Yes. But I don't want that. I wouldn't be a nuisance, I promise you. I'd be very quiet.'

64

'Darling girl, I have lived a very lonely, quite empty life. I am very, very grateful that you have accepted sharing it with me.'

'Well I didn't really accept, did I? I was left to you, wasn't I?'

'But you *have* accepted, I hope? I mean that would be awful for me if not?'

'Oh no! I accepted. I just meant that perhaps I am a trouble to you? If you want me, if you really mean it'll be all right for you, that's what I want too.'

'I want you tremendously. How will that do?'

'Very well. I can kiss you, can't I?'

'I should hope you will,' he said, and suddenly found that he was holding her body between his arms, her head buried tightly against his jacket, and that she was weeping hopelessly.

He held her to him tightly, rocking her gently, waiting for the tears and the pain, which she had held contained for so long, to flood away. He realized suddenly that for the very first time in his life he was actually holding someone in his arms who desperately needed him: might even want him to need her in return. He felt richness flood him, and bent his head so that his lips kissed the soft, tumbled black hair. He was suffused with joy. This small creature, the union of the two people he had most loved in the world, and who had loved him in return, was his. He had a long way to go, a whole life to re-plan, enormous problems, possibly, in the future, but nothing could alter the fact that for the very first time, after years and years of searching, he had found love and was loved with equal intensity. And that the love would endure. He'd see to that, no matter what the cost. Emotionally.

He squatted down, pulling her between his knees, holding her arms to her sides. 'Don't bend your head, you silly child. Don't try to hide the tears. They have to come, *have* to.'

She mumbled something, tried to raise a hand to brush her face; he held firm.

'Now look at me, be brave! Come on ... goodness! So much dribble and nose-run! You are quite disgusting!' He took the hand-kerchief from his breast pocket and wiped the ruined face before him. 'There. That's better. Frightfully good thing to be able to cry like that. I never could, just sulked. Or anyway people thought I was sulking. I think you'd better blow your nose, it's still running like a mountain stream.'

She tried to laugh, hiccupped, wiped her eyes.

'Blow your nose, woman!'

She did.

'And again. You can keep the handkerchief. I really don't think it's up to my pristine style now, do you? Cost the earth. Pure silk. Never mind, stick it in your bloomers.'

She shook her long hair back, her eyes red with tears, her lips attempting to smile, and then she suddenly threw her arms round his neck, burying her face in his shoulder. She murmured something, smothering it in the fabric of his jacket.

'You'll really have to do better than that, my dear. Can't hear a word you say. Mumble, mumble, mumble. Now come on. Out with it.'

She raised her head, but still held him; looking away. 'What shall I call you?'

'That's a frightfully good point. We rather forgot about that the last time I came down, didn't we? Well, what do you want to call me?'

'I don't know.'

'I see. Uncle is out for a start, if you had that in mind. I simply refuse to pre-age myself. And I so dislike my own name, Geoffrey, don't you? I don't feel a bit like a Geoffrey. Do you think so?'

He felt her nodding against his cheek. 'That's no answer. Do you, or don't you. You are being very unhelpful.'

'I don't.'

'Thank God for that. Would Nettles do? Just plain Nettles? Simple, straightforward, and I'm used to it.'

'Would it be rude?'

'Rude! Not in the very least, I'd be far happier if you did. You know some people, some exceptionally *uncharitable* people, Lea, say that I closely resemble the weed. Tall and stringy, with lots of little stings everywhere. Dreadfully unfair I think, but I am amazingly accustomed to it. Would Nettles do?'

She nodded again, hiccupped. 'Yes. If you don't mind. It's what they called you, isn't it?'

He held her very close. 'They did indeed! Absolutely right.'

She pulled away from him gently, releasing her grip round his neck, stood free of his arms. 'Then I will.'

66

'Excellent,' he said. 'I'm glad that we've finally got that on board.'

'Nettles,' she said cautiously, as if trying it for size. 'Nettles.'

'No,' he said. 'You were right. Obese young men everywhere jogging with Alsatian dogs, police sirens all night, rape and pillage all over the place, women shopping in curlers, quite unashamedly, even in the smartest places. Bewildering. I don't think that I'll ever get used to it, although people say one does. In time. Incredibly! After six months here trying to pump the rudiments of Roman culture and literature into classes which closely resemble a gathering of milk-fed hogs, I can't find it in my heart to agree. What a future! Half of them stuffed to the gills with cocaine, the other with junk-food and ice cream. I really know that my time is up. It was like digging the Panama Canal with a coffee spoon.'

Lea laughed, swivelled round on her cushion to face him, cross-legged, her arms in her lap, hands holding her glass. 'I think I'll be glad too. But it's been tremendous. And thank you. Thank you for a holiday beyond dreams.'

'Couldn't bear being all on my own for loathsome Christmas. Thank you.'

'No, but listen. Where on earth can you see an aquarium as vast as Marineland or a cemetery like Forest Lawn with a scaled-down, fig-leaved Michaelangelo *David*, piped Debussy, and "Where Love Lies in Beauty" as its motto! Where else!'

'Nowhere, thank the Lord,' said Nettles.

'I think it's all rather marvellous in a way. A huge Disneyland with real people.'

'Ah! I wouldn't be too sure about that. Unreal people. Not real. It's all quite desperate. People searching for identity, for roots, but at the same time destroying their individual pasts irrevocably.'

'They didn't seem like that tonight. At Alice's supper.'

'Well, we were all displaced persons there, weren't we. Russian, English, her Yugoslav lover. I think only that odd creature, Sybil Witt, was American, and if you scratched her I'm sure you'd find a Latvian, Estonian or Bulgarian underneath the fixed face, the fixed nose, the Anglo-Saxon name, the straightened hair and the

67

cosmeticized teeth. Don't you love the word? Extraordinary. Imagine poor Fowler here!'

'You are too cruel by far. I quite liked him.'

'You bewilder me. Whom did you like? The Yugoslav chap? Fowler?'

'Pool. Jonathan Pool. I was sitting beside him.'

'Ah yes. Good writer, I'm told. Very popular.'

'He didn't bring his wife, I gather.'

'I didn't know that he had one to bring.'

'Oh.'

'Are you relieved?'

She looked up at him in surprise. 'Relieved? Why? Now why should I be relieved?'

Nettles leant forward, elbows on knees. 'You're giving a perfectly appalling performance, you know.'

She turned away, putting another log on the dying fire. 'You really are rotten. I was only asking. Nothing important.'

'I know you, my child, far too well.'

'Well. Well, he was extremely pleasant. A very attractive voice, didn't you think?'

'I did. Do. I'd say he was quite good-looking too, wouldn't you. For someone in his early forties.'

'Forties?'

'Well ... somewhere about there. He won't see thirty-five again, that I know.'

'Forty. It's quite an age, isn't it?'

'Is it? Are you doing rapid calculations?'

'About what?'

'Age. You are thirty and he's about ten or eleven, maybe twelve years older. If you are anxiously considering if he would be suitable or not, I'd say that he was ... and that once he gets over his jet lag, or whatever it is, he might prove to be intelligent, too. Now what more can I say?'

'Nothing,' she said. 'We must go to bed. I was curious, that's all. Can't a woman be curious?'

'Not without motive.'

'God, you are a bastard to me.'

'Well, go carefully. I have to confess that most of your gentlemen friends have been pretty much of a dead loss, haven't they?'

68

'Dreadful. I'm a bad picker. Always have been.'

'Your last wild madcap fling with –what's his name?–Donald Upcroft-Williams, was beyond any comprehension.'

'He was very rich, very attentive, and kind.'

'A third-generation grocer with a Wilson knighthood. Madness.'

'Snob. Ghastly snob, you are.'

'If you mean, by being a snob, that I only like the very best ... of everything ... then I cannot contradict you.'

'A house in Wiltshire, flat in Eaton Square, glorious villa in Marbella ...'

'With, one imagines, a cocktail bar in every lounge, and a Jacuzzi in all the playrooms. God almighty!'

'I'm not going into all that now. It's done anyway.'

'Well, frankly, I think that Pool isn't half bad. You looked very pleasant together. Well matched.'

'Nettles, we are not a pair of book-ends. And I wasn't even thinking on those lines. But I did like him. Anyway, he's staying here, and we are off to Europe. So that's that.'

'He said only a week or so. Got a book someone wants to buy. Or has bought.'

'Oh.'

'Yes. Oh. That's stopped you in your tracks.'

'I just said Oh.'

'If I were you I'd arrange a little meeting, perhaps, before you go. And as soon as he comes out of his Atlantic trance. Somewhere easy, not dinner ... that leads on to struggles, as you know. A drink? Tea? Try lunch ... you can always get away after a lunch, hairdressers, dressmakers, dentists ...'

'Arranging my life again? I've already made a little arrangement. We're lunching at Ma Campagna tomorrow. So.'

'Splendid locale. You won't hear a single word you address to each other. It's like a cage of macaws. Claws, beaks, feathers. The claws are well in evidence.' Nettles got up stiffly, put his glass on the table before him. 'I'm off to bed. I do find dispensing wisdom exhausting. And all that wretched Yugoslav's brandy ...'

'It was Pool's actually.'

'Far too much, and I want to watch the Inauguration tomorrow ... shall I leave you here?'

'For a moment,' she said. 'Until this log goes. Time for reflection.

'Reflect well. Not unhappily.'

'I won't.'

'I gathered, from Alice herself, that Jonathan Pool was married some years ago to a quite tiresome girl called Deborah who now breeds ponies on Exmoor, or somewhere like that, that they were divorced, and that he has been deeply in love with Alice Arlington for a thousand years. Hugo put up with him because he was safe and often useful. That, just to round off the evening.'

She turned and looked down the room towards him, one hand running fingers through long hair. 'Thank you. I'm obleeged, sir. But I have a feeling that perhaps he is no longer in love with the Widow Arlington.'

'Oh?'

'He suggested that a ghost had been laid, this evening.'

'A disagreeable turn of phrase. Did he mean poor Hugo? Poor dead Hugo?'

'No. I have a feeling that he meant Alice. Poor live Alice.'

'Extraordinary thing to say. Can't work that out at all, can you?'

'I can have a damned good try,' she said. 'Can't I?'

Irina Miratova

Irina Miratova closed her front door with extreme caution. She had done so for many years, ever since someone had suggested that a good slam would bring the whole house down around her ears and spill both herself and its contents into Santa Monica Bay below.

When she had first arrived in California the house, a strange wooden building with gables, a fretwork verandah and a high brick chimney stack, had stood comfortably on the cliffs with a modest yard before it and a run-down, but quite large one, at the back. Years of storms, torrential rains, and the enlarging of the coastal road below had eroded the cliff in time so that the house presently stood almost at the edge; much of the yard at the back had long since slithered into the sea, and the winds rattled the unpainted shutters and clapboarding.

She had been warned, begged, warned again, to leave, but had stayed on. No mayor, no local authority, no priest (they had even tried religion at one time) could persuade her to budge, and so she stayed there, aware, as they were, that one day she would be tumbled into the sea and lost for ever.

At eighty-three, or about that (she really didn't know her exact age and had lost all her original papers leaving Russia in 1922 in a hurry), she didn't think that it mattered very much. She had had a long life, was in almost constant pain from arthritis, and felt that the sooner she went, really, the better. But from her own house, on her own terms. However, she was still cautious when it came to shutting the wide front door, or opening windows. There was no need to nudge fate. Death would come for her, in whatever manner, when it chose.

The high-ceilinged hall was shadowy in the dim glow of a single oil-lamp which stood on a small table in the centre, piled with books and dusty china cats. The light which it cast couldn't reach the first landing, which lay in darkness, but she was perfectly aware of the small figure crouched on the top step, its rimless eye-glasses glittering in a caught reflection. Carefully, methodically, she picked up one of the many china cats and blew on it. Hard.

There was a muffled cry from the crouching figure above.

'Dust, Mouse! Dust!' said Irina.

'Oh, Countess, you know you forbade me to touch them. I am so sorry.'

'All these things are covered in dust. Books, my cats ...'

'The front door, you see? It is directly in front of the table and every time it is opened and the wind blows ...'

'We get dust,' said Irina. 'I know. For over fifty years we have had dust.' She started to climb the stairs, holding firmly to the polished pine banister.

Mouse, who was four foot high if she was standing erect, which was seldom, servitude having given her a permanent crouch of humility, switched on a light, and hurried down past her mistress to extinguish the table lamp below.

'Why are you not in bed?' said Irina, without waiting for an answer, for she knew that Mouse never went to bed before she arrived back from wherever she had been.

'To help you.'

71

'Help me!' said Irina. 'With what, pray?'

'Corsets,' whispered Mouse. 'Your corsets.'

'Ah yes. You are fortunate that at eighty-three, or are you eighty-five? I forget ...'

Mouse gave a little cry of distress. 'Eighty-one, Countess. Eighty-one only.'

'Well ... at whatever age you are, you are lucky to be so skinny, so meagre, so small and so weak that you do not need a corset to carry your frame. I am altogether different. Altogether.'

'Altogether,' agreed Mouse, preceding her mistress along the landing to her bedroom. 'Was it a pleasing evening, Countess? Gay? There was no sadness, I trust?'

'Why should there be sadness, tell me? Why?'

Mouse opened the bedroom door and crouched aside as Irina entered. 'It was so terrible when that golden man died. So suddenly, brutally ... and we had all been so recently together.'

She pulled a small padded stool into the centre of the room and stood deferentially aside as Irina lowered her ample body on to it, and then, with fingers as rapid and as curved as the legs of a scuttling crab, she started to unpin the ruin of the chignon on her mistress's head, removing, at the same time, a crumpled snake of cotton wool, wrapped tightly in dark net, which supported the handsome edifice of grey hair, and stuffing hairpins rapidly into the pocket of her dressing gown.

The result of the removal of this halo of support was surprising to behold. Irina never did so. For she looked as if she had suddenly been capped by a half-closed umbrella of thin, wispy locks, which stuck out about her shoulders like spokes.

'A long time ago, all that. They have put the sadness out of sight.'

'In only nine months or so? They've not forgotten so soon, surely?'

'*Not* forgotten. Put *out* of sight. Undo my dress and stop whimpering, Mouse, you are an over-romantic creature with too little to do. Time passes. You will know. One day.'

Mouse, with her scuttling, crab-like fingers, began unhooking the back of the flowing grey dress. 'Countess? I remember things very well, even if I am romantic. I do not forget.'

'Dust? On my cats? Hah!'

72

'We had such happy, happy times in this house when that splendid man came to call: there was such laughter! Have you laughed so much since! What pleasure. Do you remember the time in the cellar?'

'Papers to burn. Manuscripts. I don't recall.'

'He said that our cellar was the one advantage of this house. So useful! And with a real furnace, how worried we were that he would set us all afire! Do you remember? Standing out there in the yard watching the smoke come out of the chimney after so many years; little showers of black paper sailing out to sea ...'

She peeled the dress from Irina's shoulders and arms, revealing ageing, withered flesh wrapped in a surfeit of mixed woollen vests, encased in a once white corset. Her fingers started on the hooks which ran down the back, and Irina gradually started to spill from the steel frame of her support.

'Relief! Such relief!' She murmured as each hook was eased. 'Pride exacts a price. And I think it would be wiser, Tatiana Ivanova, if you remembered *less*. It is not always wise, or convenient.'

Mouse was momentarily stopped in her industrious efforts. The use of her formal name was a certain indication of displeasure; however, she bit a thin lip and went on with her task until the corset was quite undone, and removed it discreetly as Irina rose majestically in sagging bloomers and a multitude of vests and went towards the bedside-table where, ready for her on a tin tray, stood a half bottle of vokda, a glass, and three biscuits. She stepped over the tumbled folds of her dress.

'Dear Mousie. A tiny vodka after all my aches and pains. Why not? A teeny-weeny vodka!'

Forgiveness! thought Mouse. Forgiveness in the voice! And bemused with pleasure, her glasses winking, she hurried across the room to pour the vodka herself.

'Thank you, Mousie,' said Irina. 'Thank you. So delicious ... you are a good girl.'

Mouse stooped to pick up the discarded dress, hung it over her arm. 'But this I *must* remember, and you will not be vexed. Alexi Andreyev telephoned to say that he will be delighted to see you tomorrow in the drugstore of the Beverly Wilshire Hotel. At three precisely. I had to remember that, hadn't I?'

73

'The Beverly Wilshire? It's miles from here. How am I to get there?'

'Something else I remember,' said Mouse, smiling happily as she folded the panels of the corset together. 'He said that you were to take a taxi into town and that he would reimburse you. He said that he would be most happy to! Now! There's a real gentleman for you. Of the old school. A taxi! What a treat.'

Irina had finished half her drink. 'You may accompany me,' she said magnanimously. 'Not to the hotel, I do not want you there, but you can walk about and look at the shops. We need lavatory paper. Something else which you have *not* remembered.'

Mouse clasped her hands in a mixture of delight and distress, shook her tiny head from side to side like a metronome. She had very little hair, and what there was of it she had cut off close to her skull, with a narrow fringe, and dyed an intense black.

'Oh! But I am dismissible! I was economizing. We have paper napkins left over from one Christmas, do you remember? But I'll get it, I'll get it ... Oh! My blue? The beige ... what?'

'Decide for yourself,' said Irina, heaving herself onto her high French Empire bed which often reminded her of Charon's boat, except that it was square at both ends.

'Can I assist you, Countess? Your nightgown? It is here ...'

Irina took another little sip of her drink, lay back in thick pillows. 'I may very well stay as I am. Go to bed, Mouse. Plan your wardrobe.'

Mouse bobbed about the room anxiously, looking to see that all was secure for the night, that the long dusty curtains were closed tight against the morning light, and then she came over to the bed and, with the greatest courtesy, unlaced Irina's shoes, removed them, placed them with the corset reverently and silently in a cupboard, and hung the grey dress above them.

'I will go, Countess,' she whispered. 'I *will* remember the dust on your pussy-cats, but I *will* forget the golden man and the fire that day. I will forget all sad things and times, the Good Saviour knows that I do.' She touched a little icon on a chain at her throat. 'I remember only happy things.'

'Correct,' said Irina, who was mentally starting her long climb towards another level. 'But do not forget the lavatory paper. We are not peasants. Yet.'

74

'Countess,' whispered Mouse, and closed the door.

Irina lay quite still, eyes closed, her hands holding the half-empty glass of vodka on her stomach.

I will forget the golden man and the fire. What an idiot creature I have in my life. Why would she remember that? Like a child at a firework show, one can only suppose. Irina ... he spoke my name so beautifully always. You have the great advantage of an old-fashioned furnace ... everyone else is highly modernized. Where is one to burn unwanted manuscripts? Is one to throw them into the trash can, to fly about the streets of Los Angeles like confetti! That will not do. So I beg that you will let me use your invaluable furnace?

It was a modest bundle in a plastic bag from Bullocks, Wilshire. And after we had had our little glass, I went down just to rake through the cinders and be certain that there was nothing that could set the house on fire. Useless to ask Mouse. She is afraid of the dark, and the cellar ... but there was nothing there. Warm flakes of dead paper. So sad. So much work destroyed. It seemed so sad, so sad, so sad. A little fragment. A little fragment left; black and charred. Suede, with a date in faded gold ... 1979. A journal perhaps? Notes? So sad. All gone. Nothing left.

Slowly she reached for the vodka bottle and poured herself another glassful. It is one way of forgetting.

A teeny-weeny vodka for Irina. Who said that?

I did. So sad. Nothing is left. Those fragments, just fragments. All that is left of a life. But too late now. Too late. But the child was happy tonight, with her little ladybird bracelet. 'Ladybird, ladybird, fly away home: your house is on fire, and your children are flown.' Who was at the table tonight, Irina? Remember. Remember. We have tea with Andreyev tomorrow.

3

Inauguration Day

Andrew Samuel Shapiro, of Cristal Productions Incorporated, lived in a Cotswold manor house, set on a third of an acre of land on North Canon Drive, Beverly Hills, entirely surrounded by an eight-foot-high fence of iron railings, painted white, curving lethally outwards, at the top. It looked like a bear cage.

'*Sheet!*' said the White Rat. 'What is this! You got the right place?'

On the gates, a notice. 'No Cars. Sound Horn for Identification.'

'Sound the thing,' said Jonathan.

'I am just amazed, amazed.'

The front door opened almost immediately. A tall man stood on the steps dressed in black trousers and a black-and-yellow-striped jacket with the initials A s s on the pocket. He peered down towards them through the bars.

'I'm expected. Jonathan Pool for Mr Shapiro.'

'Sorry, sir, you'll have to walk,' called the tall man. With a British accent.

A buzzer went off; one of the gates slowly opened.

'Jeez! It's like a spook movie. What do I do? You want me to drive round the block a few times?'

'No. I'm staying for breakfast. We're going to see the new President on TV. How long does that last, do you know?'

'Not an idea. Maybe an hour.'

'Well, come back at eleven, if I'm not here in the cage just go round the block until I am.'

'Okey-dokey. Have a nice time now.'

'If you'll follow me, sir, Mr Shapiro is in the breakfast room.'

'You're English I assume, right?'

76

'Abingdon, Berkshire, sir.'

'Ever get homesick?'

'Not on this salary, sir.'

They went up the flagged steps, into the high, beamed hall filled with warming pans and hunting prints. In one corner a grandfather clock, in the other a rocking chair and a hunting table.

'Mr Pool,' announced the man from Abingdon.

The breakfast room was yellow and white. Andy Shapiro rose from a wing-backed Queen Anne chair, small hands outstretched. He appeared to consist of two spheres, the smaller being his head. 'Great to see ya . . . We had a good meeting yesterday, right? Jet lag all gone?'

'About. I slept a little.'

'Sit down,' said Andy Shapiro, indicating another wing-backed chair tightly covered in white velvet. 'I reckon you'll feel at home here, everything in this house is from your country. England. My wife Shirlee will be down directly, she collects the antiques, I do the galleries.'

'Very fine,' said Jonathan. 'I can see why you have protected yourself, fenced yourself in.' He looked along the row of obligatory French Impressionists.

'Those are my little pleasures. You like my Sizzly there? And my Brack? Great little painter, Brack. I got four of his. And over the fire here, see? Well, that is just my greatest. I bought it in Paris, France. Know what? Can you guess?'

'No,' said Jonathan truthfully.

'Twoloose Lowtrek. You know what? *Unfinished.* Died before he could finish it off. See the chalk lines? No paint. Isn't that just so moving? I think it is so moving. So does Shirlee.'

'You must have a king's ransom in here.'

Andy Shapiro giggled, clapped his hands. 'This is just the breakfast room. Wait'll you see the drawing room, and my den.'

'It's very impressive.'

'But I want you to know that I worked for it! Sure as hell did. When I arrived in this country I was age five. Know what my first job was? Cutting all the buttons and things off of the rags they shipped to the pulp-mills. Buttons and hooks and things. They foul up the machinery. That's what I did.'

'You've come a long way.'

'I sure as bloody hell have. Kiev. That's where.'

The breakfast was wheeled silently into the room by the tall man and two maids, chairs set around the table, which was placed so that it directly faced the television. The smell of coffee and something toasted was pleasing. And real.

'And now we will be watching the Inauguration of our new President. A memorable day for all America, and the whole Western world. Who else is there? Who has the clout? No one. Not in Germany, nor your country, nor France. Nowhere. Answer me that?' he added inconsequentially, and without waiting for one he instructed the tall man to inform Mrs Shapiro that she was late.

'She is already on her way down, sir. She was informed moments ago,' said the tall man the instant that Shirlee Shapiro arrived at the door.

'My *timing*! See, Daddy? Right on *cue*.' And turning to Jonathan, she said, 'I never was late in my whole life for a single cue ever. I was a dancer – I may not look it now, but I was really hot, really good, wasn't I, Daddy? Good?'

'Right,' said Andy Shapiro. 'This is Jonathan Pool. He wrote *The Familiars*.'

'Oh! Oh, of course! I'm so pleased to meet you, now come and sit down and have some chow. You sit between Daddy and me, Daddy at that end, me here. Can we all see the TV okay ... I don't want to miss one itsy-bitsy second.'

The television was on, without sound; people milling about on a cold day in Washington.

Shirlee Shapiro had had her face hauled up and dragged behind her ears so many times that the skin was drum-taut, and she was unable to smile; enamelled in ivory and peach, small blue eyes rimmed with heavy fur lashes. Her hair was an astonishing confection of golden loops and twirls, towering over her bland face like a cushion, and must once have graced the heads of at least ten novice nuns, judging by its size and weight. The hands were long, thin, bony, like those of a mummy, liver-spots showing through the white make-up, her nails crimson plastic, an inch long.

She wore too tight Pucci pants and a Hermès shirt which was dragged down from one shoulder by a giant diamond clip with an emerald centre, which matched the ring on her left hand; gold

78

bracelets hung heavily from both wrists, knuckle-dusters in weight, clonking and clanking against the porcelain on the table as she started the breakfast.

'Daddy and I just take fruit juice and yoghurt. But Arnold has a real traditional English breakfast all ready for you, isn't that right, Arnold?' Arnold admitted that it was, and started to serve Jonathan bacon and eggs and a toasted muffin, which surprised him. His surprise must have communicated itself to Arnold.

'A toasted muffin, sir. *Very* traditional, I would say?'

'Very. Thank you.'

'And we have sausages, sir, if you would . . .'

Andy Shapiro gave a shrill cry of terror. 'It's starting! It's starting! Arnold, get the damn sound on right this minute!'

Jonathan realized that his breakfast was lost. He dare not move.

'It's Ronnie! There he is! Oh Ronnie, I love you!' cried Shirlee, blowing kisses.

Andy grunted, 'Hold it Shirlee, hold it.'

'But he's for the *Right*, isn't he?'

'I'm trying to hear what's happening, Shirlee.'

'Well . . . I am too . . . and I'm for the Right. He looks so great!'

They listened attentively to the swearing-in of the new President. Shirlee, at the end of his speech, had pressed a yellow table napkin to her mouth; it was the nearest that her face would allow her to show emotion.

'His make-up,' said Andy Shapiro. 'Why did they finish it at his chin, for Godssakes? Looks like a turtle.'

'He looks just great. Inspiring. And there's *Nancy*! She's so damned smart, so neat! Everyone else in black, or dark blue, and Nancy in pink! . . . That's so *damned* clever; *she's* going to get noticed.'

'She will,' said Andy.

'Would you call that pink, Jonathan?'

'Coral perhaps? Bright coral?'

'She looks like a fire hydrant,' said Andy. 'And what's on her head?'

'At hat, that's what, isn't that the cutest hat you ever saw?'

'Looks to me like one of those French things you get for breakfast . . . hot . . .'

79

'A croissant,' suggested Jonathan,eyeing his congealed eggs and soggy muffin.

'That's what it is. You get them hot.'

'It's neat,' said Shirlee. 'So everyone can see her from *all* angles. Nancy knows all the tricks.'

'Betcha,' said Andy. 'Hey! What did he just say, that guy ... you talk too much, Shirlee ... did he say the hostages were going to be freed? That's what he said to the President? Did he say that? Christ!'

'I think he did ... I didn't hear properly,' said Jonathan. 'But that's what it sounded like.'

'We are seeing history in the making,' said Shirlee.

'But we can't *hear* it being made,' said Andy Shapiro, 'because you talk all the time.'

Arnold returned silently, removed Jonathan's untouched plate, replaced it with a new one under a metal cover.

'Very hot, sir,' he murmured.

Andy Shapiro took a long cigar from his breast pocket. 'That's what it is. They have released the hostages! It's fantastic! Two great deals on the same day. This is a solemn moment for the United States.'

'I beg your pardon,' said Jonathan as Arnold removed the metal cover to reveal a freshly cooked breakfast: without a muffin. 'But I think it is an unconfirmed report at the moment.'

'Maybe,' said Andy Shapiro. 'Maybe. But it'll be confirmed, you'll see. We don't get kicked around by no Ayatollah. Arnold, you can kill the picture, we seen all we need to ...'

'If there's a motorcade hold it!' said Shirlee.

'What's the big deal with a motorcade?' said Andy, lighting his cigar.

'That's where they'll have a shot at him. Remember? Kennedy and Dallas?'

'Who the hell is going to shoot Ronnie? They just elected him! He's the President!'

'Well, if they did, it would be in the motorcade.'

'Turn the damn thing off.'

The room was suddenly silent apart from Jonathan's knife and fork.

'I think that was really mean, Andy.'

80

'You're gruesome, Shirlee. Sometimes you are just gruesome.'

'Oh! You and all your big words. Didn't you get a muffin, Jonathan?'

'I'm fine with this, really. Thank you so much.'

'You get my messages I left at the hotel last night?' said Andy suddenly.

'I did indeed. I'm sorry. I was out.'

'It's fine. No problem. I just had some ideas about the script ... we can talk when you are through with that.'

'Did you go to a great party?' said Shirlee, looking anxiously at her lips in a small hand-mirror which had lain concealed beside her bowl of yoghurt. She flicked the tip of her tongue about like a basking adder.

'Not great. Just old friends. In Brentwood.'

'Brentwood?' Shirlee slid the compact under her plate. 'And where is Brentwood?'

'Well ... we went down Wilshire, then on to San Vicente, and then ...'

'I never been there,' said Shirlee.

'It's towards the ocean,' said Andy. 'Santa Monica, thataways.'

'You mean west of Sunset?'

'My wife,' said Andy heavily, 'does not know where she lives. Sunset Boulevard, honey, runs right through Hollywood: you know *that*. Then it comes along through here, Beverly Hills. Right?'

'And it *stops* right here.'

'It does not. It makes a turn north by the Los Angeles Country Club and then goes right on down to the Palisades.'

'I don't know that part. I never even been there. Anywhere after Beverly Hills is west. I don't go beyond that. Who lives in Brentwood anyway?'

'People,' said Andy. 'All kinds of people. Writers, painters, ordinary people, people in television.'

'Television!' said Shirlee, with withering scorn. 'What do I know about television people? We're picture people.'

'You finished?' said Andy to Jonathan.

'Just my coffee ...'

'Bring it with you, we'll go to the den, I got some ideas I'd like to kick around with you. We had a great meeting yesterday, right?

81

Very fruitful, constructive. I think we have something going for us with a truly great potential.'

'Television,' said Shirlee, getting to her feet, touching her piled hair with care to ascertain that it was still a part of her, 'television is the asshole of the business.' She put out a hand towards Jonathan, which he took.

Unable to muster any muscular expression on her enamelled face, she concentrated on a flashing of fur eyelashes which signified, for her, a smile of welcome and pleasure. 'And when Daddy and you are through with putting your heads together in the den, maybe we can fix a date for dinner here? A six or an eight or a twelve . . . you ask any and all of your friends from, uh . . . Brentwood . . . I'd be so *interested.*'

The den was pine panelled and full of buttoned-leather armchairs grouped about a vast partner's desk with a scarlet leather top, and a bank of five telephones. Red, green, ivory, blue and black. In the centre Jonathan saw his buff-coloured script of *The Familiars.* He also saw the Picassos on the pine walls.

Andy hustled himself behind the desk, took his seat in a swivel chair, pointed to one in front of him. 'Sit there, Jonathan. Right there. Good and close. Partners, eh?' Apart from the lonely script in dead centre, and the telephones, there was a brass student lamp with a green shade, a Lalique sea lion, and a small pot of artificial marigolds. 'Quite comfortable? You want more coffee?'

'Quite comfortable, thank you. No more coffee.'

'Right,' said Andy, and leaning over the width of the desk he addressed the small pot of marigolds. 'Okay, are we running, Ellen?' A green light flashed on the blue telephone three times. 'Now . . .' he sat back, clasped his small pudgy hands together. 'Well. Like I said, Jonathan, this,' he tapped the buff-covered script with one immaculately manicured finger, 'has a lot of potentials. I say this in the plural you understand: potentials, not potential. That's good, right?'

'It sounds good, yes.'

'But a lot, and I hate for to say this, Jonathan, has to go from this script of yours. A lot.'

'Oh.'

'As it stands, it doesn't.'

'Ah.'

'You see what I mean?'

'Um ... yes ...' said Jonathan. Who didn't.

'Now we had a great meeting yesterday, right. You, me, Don, Mel, Art ... they were very enthused, you could feel that, couldn't you?'

'Ummm. Yes.'

'A great bunch of guys. We've been together a long while. And Art got the Oscar for *Moonride* two years ago, we don't forget that easy. Right?'

'Right.'

'Well, thing is, after you left, after we had had that very constructive, very informative, ongoing discussion, we got to kicking things around, you know the way fellers do? We started taking it all apart.'

'I see.'

'Well, you have to take things apart to see if they'll go back together again.'

'And?'

'They didn't.'

'They didn't?'

'No. In this form, at this moment in time, as it stands at present, it is not of today.'

Jonathan shifted uneasily in his chair. 'It's only a first draft, you know? It's not a final one.'

'Shit! I know it's the first draft. I been in this business a million years, think I don't know a first from a final for Chrissakes? But it just will not do.'

'But yesterday you all seemed to agree that it would.'

Andy leant back in his swivel chair, swung a little to the right, a little to the left, his fingers to his lips in thought. 'Jonathan,' he said finally. 'Something you got to learn. Yesterday is not today. It is not tomorrow. It is *gone*.'

'Well, perhaps you can tell me where I've gone wrong ...'

'I can do that, sure. First. The title. *The Familiars*. It is confusing to an audience, what the hell does *The Familiars* mean?'

'A sale of sixty-five thousand in Europe, one hundred and fifty thousand in America, and a big paperback deal. That's what it means.'

'Look, I know it sold well. Why do you think we made a handsome offer for the first option? I know you're into paperback, but it is not a viable title for Americans.'

'It was for one hundred and fifty thousand of them. And a paperback deal.'

'As a book.'

'As a book.'

'People who read books do not, I repeat do not, go to the movies. If they went to the movies they wouldn't read books. Is that quite clear?'

'Almost.'

'So we all agreed that we will have to change the title, and for another we feel that the character of, what in hell is the girl's name, the one who gets the heebie jeebies all the time?'

'Rose?'

'Got it. Rose. We lose her.'

'Lose her? But she's the main character.'

'Lose her and make her someone different.'

'Different? Like what?'

Andy leant on his desk, hands still clasped, little eyes sparkling. 'Like a man!'

'A man!'

'Yeah. In one. Great chemistry. Don had this idea last night. Remember the Hitchcock movie, *Psycho*? Great movie. Made a cleaning. Now *he* used a man for the main character. Great innovation!'

'But Rose is a simple country girl who sees visions and ...'

'I already read the script!' said Andy, thumping it hard.

'But it wouldn't work with a man, honestly. A simple, peasant girl in Ireland ...'

'That's out too.'

'What's out?'

'Ireland is out. It has dangerous connotations here in America. We'd lose all the Irish, they'd boycott it if it was made in Ireland. There's a strong feeling about that country here and what your country is doing to it. Excuse me if I'm rude.'

'But Andy! It's not a political story! Nothing happens against Ireland or the Irish, they are the centre of the story for God's sake ... It *has* to be Ireland.'

'No. It does not have to be.' He winked knowingly. 'Haiti!'
'Haiti?'
'Don't you see it? We lift the whole story, reverse it, set it in the jungle, Papa Doc, and all the voodoo. I mean it's just there ready and waiting to be put on screen. And all those Tootoo Macoots, you know who I mean, the Secret Police, guys in black glasses, wonderful touches we get there. Menace.'
'It has nothing to do with the book.'
'Correct. Now look. We change books around in the movies. If they don't work for us we make 'em work. Our way.'
'But you're talking about Graham Greene ... he's already done it.'
'No, no, now don't get uptight with me, Jonathan, I never heard of this Graham Greene. Forget him. What's bugging you suddenly?'
'Why did you buy an option and why did you ask me to write the first draft of the screenplay?'
Andy unclasped his hands, studied his nails, counted each one to be certain they were still there, and that he had, perhaps, not grown another. He looked up at Jonathan kindly.
'Good manners, Jonathan. That's what. We liked the book, read the reviews, Shirlee was very, very high on it. She is my reader. I don't have time to read books, I read scripts and minutes, that takes all my time. But it had great reviews, she was very enthused, so we made the offer. If you will forgive me, every British agent gets ants in his pants when Hollywood makes an offer for the option on a book. They got a great respect for Hollywood. They want the most so they settle for a small financial outlay. We, frankly, buy cheap from British agents. They stand in line to sell us anything. See? And so we thought, hell, the guy who wrote the thing would be great at writing a first draft screenplay. Right?'
'Right.'
'But last night, after our great meeting together, after you had gone, Don and Art realized that it wasn't feasible. It doesn't work in visionary terms. So, well, we put our heads together and Art suggested a whole new outline. The voodoo, steamy jungles, this guy who is trapped with his visions. It is *irresistible* ... and you have to remember that Art won the Oscar just a few years ago, for *Moonride*, and that counts. He knows. He's the director after all.

85

We'll have lotsa mystery, fear, visions, so on ... it'll be a smash.'

'Well. It seems that I have wasted your time ... everyone's time.'

'Oh, Jonathan, don't *be* like that! This is movies! We just start in all over again; we got a good idea from you, we re-do it all over. Like the title? *Voodoo Death.* How's that? Of course it's only a working title right now. We have to try it on the distributors, they say that "Death" is death to the box-office. They need sex, but I don't see how we can work sex in, just at present. The Story Department are right this minute working on that.'

'Story Department?'

'We got eight great writers busy hammering at their typewriters on your story.'

'But it won't be my story.'

'You had the idea, didn't you? And we keep the priest, by the way.'

'The priest?'

'Yeah, this Father Whatever. He's good. We won't junk him. I would have suggested some time ago that Charlton Heston would have been terrific in the part, just terrific, but we do things a different way now. Know what? We feed all the data about the characters into the computer, plus – mark this – plus the names of the players we all think would be great for the parts, and the computer delivers its chosen list. That is what we use. The computer knows the bankability, and suitability, of every actor and actress in this town.'

'You mean you cast by computer?'

'That's what I mean. Today is today. Right?'

'So I'm out, I mean you don't need me any more?'

'Well ... I'd be glad if you just hung around town for a week. We paid a lot for this book, your work, the fare, you know, all the little incidentals ...'

'The fruit basket from Gourmet Heavens?'

'You got that? Great. Our little welcome to Hollywood and Cristal Productions. A snack if you got hungry, it was a courtesy, think nothing of it ... hope you enjoyed it anyways.'

'The processed cheese was like soap, the brandy was fine, the crackers were damp, and the wine tasted of piss, the apples of wet felt. Otherwise it was a sweet gesture.'

Andy looked startled. Unable to think of a reply he hurried back to the subject which he knew best. 'Just hang about until the end of the week, have some fun. We might want your advice here and there, maybe you'll come up with a great idea.' He cocked his head to one side. 'We get our money's worth that away, right? Business is business. Stay till we say. When are you booked out?'

'Sunday night.'

'We'll call you Saturday unless we call you before.' He got up from the desk, bent down to the pot of marigolds. 'Ellen? You got all that?'

The blue telephone blinked its fierce green eye three times.

'Great. Just cancel out Mr Pool's remarks about the cheese and the wine, right? Keep in his remark that it was a "sweet gesture" ... otherwise wipe it. "It was a sweet gesture", okay?' The green light flashed, Andy came round the desk, his little hand outstretched. 'Jonathan, it's been great talking with you. So constructive. Now I have to go and freshen up a little. I got Moses Steenberger coming along, know Moses? Great guy, he did *Ash Wednesday*, and we want him for another project real soon ... come and say goodbye to Shirlee ...'

She was sitting in the breakfast room at an enormous tapestry frame, to which was fixed a magnifying glass of some proportion, so that she could look at her work without wearing glasses. She pulled a length of thick wool thread upwards as they entered.

'Jonathan and I had a great time. Great conversationalist. Your car here?'

'He will be.'

Shirlee shook the hand which held the needle and thick wool in his direction. '*I* know where you were having your party!' she said roguishly. Or giving a near approximation of that.

'You do? That's clever ...'

'At Hugo Arlington's house. I didn't know he lived down *there*.'

'He doesn't. He's dead.'

'But ... oh yes ... I remember. Anyway it's in the *Hollywood Reporter*. You were with Sybil Witt, and Boris Kragujevac ... *very* international.' She stuck the needle back into the canvas. 'Sybil Witt is a supporter of Castro's, did you know? Cuba. She's nuts about Cuba.'

'Ronnie will get all that changed,' said Andy heavily.

'Oh sure! Ronnie and Nancy are *Right*, real Right. No gays no

Commies no Democrats. You should be careful, Jonathan, but of course you are a stranger in town, how would you know? But watch your step, honey, the people you mix with. It gets around. Fast. And that's not good. Things are going to change in this place. Now I know why I didn't know *Brentwood*! It's full of Radicals ... and Miratova was there? I mean it was all Middle Europe!'

'Alice Arlington is a very old friend,' said Jonathan. 'From England.'

'I remember: she was so upset when he got killed in that crash. Now I remember the pictures of her, she was upset, poor woman. Perhaps they were people *he* knew.'

'Who?' said Andy, starting to feel restless.

'That Hugo Arlington. He had some of the weirdest people around him. I mean weird.'

'They really didn't seem weird to me,' said Jonathan hopelessly, watching her stab the canvas, drag the wool towards the magnifying glass.

'Sybil Witt has to be weird. Has to be. She marches for nuclear disarmament, she's against the death penalty, she even went to that black's funeral, who was he Daddy? Martin Luther King ... she'll do anything. She even gives interviews about the dissidents in Russia. Now, if they don't like the Commie government how come they voted them in? She's weird. Talented, I agree, but weird. And now Cuba. The new chic thing, and they are right across from Florida! My momma stays in Florida ... I mean, I worry.'

She stabbed the canvas again and again. Andy, who had anxiously sat down (he found that standing for longer than five minutes fatigued him), suddenly got to his feet. 'Moses Steenberger must be late. He's always so punctual.'

'Moses is a darling man,' said Shirlee firmly, and turned suddenly towards Jonathan as if he had contradicted her, the needle raised aloft like a poisoned dart ready for throwing. '*So* darling. All his family were sent to that place in Poland, Auswich ... he has no one left.'

'I'm dreadfully sorry.'

'But he was very brave. Do you know that every week for three whole years he sent them a food parcel from here to that place. Candy, pineapple chunks, canned milk. God! He was so kind and brave. He gave them happiness before ... well, before those damned Polacks got them all.'

88

'*Germans*,' said Andy miserably, looking through the window.

'What's the difference?' said Shirlee. 'Only the name.'

Outside a horn sounded, Andy hurried from the room and collided with Arnold who was struggling into his striped jacket.

'Is it a baby-blue Rolls?' cried Andy, hands clasped.

'An orange Ford, sir,' said Arnold.

'That's mine ...' Jonathan turned to Shirlee. 'I'm leaving, Mrs Shapiro. Thank you for such a splendid breakfast, and the television and so on.'

'That's nothing. We were so happy you came. Don't you think the new title is just great? *Voodoo Death*. I hope they get to use that, and I think changing the girl for a man is a brilliant stroke of ... well ... it's brilliance.'

'I'm certain it will be.'

'It was very nasty of you to speak so badly about Daddy's little present to you. About the wine and the apples. That was not kind.'

'No, it was not.'

'We're booked clean through till Sunday, Jonathan. When did you say you fly out?'

'Sunday.'

'Oh. Too bad. That's real sad. But it was just darling of you to come this morning on such an historic day. You made it complete.' She turned back to her tapestry, and left him to go alone into the hall, empty except for Arnold.

'Mr Shapiro had to take an urgent ... telephone call, sir. He sent his regards.'

'Thank you. It's been a very historic morning.'

'Very. If you'll excuse me, sir, my grandmother used to say, "It takes all kinds ...".'

'Arnold, she was dead right,' said Jonathan, and hurried down the flagged steps to his orange Ford and the White Rat. *With joy.*

'Biff, bang, wallop, and finally slam!' said Jonathan. 'It really was the most extraordinary morning. A house enclosed in a bear's cage, literally. Breakfast while the President got elected in a room chock-a-block with Impressionists which would have made the directors of the Tate ill with envy, my entire script rewritten overnight by three hustlers – I met them and I know – and the whole business recorded on tape, while Medusa sat doing her tatting and listening to every word in another room.' He took a long drink of iced water. 'Then she gave me the choke-off for dinner because I made some ungenerous remarks about that God-awful basket the children opened at Alice's last night. Goodness! I *am* glad to see you ... be with you, away from all that.'

'Were you very uncomplimentary? About the basket of groceries?' said Lea.

'I was rather. Said the wine tasted of piss.'

'It did.'

'The cheese of soap.'

'Correct. The brandy was all right, though.'

'I said that. Anyway, I won't have to dine with them. I'll probably never see them again in my life.'

'But what about your script, book, whatever it is?'

'They took an option for a year. It's up in two weeks ... I'll do my best to block another, if it comes. Otherwise ...' Jonathan shrugged and stared up into the struggling vine above their table. 'This is a rum place,' he said.

'This place? Or Los Angeles?'

'Both really. Cultural shock, I suppose.'

'Good job we were given the worst table in the restaurant, stuck in a corner. We can watch and comment.'

'I hope we'll get fed.'

'They might forget. Possible. We aren't famous, you see.'

Jonathan looked out across the brilliant, chattering mass. Jammed under high umbrellas and some wispy palm trees. 'There are famous people here? Really?'

'Well, no Garbo, no Bergman, no Dietrich or Cary Grant. But these people think they are. To themselves anyway. They are called The Beautiful People. Can you credit that?'

'It's like a monstrous aviary.'

'Just what Nettles said. A cage of macaws, were his words. Apparently this was a parking lot originally, then they paved it, built the kitchens and a very plush bar, planted a few sad creepery things, stuck in the parasols and it's become the absolute "in" place for wheeling and dealing, ditching and bitching.'

'Macaws,' said Jonathan. 'And parrots. Preening and screeching.'

'The noise goes up a decibel or two with each martini. I don't know why.'

'Panic, most probably.'

'Panic?'

'Like the British abroad. They have to shout to be understood, to dominate. If these people don't keep talking they might be forced to think. And that frightens them.'

'You *are* clever. Goodness.'

'I am sometimes. I wasn't very clever this morning, I'm afraid.'

'Make up for it now, astonish me with your wisdom.'

'No, you do that. The macaws and the parrots, tell me, who are they?'

'Ummm. Actresses, actresses who have been forgotten, or begun slipping. Producers' wives, directors' wives. Hopeful actresses. And some tarts, of course.'

'Good. The sparrows?'

'Can't see any.'

'There are one or two. At the back tables like us.'

'Out-of-town tourists.'

'The rooks and crows?'

'Agents, columnists.'

'The birds of prey? The kestrel crowd? Trim, tweedy, bright-eyed ... clawed?'

'Producers, lawyers, divorce attorneys, smart doctors, directors.'

'The magpies and the jays?'

'Publicists and press. Anyway, carnivorous.'

'Very knowledgeable. I'm amazed.'

'Only three weeks in this town, and you learn fast. Of course, it's terribly easy to send this place up, make fun of it, Los Angeles, or this part anyway. But I have met some of the kindest people here I've ever met in my life. Warm, affectionate, longing for one to like it here, to share it, to be happy. I suppose that if one does, it makes them feel reassured that *they* are happy too. It's easy to kick the place in the shins because everything is so absurd, so pretentious. It's all wrong and all fake, but I'll look back on this trip with perhaps some bewilderment, but a certain affection.'

Jonathan pricked a series of holes with the prongs of his fork in his empty avocado pear skin. 'Where do you live? In England, I mean.'

91

'A small terraced house near Sloane Square. Which I can't afford.'

'Married?'

Lea, who had placed her elbows on the table and cupped her chin in her hands, suddenly withdrew them sharply, as if in response to a silent rebuke. 'No! Goodness no. I'm a maiden lady. Bit over the hump, if you follow me. No longer in my spring. Shades of autumn on the way.'

'Balls! Terrible connotations of those wispy crocuses and September morns ...'

'Don't you loathe them?' She had pulled a length of hair across her lips and was chewing thoughtfully on it.

'Loathe them. Are you fearfully hungry?'

'Starved. Are you?'

'Starved.'

'No. I meant married?' She pitched the question casually into a chatter of parrots beside them.

'Was. For a short time. Nice girl, not her fault. Entirely mine.'

'Sorry.'

'Not at all. She wrote children's books, not half bad as a matter of fact. If you happen to like children's books.'

'I don't.'

'No more do I. But she was very pretty in a wimple-and-hand-embroidered way, you know? We had a cottage at Faringdon, so that we could both write in peace and contentment.'

'But no go?'

'Well ... I got a bit fed up with natural foods and real compost and lots of roughage and bloody pulses and prunes.'

'Goodness! But didn't you know about those before?'

'Not really, no. Isn't it odd? One really doesn't until it's the Death Do Us Part bit ... I can't imagine why. She was warm and sweet, wonderfully loving. Except that the loving extended to every stray dog and cat between Oxford and Reading, plus Shetland ponies. She won lots of cups and rosettes with her ponies ... and wrote her books as well.'

'About Shetland ponies?'

'There were quite a few I think.' He folded the pulp of avocado skin into a neat package with his fork. 'Ill-matched, I think was the phrase she used, and of course she was dead right. Anyway, we packed it all in after a couple of years. My fault entirely. I married her because I was desperately in love with Alice and knew that I could never have her, because she was more in love with Hugo Arlington than life itself. So really I did a pretty foul thing. Married a perfectly nice woman on the rebound and after three weeks, three weeks mark you, I was ready to slit my throat.' He looked up at her and smiled suddenly. 'I don't know why the hell I'm telling you all this.'

'Because I asked.'

'I suppose so. Full disaster anyway, two perfectly incompatible people joined together in holy matrimony. Guilt on my side, bewilderment on hers. Anyway she's now exceedingly happy in Devon, writing away like billy-ho about fairies in harebells, squirrels in polka-dot skirts and talking badgers. And breeding ruddy ponies. Good luck to her. She deserves it all.'

A slender waiter eeled his way sinuously through the too close tables and stood before them, swaying slightly. 'You wanna cold chicken and beefsteak tomato, right? And one Garden Salad, okay?'

'Right,' said Jonathan.

The waiter, singing under his breath, cleared the first course, set the second. 'And two glasses of buttermilk, right?'

'Wrong,' said Jonathan.

'Wrong? Who's wrong?'

'No buttermilk. We didn't order buttermilk, sorry.'

'You did too! It's on the paper. Wanna see the paper? The order paper? Is here, right here, you take a look.' He thumped the piece of paper on the table.

Jonathan cleared his throat. 'This is for table eighteen.'

'So what's this table?' He found the plastic disc, read the number slowly. 'Seven! Hell's a virgin!'

'Sorry. But everything else is just fine.'

'Everything else is just fine,' said the waiter. 'Holy cow! Two buttermilks . . .' He twisted his way back to the restaurant.

Lea started to eat her Garden Salad in a preoccupied manner, picking out odd bits and pieces with her fork, a round of radish, a sliver of chicken, staring before her absently.

'You gone away for good?' said Jonathan.

93

She looked up at him in vague surprise. 'Not good. No. I was thinking.'

'That came across. Food all right?'

'Well, it's green, shall we say? I was thinking how odd it is that I am also a bad picker. Gentlemen, I mean. I never actually got married though. Thank God. When I see what the "husbands" have become. I mean the ones I might have swooned at the altar with. Always the Flash-Harry type, do you know? Always older too. I suppose that's because I am a poor, lone Orphan Annie. Looking for a father.'

'Are you?'

'An orphan, yes. But I have a perfectly amazing man who loves me and puts up with me to an incredible degree. Geoffrey Nettles – well you know, you met him last night.' She speared a small piece of something green, put it in her mouth, chewed for a time. 'No, what I mean is, that it was always *me* who got left. I do think that a bit peculiar. I'm not all *that* bad looking, am I? Would *you* say I was all right? Impersonally speaking, I mean?'

'I couldn't speak impersonally on that subject.'

'Couldn't you? Oh. Oh well, that's quite nice. Thanks. But the thing is … I'm finding this very difficult to put together … I never left the men I thought that I loved. They all left me. And now that you have told me about your ex-wife, I have a feeling that perhaps I was a bit like her myself. Oh no! Not pulses and dreadful prunes …'

'Or fairies in harebells?'

'Or those. But I have a hideous feeling that I did perhaps cling a bit. Bindweed. I think I put them off; strangled the plant of life. Goodness! What a time to find out!'

'You honestly don't look the bindweed type. Clinging. Far too cool, elegant, cautious.'

'I'm not cautious at all! I charge in where angels fear to tread. And that's what it is, of course: fear. A woman hitting her thirties gets panicked. Visions of that shelf, on which one is left, start to loom. I think that I could do with another glass of wine, is there more? Oh dear, this is true confession time.'

'Masses.' He filled her glass. 'You know, in this extraordinary aviary you look just like an egret.'

94

'Do I? I'm not certain if that's a compliment or not. Are you still suffering from culture shock?'

'No. I mean among all the macaws and parrots. So elegant, white, so graceful. You really are.'

'It's a compliment I begin to gather? My white Givenchy cotton and no make-up?'

'Perhaps. No. Not as simple as that.'

'Egrets have fearful pointed beaks, don't they? Splash about in the paddy fields?'

'I think so. But they are very beautiful.'

'It *is* a compliment. You *are* nice.'

'That's all right. They have long legs too. Slim, long legs ...'

'Mine are! *Isn't* that convenient! It's the beak that worries me: I mean, do tell me. Honestly? Have I got a long nose? Is that what it is?'

'Christ, no!'

'It could be a reason for every one of my chosen mates to leave, couldn't it?'

'You are a lunatic. You must know.'

'Know about my nose? One doesn't. One has had the thing for so long that one gets quite used to it.'

'No, not that. But that you are beautiful. Amazingly beautiful.'

She looked at him through narrowed eyes, the glass at her lips. 'You've been boozing with Mr Shapiro, I do declare.' Her heart stopped. Restarted.

'Coffee. I speak with the full authority of a man who has, for years, been besottedly in love with one ravishing creature. Alice Arlington was my air, my water, my sun and my rain. She was my whole existence. I yearned and yearned for her.'

Lea placed her glass on the table and took a forkful of mangled lettuce.

'Isn't it sad how "yearned" rhymes with "spurned"?'

'And I was. Thoroughly. But I hung about mooning, hoping for any little crumb from her table ...'

Lea looked up at him directly, eyes smiling, long fingers stroking her hair. 'Get any?'

'Once. I reminded her of it last night, in the most oblique way, and all that she could remember was the meal we had.'

95

Lea covered her eyes with both hands, shook her head. 'Oh Lord! Isn't it simply awful being in love? I am sorry, really.'

'Frankly, I think it's pretty marvellous.'

'Well, you're very brave. I mean with that Yugoslav man, Dubrovnik, who drank all your brandy ... perhaps I mean patient, not brave, do I?'

'I don't know. But I'm not speaking of Alice actually.'

'Oh.' Lea laid her fork at the edge of her plate. 'I wonder if they perhaps have any cheese here? They don't in America, isn't that strange? Could we get hold of that dancing waiter again, and ask?'

'I was talking, if you want to know, about you.'

'But not that shiny orange processed stuff, real cheese.'

'I told you last night that I had laid a ghost, didn't I?'

'So you did. Rather a coarse remark, I thought.'

'Perhaps it was. It was the only thing I could say under the circumstances. When you came into that room last night, I knew instantly that the mooring ropes had been cast off, the sandbags chucked out. I was a balloon, soaring away, adrift, full of helium ...'

'Hot air.' She was laughing, but aware of a growing sense of unease within herself.

'What do you mean, hot air?'

'For balloons. Airships use helium, don't they?'

'Look, Lea, this is not a discussion on aeronautics. A ghost had been laid. I am released ... free.'

The unease grew rapidly into panic. She became, instantly, distracted. 'I do wish we could catch that dancing waiter. For some cheese. Every time one needs them they fade away ... perhaps if you shouted or something?'

'And it was you who did that. Understand? Can you?'

She sat looking at him in silence, heart thudding in her throat, daring not to speak for fear that her voice would sound as uneven as her pulse.

'Can you? Do you? Say yes or no. Say *something*, for God's sake!'

'I don't know what to say. I ... well ... thank you.' She cleared her throat, shook her head, pulled a strand of hair from across her chin.

'I don't think that you have taken it in.'

'I have! I have. I was thinking of ... not that shiny orange stuff. In cellophane.'

'You're *still* on that bloody cheese!'

'Because I'm terrified.'

'Of what?'

'Of what you'll say next.' She started picking industriously at the side of her thumb. 'I'm only talking about cheese because I'm trying to change the subject ...'

'Well don't! What's the matter? Is it me? I'm not Flash Harry enough, is that it?'

'No! Don't be so silly. So idiotic. What a *ridiculous* thing to say.'

'Well what ...'

'Jonathan, do shut up, please. I know what you're going to say, and I don't want you to ...'

'Why?'

'Because if you said it, and you didn't really mean it, I think that I'd ... well ...'

'Well what? Look at me. What?'

She looked at him, and he was surprised to see that her eyes were bright with tears.

'I'm going to say it, Lea. I don't know where it'll take us, but I'll mean it.'

'You don't know anything about me ...' she said.

'Enough.'

'Nothing *really*. My mother was Eurasian.'

'Mine was French. Worry you?'

She shook her head, pulling at her thumb. 'Don't even know what I do for a living, how I live, anything.' She shrugged hopelessly.

'I don't honestly think that it matters, do you? Unless, of course, you are vastly rich with great estates, terribly social, bully me, hold the purse strings. So on. Wouldn't care for that much.'

'No. But you didn't know about pulses and prunes with your other wife.'

'Ex.'

'Ex, then. Sorry. You said you didn't find those things out until Death Do Us Part.'

'Did I?'

'Yes. And that would be a bit late to change your mind, wouldn't it, a second time around? For both of us. At our ages.'

'Couldn't change my mind. Nothing will.'

'We could be incompatible. Your word.'

'Possibly. I doubt it. I don't feel incompatible ... do you with me?'

'No. Oh no!'

'After all, you are doing all the whimpering and sniffing and I'm the one who has the most reason to.'

'Why?'

'Well, you know how I feel about you but I don't know how you feel about me.'

'I don't know how you feel either. You haven't said.'

'You wouldn't let me. I love you. Am in love with you. There you are. On a plate.'

'I'm a children's psychologist. Queen Alexandra's.'

'I am grateful for the information. Riveted. You are exactly what I need.'

'I'm quite good at it.'

'And you are as stubborn as a bloody mule. You won't commit, will you, or say it?'

She placed her hands on the table, fingers spread wide, palms down, and noticed that they were instantly freckled by the shifting patterns of sun falling through the weary vine above. 'I've never said it before in my life ... not meaning it truthfully, I mean.'

'You must have said it to whatsisname? Nettles? At least once in your life?'

'Oh yes. To him, of course, of course I have. But that's not quite the same thing, is it?'

'I'd rather hope not.'

'No. You see, that's quite a different kind of loving. But when I have said it before to the, well, Flash Harrys, I only thought that I meant it at the time, but it didn't sound very good. Not really.'

'It probably wouldn't if you didn't mean it. But if you said it now, "I love you", here at this table in this macaws' cage, do you think it might have a different flavour?'

'To you?'

'Well of *course* to me, for God's sake.'

'Don't know. I'm simply terrified of trying.'

'Now look here, this is taking *far* too long. Be wildly abandoned, risk it, be reckless. If it sounds terrible, stale on your lips, like kissing dust, you know? then bad luck for me, we'll forget all about it and I'll try and catch the dancing waiter. Not shiny orange. In cellophane. Real cheese. That a bargain?'

She pushed aside her plate of wilting garden salad, folded her arms on the table. 'I love you,' she said.

He waited for a moment, letting the chattering and laughter around them fill the silence. The paved floor at their feet was barred with sun-stripes, a lavender-rinsed toy poodle with a diamond collar scurried past.

'How was it, then?' he said.

'How did it sound to you?'

'I'm stunned, frankly.'

'Good. I quite liked it myself, as a matter of fact,' she said.

Irina Miratova's journeys into Town, as she called the urban sprawl around her, were rare. For one thing she no longer had a car of her own: that had long been given up after countless minor accidents which proved, conclusively, that she really was not capable of driving anything faster than a flock of geese. It infuriated her, for she always considered that the other driver was to blame, never herself, and put aside, with a hard physical slap, any gentle suggestion from Mouse that she was 'too impetuous'.

The taxi fare was prohibitive, for the distance was long, and she found it increasingly difficult to cadge lifts from her neighbours, and even harder to persuade them to bring her home: at a time convenient to herself. And although she was usually very alert to the possibility that someone close by was about to make the trip, they somehow appeared to become aware of the fact that she would request a lift, and made excuses, or simply left earlier than they had said, leaving her white with anger on the verandah. Another thing which vexed her was that most of her old friends had died, were dying, or had given up and moved away, and younger people, she found, were not obliging.

She was, therefore, to all intents and purposes marooned in her wooden gothic pile on the cliffs, for with her arthritic back and general heaviness she found it difficult to hurry, and impossible to mount an ordinary bus. The thing which really infuriated her, which she carefully concealed, or at least so she thought, was the fact that Mouse was still driving: a battered Volkswagen which she conducted with care and efficiency, sitting high on a sandbag on the seat, just managing to see over the top of the steering wheel. In some extraordinary manner she got her feet to hit the accelerator and brake when either were needed.

So irritated did this make Irina that she refused to make a long journey, contenting herself with a grudging trip to the local shopping centre where Mouse, with strictly controlled amounts of money, was dispatched to do the local marketing. Nothing would have induced Irina to enter such a place: she had once, and it had so bewildered her that she never went again. But her vodka was of prime importance. So the shopping had to be done: and Mouse was sent to do it. Irina was certain that it was good for Mouse to stir herself a little from time to time, for she spent the major part of her life scuttling about the house like a black beetle, accomplishing little in the way of housework, less in cooking, but at least providing a semblance (Irina would accord it no more than that) of company and life, which as the years drifted on she found essential. The gathering memories were like shadows in the bleak house, and the silences sometimes unbearable.

There had once been days of glory; conversations of rare distinction, laughter or violent discussion. But those had been during the time when Miratov was still alive; when the Manns, Lenya, Brecht, Weill, Auden and Huxley and many others had come to sit about in the big room while Irina presided over her samovar. On one magical occasion Einstein had come, and so enjoyed his conversations that he came again, proposing irresistible, if incomprehensible, sciences and laws, and calling Mouse, Mouse. Indeed it was he who gave her the name, for she sat always removed from the direct flow of conversation, but clearly a part of the group, in a corner with some piece of hemming or stitching, her neat ankles crossed, her head nodding and bobbing with agreement and delight at the words which tumbled about her ears. But she seldom spoke: it was not her position to do so. She listened carefully, in raptures, proud that she had done all the arrangements for the tea, and that it was her hands which had given the great samovar its lustre.

House-Mouse, she was known as; and Mouse stuck.

And Mouse could still drive. It was infuriating. Of course one could have removed the wretched little car, and that would have been that. But in many more ways than one, the car was essential. In the deepest recesses of her heart Irina knew that Mouse was also essential. Death had reaped across her small field, there was little left, and less time. Vodka was the one great solace, being with tiresome Mouse the only other she had left: the two barriers which held back despairing loneliness.

On the occasions when she and Alexi Andreyev met, Mouse would drive her down into Santa Monica, according to Alexi's instructions: either they would meet at the entrance to the Pier, four concessions along on the left or the right, or at a seat on the promenade where, among the roller-skating youth and the heavy odour of 'pot' and pizzas, they could talk without restraint. She didn't care for Andreyev. A common man. A man with all the pretensions of good manners and grace, but with none of the charm, without which, she thought, neither was of the least use at all. However, beggars could not be choosers, and he was exceptionally polite, even on the occasions when she brought him little, for as age and lack of mobility slowed her down and invitations grew fewer and fewer, she became less and less useful. The idle gossip, for that is how she chose to consider it, was beginning to fail; the wells were running dry.

Now, today, he had made an exciting alteration in arrangements, and they were to meet in Town. An adventure. A taxi. Which she sincerely hoped that he would reimburse her for, for the pennies were clinking in her purse.

'I hope, Countess, you think that what I am wearing is suitable?' said Mouse suddenly, as they drove under the San Diego Freeway. 'It's so difficult to make up one's mind in a hurry.'

'You have had all night to make up your mind! And as you possess but two possible garments, apart from that loathsome black thing you rot around the house in, I should have thought it could have been a very small matter of concern to you.'

'Well, Countess, there *is* a difference between my blue and this beige. The blue is more formal, for evening occasions perhaps?'

'When have you been to one of those, may I ask? Since nineteen-forty-one?'

'Well, I feel that this is less formal, more suited to a trip to Town.'

'You are not visiting St Petersburg.'

'Ah no ...' sighed Mouse. 'Not there. But the beige I have chosen is best, I feel.'

Irina grunted, eased her back, placed both hands flat on the silver knob of her walking-cane. 'As you will be spending most of your time in some hideous supermarket, I can't see why you make the least fuss. You are an anonymous creature, quite lacking in any individual characteristics. Beige is the same: it is a forgettable colour. It would seem to me that no one will ever know that you are there, and should you fall to the floor in a fit they would step over you. Altogether anonymous.'

'My hat,' said Mouse undaunted. 'My hat is new.'

Irina looked at her with pain-filled grey eyes. 'New?'

'Well, almost. Do you notice something different? Oh, I pray that you do!'

'I have known the hat for more than twenty years. What is new?'

'This,' said Mouse, touching a grey net bow stitched to the brim. 'This bow. I made it last night. From a scrap I found in the work-basket, and then, if you will notice, I put the feather in. A feather from a dove. We picked it up years ago, I kept it for luck. A dove's feather. It is stuck through the bow, you see? Now that's different, isn't it?'

'Marginally. Not altogether different.'

'But it perhaps gives the hat a little ...' Mouse hunted about for a word to use that would satisfy her mistress. Last night the word 'chic' had presented itself, but now she dismissed it quickly before the unblinking grey eyes. 'Style?' She finally said anxiously. 'Do you not think so, Countess?'

Irina opened the big black handbag on her knees, found a folded paper napkin, one of those left over from Christmas, and blew her nose. 'If you think so, if you think so. Don't start to flirt with the man in the liquor store and drop my bottle. Remember!'

'Oh!' cried Mouse with joy and smothered the sound with her hand.

The taxi, on Irina's instructions, stopped at the side entrance of Brentano's book store, and they alighted; she paid it off, counting each bill and coin with the greatest care, and started towards the doors.

102

'It is not at all like an hotel,' said Mouse.

'It is not an hotel,' said Irina. 'I do not want people to know that I am going to an hotel.'

Mouse looked about the wide boulevard. 'No one is looking.'

'How can you tell, pray? Telescopic lenses? Secret cameras in windows ... how are you so certain? I am, to all intents and purposes, walking into Brentano's book store; if I walk through the length of the shop it will bring me directly into the lobby of the hotel. And no one will be the wiser. I'm not a fool.'

'Indeed not! How clever you are, Countess.'

'And you will meet me here in one hour, at this door. You may have to wait, I don't know how long Andreyev will keep me. Remember the lavatory paper, and remember that you must, on no account, cross the road except at the traffic lights and then only when they light up and spell W A L K!, do you remember all that?'

'I remember. W A L K!'

'And there will be change from the twenty-dollar bill which I have given you. I ask you to remember that too.'

Mouse watched her mistress make her way into the store, tapping ahead with the silver-knobbed cane, and then she turned and walked quickly to the nearest traffic lights, muttering W A L K! under her breath, feeling exceptionally light-hearted in her almost new hat with the net bow and the feather of a dove.

Alexi Andreyev was standing at the newspaper rack in the drugstore as Irina entered; he turned and came to her with a welcoming smile and a copy of *The New York Times*. 'Always on perfect time. You can be relied upon for that. I trust that you are well and in good health?'

'Do not put your trust in my health. I become older and older, I have almost overstayed my welcome in the Good Saviour's taxing world.'

'That saddens me. Now, I am about to buy a package of candy for Tatiana Ivanova ... advise me? What does she prefer? There are all kinds here, as you may see.'

'She cannot eat those. She has no teeth. Buy her a Mars Bar, she will melt it in a saucepan, and pour it over a measure of ice cream. Sometimes I know that she only sups it from the spoon. It is disgusting. But if you wish to make a gesture ...'

103

He had reserved a table at the far end of the café adjoining the drugstore, and ordered tea. 'I regret that it will be tea.in bags, but I have no doubt that you are long accustomed to this vile practice ... you will have heard the good news, I assume?'

'I have heard no good news for a long time.'

'Then this will please you. The hostages. They are being flown out of Iran to Algiers tonight ... it is all over.'

'Hah! A most important day for America. How *convenient* for the new President. God is showing him that He is on his side.'

'Little to do with God, I imagine. More to do with pennies.'

'We must hope,' said Irina, 'that they were not silver. Thirty pieces, eh?'

'An important day for America. A new President, and the release of the hostages. The reasons why I had to send for you, and could not come to Santa Monica as I normally do. I hope that the journey was not too exhausting? But I could not get away. So much to listen to, to watch, to note. It is useful to have one's finger on the pulse of a nation at such a time, even if California can hardly be considered the nation entire. But one gets an incredible reaction. One hears, and notes, opinion. Very useful.'

Irina opened the black bag, took from it a small bottle which once held two ounces of scent and now contained the same quantity of vodka. Expertly, and without losing one precious drop, she poured half of the liquid into her cup of milkless tea, replaced the stopper tightly. Andreyev made no comment. He had seen this operation before.

'I beg you not to apologize. I know that you have your ... work ... to do, and this has been a minor pleasure. I shall go and look at the yellow ribbons of welcome. I am vexed only that I have not put up my own; but I was not *certain*.'

'They are putting them in the trees along the boulevards. A palm tree with a yellow ribbon bow is the strangest of sights.'

'And no one will notice,' said Irina. 'Except you. You, who have been looking and listening. The faithful watch-dog?'

Andreyev looked about the crowded room. 'One does one's best. Every tiny morsel can be of use, as I have told you so often. Just one little piece of apparently irrelevant conversation, one comment remarked upon and noted, things which may have no political meaning to you or to me, trivia we would perhaps say, but one tiny piece of trivia could fit into the greater puzzle and clarify a picture for those who, far away, are working hard to keep informed. We watch-dogs as you call us with such humour, are vital; and we are wide spread.'

'I am surprised,' said Irina carefully, 'that you have chosen such a popular rendezvous. But I assume that you have perfect reason? And faith in your judgement?'

'Perfect. We think it unlikely that the Pink Turtle Café has any "device". We could plan a Second Coming here and no one would be any the wiser, the noise is far too high, and the CIA are heavily occupied in Washington and, probably, Algiers.'

'The taxi fare was enormous,' said Irina suddenly.

Andreyev removed the copy of *The New York Times* which concealed the Mars Bars for Mouse and a small, silver-wrapped box, which sat beside them. 'I have added enough here to the normal amount to cover the taxi handsomely,' he said, tapping the box with a nicotined finger.

'You are most thoughtful,' said Irina. 'Good watch-dog.'

'A cog,' said Andreyev. 'Just as you are. No more, no less.'

'A cog?' said Irina.

'We are not important, you and I.' He poured himself another cup of hot water, swirled the sodden tea-bag around, pressed it with a spoon to release flavour. 'Cogs. And when a cog wears out, it is of course replaced. And must be.' He suddenly smiled at her, tapped the silver-papered box once more.

Irina understood what he meant perfectly well. She was wearing out.

In the early weeks of America's entry into the war she had been convinced, by subtle, coaxing tongues, that as a Russian by birth, although now an American citizen, it was her patriotic duty to do all that she could to assist her native country in its desperate fight against Nazism. To this she, at first reluctantly, and then with growing fervour, agreed. Russian she was: and, after all, both countries were now Allies in a common cause.

Her popularity, wit, the elegance and erudition of her Sunday *salons* were, it was thought, just the weapons needed. All that she would be required to do was collect any little bits of gossip, conversa-

105

tion, opinions, comments made and sympathies, or even the lack of them, expressed, by people in the mainstream group, of which she was part.

She was gregarious; a perfect listener, an observant woman in all respects, and the effort of her patriotic duty was borne lightly on her shoulders. No one could possibly have known; no one did.

So she collected up bits and pieces, noted them down carefully, dates, names and provenance, and once a month would be bidden, by telephone, to meet a messenger, as they were called, at a given rendezvous where she would hand over her little packet for the common good.

It never occurred to her that she might cause anyone harm; except, of course, the Germans, or the pro-Germans in America, and there were a fair number of these, she knew only too well; equally she was perfectly certain that when the war was over and won, her duties would end.

But they did not. Irina found to her surprise that she was too far in to back out; she was also broke to all intents and purposes. Miratov had died suddenly and, she thought, inconsiderately, leaving his modest but fine collection of paintings to his adopted land, and a small settlement and the house to his wife. Which infuriated her; for she had long had her eyes on the paintings, and had thought that when the time came she could manage to exist perfectly well by selling off one or two. There was a Poussin of great beauty, a greatly admired Ribera, and a Ruysdael which, on its own, could have settled all debts, made sound the house, or, which was far more attractive, allowed her to live in great comfort in San Francisco . . . for she felt that Los Angeles was now becoming shabby and vulgar, and the house would very shortly slide down the cliff. It was typical of Miratov to redraw his will without her knowledge. As she wretchedly watched these works of infinite beauty, not to say value, being crated and shipped off to a grateful Metropolitan Museum in New York, she knew that she would have to continue with her war work in peace-time, and for a fee. This was agreed instantly, for the quality of her gossip-gathering had been high, and the information often revealed in the irrelevant comments she had passed on had been invaluable.

She could never be certain, nor was she ever told at any point, if she had actually contributed anything which would have proved to be the 'one tiny piece' missing in the great jigsaw puzzle of International Diplomacy, but she felt reassured that her work, humble as it was, must have borne some kind of fruit, for each month the little silver-paper wrapped box of bon-bons contained, beneath the glossy sweets, two hundred very acceptable dollars.

She worked well, quietly, dutifully, and then, almost imperceptibly, the pattern of things began to change around her. She grew older, became less mobile. Her *salons* had long since ended, for her cast of players either returned to Europe at the end of the war or went to New York, her fields became harder to glean from, there were fewer invitations, new people moved into the city, new faces were in charge of old businesses, no longer was her company much sought for concerts and first nights, and she rapidly discovered that the parties, which had always supplied so much of her material, had almost completely altered in tone and style, and that she was no longer invited. For no other reason than that the hosts were newcomers, and had never heard of Countess Miratova. There were few of the old crowd left, and they had given up parties for home movies. One couldn't pick up much at a first screening: no one spoke, except to make some comment, kind or unkind, on the current film showing. And she usually dozed off anyway.

However, one of her old cronies remained true, and still held gigantic brunches or buffet suppers, to welcome the latest arrivals in town.

Peter Clivden had arrived in Hollywood in the very early thirties, after one staggering success on the London stage to which he never returned. His house was known locally as Ye Old Curiosity Shoppe, although whether this referred to the owner and his friends, or simply to the junk he had amassed over the years, it was difficult to know. Every evening he lowered his Union Jack; each morning it rose into the smoggy air of Bel Air where he lived in some style with an ex-truck driver for a lover and three aproned crones as his maids. He bred Pekinese dogs, played the piano by ear, Coward, Novello, Ellis, and worked only rarely; for the clipped accent which he had diligently cultivated since he had left his family home in Pudsey, was no longer in demand, and his age was, frankly, placing him in a difficult category. However, he had saved prudently, invested wisely, and was still able to hold his brunches and suppers in the house which he had built in 1933, which was closely modelled, outside anyway, on Pauline Borghese's villa in Rome.

It was here, amidst the splendours of early thirties-modern furniture and some extremely suspect Utrillos, that Irina met Alice and Hugo Arlington at a brunch given in their honour and to welcome them to California. She latched on to this glittering pair shamelessly: the Arlingtons were young and attractive, were looking for a house to rent for at least a year, they were determined to have the greatest fun; they needed help in a hundred ways. Irina took them both in her capable hands and got to work. She was making a determined bid to renew contacts.

It was a short spell of happiness. Hugo died, the parties stopped, Alice moved away from the splendid house in Bel Air to the more modest and unfashionable area west of town. Irina knew that she no longer had the strength to fight on: the effort was too great, she had used up most of her time, what was left she really had no need of.

'Cogs,' repeated Andreyev slowly.

Irina opened her black bag, removed a small packet which she placed on the table before him, took her scent bottle and filled her cup with the remainder of the vodka. 'It has been a quiet month. Christmas was not at all amusing, I don't know why. Age, I suppose? One likes it less and less. So your packet is not very fat. The cog,' she said, raising the cup to her lips, inclining her head politely towards him, 'is wearing out. Just as you say. However, you may find one or two things in there which, while not pearls of great price, have a certain curiosity value if nothing else. Sybil Witt, Boris Kragujevac; such useful conversationalists.'

She finished her vodka, replaced the cup in her saucer, reached across the table and took the silver-wrapped box. 'If I may?'

Andreyev nodded. 'Of course you may. Do not forget Ivanova's Mars Bars ...'

'I will, I suppose, hear from the Bureau, sometime ...?'

'As you know, that is not for me to say. I too, I must remind you again, am only a cog.'

Irina stuffed the packages into her bag, snapped it shut, slung it over her arm, took up her stick. 'I suppose the next thing that you will say is that we are both just a part of the Greater Machine?'

Andreyev spread his hands wide. 'Why should I say that? When you have already said it for me?'

He slipped her small packet into his pocket and signalled for their bill.

4

Friday, 23 January

Jupiter didn't much like her sister Etty. She didn't like the way that Etty conducted her life generally: take a look, as she was now doing, at Etty's front yard and you'd know her for a slut.

Desolation, indifference, dusty, junk-jammed.

In a corner a bird-of-paradise plant, tattered leaves drooping, dead flowers spiked like twists of orange paper. In another the hulk of a car; wheelless, doors hanging wide, rusty. A pile of worn-out tyres spilled, a battered baby-carriage. Tin cans.

In the middle of this the single-storey wooden house crouched behind its sagging porch in shame. Paintless, the wood long silvered by years of exposure to wind, sun and sea. It had once been tight and proud in a tended plot, contained by a neat picket fence, shutters fresh painted, screens at the windows to keep out the evening bugs, because Venice was built, they said, on swamp and marshland which had been drained into little canals, or wide ditches, when it was a place to come to retire, or to escape the summer heat of the desert sprawl to the east. But that had been many years ago. Maybe fifty, sixty even.

Now it had almost crumbled into a shanty-town.

Somewhere there were still traces of the Venice which had been; the Venetian arches and colonnades survived. The pillars cracking, the iron supports bleeding rust into scaling concrete, walls covered in spray-bomb graffiti. On Ocean Front Walk, which as its name suggested ran along the ocean edge, things were less derelict, but behind lay the black area, and no one much went there. The black people had moved in as the whites had died off, or moved away. It was lost land. Wasteland. There ain't much joy in this place, thought Jupiter as she picked her way among the scattered cans and fallen tyres. Etty is just one slut. One big slob.

She reached the porch, the four wooden steps up, creaking under her weight.

'Etty? This your sister Jupiter. You got a cold beer there?'

Etty's voice was flat with years of indifference. 'I got beer. Right here. All cold. Come and get it.'

The front parlour was darkened by lines of washing which criss-crossed the room from one corner to the other, stealing the light from the window. Etty was ironing at a fold-up ironing board in the middle of the room, a pile of tumbled clothing on a chair at her side. She didn't look up when Jupiter came in.

'You wash and iron all your given life,' said Jupiter, opening a can of Schlitz with a pull-ring.

'Some people got to work,' said Etty.

'Some people got too many kids.'

'If you want a cup or a glass they's in the kitchen.'

'Your kitchen is full of roaches.'

'You a roach yourself, gal, don't I know it,' said Etty, folding a shirt.

'I admit you iron pretty. Should do, so much practice.' Jupiter went into the kitchen and found a glass.

'This glass is so dirty I could grow corn in it,' she said.

'Whyn't you try? This *aint* kids' stuff. It's grown-ups' . . . see this label? Fancy.' She held the folded shirt towards Jupiter who read slowly.

'St Michael. Made in England. What's so fancy?'

'All his stuff is fancy, he got things from Paris, France, Rome, Italy, all over.' Etty put the folded shirt on a pile, picked up another from the heap beside her.

'Who this he when he is home?' said Jupiter.

'And shirts. Real fancy names. He's that white fella. European, lives on Whitecrest, friend of your widder lady. I do all his laundry, won't trust no one else. Very particular.'

Jupiter moved a pile of shirts from the davenport and sat down. 'I'm getting old, Etty. Old is what I am. Carrying the burden the Good Lord has given me.' She poured her beer and took a long pull,

111

wiped her lips with the back of her hand. 'My widder woman is right there now. Whitecrest Avenue. With your fancy European. They call him Dubrovnik, I don't know for real what name he has, that's all the kids call him, Dubrovnik.'

'She there with him now?' said Etty indifferently.

'I always know when the kids go away for the night and she tells me to finish real smart so she can lock the house and get away. He don't never stay in the house. I seen the sheets 'cause I make the beds. He ain't never there. Never no smell of a man, I can tell.'

Etty sprinkled water with tired fingers over the shirt on the ironing board, rolled it neatly into a bundle. 'Never no smell of a man in this house neither,' she said. 'It gets lonesome.'

'Don't know why he left you-all,' said Jupiter, and belched.

'No work in Venice. It's hippies, junkies and crazy kids. He said he could do better down San Diego, a whole lot. He sends money every week, never forgets, and the kids.'

'Sends the kids money!' said Jupiter.

'No. A card. Real pretty card, there was this battleship and a blue sky and it said, "Hi Folks! From San Diego!" In sparklers.'

'That was nice.'

'The kids was loon-happy.'

'I didn't know Daniel could write. He write?'

Etty switched off the iron, stood it on a brick to cool. 'His name. He does that okay. Not a message. You a real roach, Jupiter.'

'Hey! You lost all your joy, you know that Etty? You don't laugh no more, that's sad. You had real pretty laughter, real sweet as I recall ...'

'Those days is gone,' said Etty, lifting the bundle of clothing from the chair and sitting down. 'They's gone. You lost your joy too.'

Jupiter stared into her beer glass. 'Julie-Mae. I ain't cracked a smile since that day forward. I lost my joy, you right.'

Etty rose, put the bundle of clothing on the ironing board, opened the ice box, got a can of beer. 'A sad time. That May-time. Julie goes wandering, then the Duke gets smashed up in his big white car.' She pulled the ring on the tin, it opened with a pop and a hiss.

'They was real bad days. Real bad,' said Jupiter. 'More tears shed in those two days than the Good Lord could have used for his Flood.'

'Maybe, one day, Julie-Mae will just walk in, all happy, and you

112

won't scold, you be so glad to see her. But the Duke ... ol' Duke Ellington, he won't never walk back into anyone's life.'

'Is true. Is true. You call him Duke?'

'Like Ellington, I never did get his name right. He liked just we called him Duke.'

'*Arlington*,' said Jupiter. 'That's his name.'

'She ever know, the widder, what he did down here?'

Jupiter emptied the last of her beer into her glass. 'What he do? I mean except for black girls and a pinch of snow? I reckon she knew about the girls. I heard once. They had a shout and a hollering, and she knew about the snow, I guess. Ain't so difficult to see when your man has done a little sniffin'. She knew that. What else he do then?'

'Black meat. That's what he liked to call it. Having those girls down at Minty's ... sometimes he was so gone on sniffing coke they was over him, three or four maybe, like bed-bugs. He liked that. He just crazy for that. Hoomiliation. That's all he wanted, hoomiliation. And he paid lotsa dollars ...'

'Hoomiliation? You never said about that,' said Jupiter. 'Why he want that? That's crazy stuff.'

'He *was* crazy,' said Etty and poured the beer from her can into her open mouth, head far back.

'You just plain disgusting, Etty. You make me sick to my stomach you do that.'

'Ain't no party manners in this house.'

'So I see. What was all the hoomiliation for?'

'He said he wanted to apologize to the black prolotariat for the wickedness of the white man. Do you believe!'

'I didn't know,' said Jupiter, 'there *was* any other kind of black but prolotariat.'

Etty shrugged, looked at her feet. 'That's what he said. I don't rightly know what he meant. Daniel told me, but I forget quick. You think these two feet of mine are getting bigger? 'Cause I don't wear no shoes? Think they spreading wider? Seems to me they are.'

'You a real stupid nigger, Etty. Your ass spreading 'cause you don't wear no pants? I'm goin' onto the porch. This room's too dark and gloomy. Come in the sun awhile, huh?'

They sat together on the porch on the battered seats from the wreck of the car.

113

'You got to tread mighty careful on this floor. The wood is all rotted away. One day someone will fall in a hole,' said Etty.

'How you meet the Duke?' said Jupiter. 'I don't recall exactly.'

'Mr Boris brought him one night to Minty's. God! That was a evenin' ...'

'Who's Mr Boris? Your fancy shirt man?'

'Is who. You call him different.'

'Dubrovnik. I don't know no other name.'

'He brought him down, oh, couple of years gone now. One so fair, the other so dark.'

'Dubrovnik?'

'If that's his name. He was tall as a mountain. First time he ever came in we all just stopped talking. Stared at him. This great man, eyes so blue they darted about like kingfishers, this curly brown hair. He was something.'

'You ain't never seen a kingfisher.'

'I read about them once. I seen pictures. His eyes were like so. Skipping from one to the other of us so fast. Laughter there. Polite. "If you please" and "Thank you", can you believe? In Minty's!'

A thin ginger cat uncurled on the sagging board floor, trod lightly down the four steps, stood with its back against the post, tail erect, quivering; ambled off into the junk-yard.

'That damn old cat,' said Etty. 'He sprays that stink like every-where.'

Jupiter laughed softly. 'You just said ain't no smell of a man in this house. Sure is now.'

'Man, I said. Not male. Is a different stink anyways. This Dubrovnik, right? he just moved into that warehouse loft up on Whitecrest, he didn't make no trouble, looked so good, so big, quiet, smiling. He talked funny, with an accent so we couldn't really understand him, but he meant kindly. Among all those punks, the gays in leather, all Minty's gals, the juke-box bouncing, he was something different. Didn't make no difference he was white and we was mostly black. He paid no attention to that.' Etty threw her empty can into a dusty bush over the porch rail.

'You a slut, Etty Baker.'

'Don't deny it.'

'What he do, this Dubrovnik, at Minty's?'

114

'He drank a lot. So we all did, so what? Sometimes he sat up at the bar and he just drank, or maybe sometimes, he wrote things in a little book. I don't know what.'

'He makes movies. The widder said.'

'I didn't never ask. The night he came in with this Duke Ellington. So funny the two of them. So goddamned different. The big black one and the blond one, he a bit scared, I could see that. The blond, the Duke, licking his lips so hard, his eyes so wild, I knew he was sniffin'. He was sniffin' for black tail too. But I didn't know that for sure the first time. Minty liked him. She said he was real class.' She laughed, shook her head. 'She a dumb fool, that Minty.'

'She get busted I recollect.'

Etty sighed, got to her feet, looked down at them worriedly. 'She got busted. Sure. Something had to give.' She started back into the house. 'My feet sure is spreading. You want another beer, you pressed for your time?'

'I got time,' said Jupiter. 'Time for one more can. You bring me one?'

'I bring you one,' said Etty. 'My bladder is pressed is the trouble. Be right back.'

'I want to know about this hoomiliation some more,' said Jupiter.

Etty stopped at the doorway, turned back. 'That? Oh, it wasn't so much, just a gas; don't pay no attention. He was just high on speed or coke or whatever he took. I never saw anything, and right now, Jupiter, I'm pressed.'

'You scat then, otherwise we'll be sittin' in a lake,' said Jupiter and threw her can over the rail into the bushes. It wasn't her house, nor her yard. So what?

There were some things, thought Etty, that you didn't tell anyone: not even your own flesh and blood. Some things better left still, not raked about. She wandered into the kitchen and stood a moment by the cloth-covered table, hands to her face. Things best left unsaid. She leant her weight against the table, felt the hard edge pressing across her thighs.

Ain't nothing wrong with my bladder: it's just the remembering. Sometimes people got to get away by theirselves, shake their heads, get rid of all the little bugs of memory. Jupiter talking about Duke and Minty. Oh, sweet Lord! Minty. High yallar, and mean as a cornered rattler. Sometimes meaner even. Minty in that green beaded shirt, the red wig, laughing, head thrown back. I recall her like that. Always will, I reckon. You want a packet of snow, she's got it; you want angel dust, she got that too. You want a boy or a girl, black or white. You want a fix; she can fix it. Anything for the dollars. 'One day,' she said, 'I'm goin' right out of this shitty dump, and when I go I'm goin' rich, I'm goin' to be richer than any Madam in the whole of America. Get myself the biggest Caddie you ever saw, a real smart apartment, real good address, people want to play games? Okay. I'll give them games, at a price. I'll get a real good bunch of girls who'll work their butts off for me and I'll be "Minty", I'll be famous all over, I won't be dealing with trash. This place is an asshole and I want out. I want real classy things. People like the Duke, that's what I mean, that kind of client. Only I'll call them "my gentlemen". I'll be so rich, so famous they'll print my picture in swank magazines, maybe even I'll be put in songs, like Cole Porter did. People will know who I am and no one ain't goin' to get in my wig. No one. No way.'

Etty leant away from the table, smoothed the rumpled cloth, went into the laundry-scattered room and got a couple of cans of beer.

'You peein' all night in there, Etty? You faint or something?' Jupiter called.

'On my way. On my way. Ice cold beer.'

Poor Minty. That's how she talked. So fine. So sure. So damned certain. She never got it. All she got was twenty years for pushing dope and, what they call it? Moral Depravity. That's something I never could understand. Daniel told me, but I forget quick.

Jupiter was sitting heavily on the battered car-seat, legs apart. She took the beer from Etty, pulled the ring, threw it into the yard and drank. 'Thought you'd gone clear to nowheres,' she said. 'Sure took your time.'

Etty sat down carefully, looking with interest at her feet, the beer can held aloft.

'What you looking at,' said Jupiter, 'like you was holding a lamp?'

'I am sure as hell sure they's spreading. These two feet of mine. I reckon it's standing at that ironing board all day, maybe I should sit? Get me a chair.' She tipped the beer into her open mouth. 'Jupiter? You know why sex is so dirty?'

'It is?' said Jupiter. 'I didn't know. Depends on the way you take it, don't it?'

'I reckon. I reckon sex and drugs is just about the most important things you can trade in, everyone in the whole wide world wants them.'

''Cause why?'

''Cause it makes people feel good. High. They have fun. And maybe it's more fun if it ain't allowed, you know?'

'I don't know. I turned off sex a while back. Sex is kids and I got enough. I lost one, my treasure, and I don't want no sex after that. That just closed me up.' Jupiter looked across at Etty suddenly. '*You* still have it?'

Etty shrugged, drank again, wiped her lips with a spread of fingers. 'I ain't turned off. Daniel has some cute notions when he comes back home ... he always did. He full of fizz.' She looked up at Jupiter with a gleam of malice, for a second the habitual indifference fell away. 'I'm younger, remember, than you.'

'Roach,' said Jupiter. 'Younger and a slut. Always was, always will be. You love your man? Or you just love the sex you have?'

'What's the difference? Sex can be real good for the soul.'

'You remember that I am Chapel, Etty Baker, that ain't no part of our teaching. I love the sweet Lord who will cherish me, amen. So hold your hush about dirty things. You got no dignity.'

'I don't need no dignity. What the hell I need dignity for in this dump?'

'You have just let slide. Everything. You should come with me to the Chapel, sing the praise of the Lord, feel His love, sing loud for Him, let Him reclaim you from your wicked ways. Sure you are younger than I am, I know that. Last born you were. Know what they call that? The last born? They call them runts. You a *runt*, Etty, the runt of the family, you is way past redemption, way past.'

Etty nodded, finished her beer, threw the can into the bushes. 'I'm way past redemption, but I sure as hell can iron a pretty collar, and I got a few other tricks I ain't forgotten.'

Jupiter finished her drink, placed the glass and the can tidily on the porch plank floor beside her. 'I'm goin' now. I jest came for the

117

beer,' she said. 'I don't want no more. I'm goin' to the Meeting. We'll pray for you Etty, sure as I'm sitting beside you, we'll pray. I'll ask the Reverend Cheever to make a special announcement to pray for the lost soul of Etty Baker, my sister. That's what I'll do.'

'Sweet in you, Jupiter, just so sweet.'

Jupiter eased herself off the car-seat, stood up, straightened her skirt. 'And there weren't no hoomiliations? Just a gas? That Duke fella?'

'A gas,' said Etty. 'Is all.'

'You are tight closed as a clam.' Jupiter started down the four wooden steps, at the bottom she turned. 'But we'll pray. Pray for that lost, sweet soul of bygone days,' she said.

Etty was looking at her feet. 'Prayin' don't bring back no sweet soul from bygone days. They gone, they sure as hell are gone. They wasn't so much anyway. Just small change. That's all,' she said.

She watched Jupiter cross the cluttered yard, push her way through the gap in the sagging fence where, once, there had been a gate, and walk heavily away down the street.

Big Bessie had him first. She was the beginning. She liked it with him, the things he wanted her to do. Wild! He was crazy, but he knew the tricks, liked being taught some as well. But you had to play real careful with him, he was serious. Everything was for real. No giggling. That made him so mad! No kindness, didn't want no sweet words, no affection. 'Punish me,' he'd say in that English voice so strange, 'punish me for all the evils we done to your people. Hate me! Hate me!'

Etty leant back against the worn fabric of the seat.

Sometimes it was tough not to laugh at him, but hating wasn't so hard to do at fifty bucks a throw. We all joined in, the boys as well as the girls. Screwed him from Alaska to Arkansas. Till he was near dead, spread out on that old billiard-table back of the bar, naked as the day he was born. Sometimes the studs, the real tough ones, damn near did him injury for life, and Bessie and Annie gave him thrashings so's he couldn't hardly walk, but Minty always cooled it, just in time. She knew what he wanted all right, saw he got it, saw the dollar bills, treated him good.

Etty laughed softly, shook her head, brushed her face with her fingers, laughing through them, biting them gently as the memories came drifting back across the dusty yard. The Duke, crawling naked round the room, Annie sitting on his back like he was a mule, whacking him hard, and him with a rope between his teeth, she jerking it back and up, so he was bug-eyed with fear at the punishment he wanted. And got. Hoomiliation. There was lots of hoomiliation, Jupiter, you'd have died laughing.

Only maybe you wouldn't.

He tied up there, in that old room, like a sack of mail, the girls kickin' him, the studs pissin' on him, and he screaming for mercy. 'Forgive me!' he's yelling. And Minty, standing there in the shadow, arms folded across that green shirt, the little beads glinting in the light, a cigarette. Smilin', smilin', watching it didn't go too far. Ready to call Mr Boris to lug him home, 'cause Mr Boris never came down to those evenings, he never was there. Just the Duke. Soon as Mr Boris got the idea what was on with the Duke, he just scrammed, he never once came into that old billiard room. Almost no one knew it was there, way behind the bar. Just a empty room with the seats all round and the table all torn-up, and the Duke beggin' us to hate him some more.

Funny times, she thought, looking down at her feet, memory fading, the present coming into focus. Funny times, all over and done with now. The hating and the forgiving. Funny what people wants you to do to 'em. Funny the way they get their kicks. Funny, but you don't laugh. Kids'll do anything to get a fix, just any old thing you want long as you pay. And he paid good. I reckon beating the life out of a crazy loon 'cause he wants it that way's a lot easier than robbin' a store or hittin' some gal on the head and grabbin' her purse. Safer. Stands to reason, and some of those kids. Big Bessie, Annie, Joe Judas, Catface, an' a few of the others, really got a kick out of pissin', and worse, on old Whitey. Vengeance and revenge; wasn't no difference, they went high for that. Somewheres inside of themselves it's what they wanted. Years of hate they let go. Years they didn't even know they knew about. Him lying there, helpless, pleading to be hated. And they did. Sure as hell is frying, they hated.

But he was scarey too, as well as all the rest. Real creepy. Time he said to Minty, 'Minty,' he said, all low and sweet like, 'one day

119

I'm goin' do something so bad they'll kill me, you see. They'll stomp me to death.'

She got up stiffly, looked down once more at her feet. 'They's spreading,' she said aloud. 'Seems to me that way.' She picked up Jupiter's glass, threw the can into the bushes, stood arms akimbo, looking into nowhere.

He never did. We never saw him again, I recollect. No one stomped him. He got minced up on the Freeway. They had to use a hose to wash him out of the wreck.

Funny.

There was a tremble of beer in the bottom of Jupiter's glass, she swallowed it, shook the glass across the porch planks. Pissin' on Whitey. Well, one way of getting it out of your system, I reckon.

The towel was too small, slimy with water. Alice rubbed her hair with it briskly. 'It's too small. This towel. And wet. Don't you have another one?'

Dubrovnik was in the studio part of his loft. He heard her voice from the bathroom, lowered the sound on the record player. 'I don't hear you? What say?'

'Too small. This towel.' Alice stood naked in the doorway of the bathroom. 'And wet. I can't dry myself. And my hair . . .'

'Only one towel. The other is being washed.'

'I suppose I should have had *my* bath first. Shower, I mean. You are too large for this rag.'

'Maybe. You are a lazy creature. It's been wet for days anyway.'

'How can I go to supper with hair like this? It'll never dry.'

'You look, you know, like Ophelia! Maybe Ondine!'

'No consolation.' She turned and went into the bathroom again. He watched her as she walked, the small buttocks, high bones at the hips, the slender back, vertebrae a line of buttons under her skin.

'But you are very beautiful. Even from the back,' he called.

'Bugger off. I'm miserable.'

'There is a dressing gown in the cupboard, I think.'

She took the faded garment from a hook, saw a pair of jeans hanging by a belt-loop. Looked at them for long seconds. Shrugged herself into the dressing gown, came back into the studio, tying the stringy belt about her waist.

120

Dubrovnik had dressed and was pulling on a sweater. 'You get it? Great. I put the heating up real high. Is better? Why you miserable?'

'That towel is disgusting.' She sat on the edge of his wide bed. 'Those jeans.'

'Jeans?'

'In the cupboard. They are too small for you ... not yours, right?'

'Oh shit,' he said. 'I'm very sorry. You find them?'

'Under this.'

'I don't wear it.'

'Obviously. They're his, aren't they? Hugo's?'

'I imagine. I think to myself I clear all that stuff away. Sorry.'

'Did he have much here, in your sanctuary?'

'Not so much. A change of stuff just to go ...'

'To go off on his little trips. I know. He'd look pretty odd in his Turnbull and Asser shirts and all the rest.'

'I don't follow. Who is ...'

She brushed the conversation to a stop with a gesture of her hands. 'Leave it. Give me a scotch, will you?'

He poured her drink. 'I'll go and take them away. For the trash. I am truly sorry.'

'It doesn't matter. A sudden jolt of remembrance. Not your fault.'

In the cupboard he yanked the jeans off the hook, felt quickly in the pockets, found a small square of cardboard. A flashlight Polaroid of two coloured children, obscenely naked. He crushed it instantly in a strong hand. Felt through the other pockets. Two five-dollar bills, some small change. He put the jeans in the basket of dirty clothing for Etty Baker, went back into the studio stuffing the crushed cardboard square into his trouser pocket.

'You want ten dollars? I found ten dollars.'

She shook her head, lay back in the deep settee, stared up at the rice-paper Japanese lantern hanging from the ceiling. 'I just wish that you had told me before.'

He was pouring a drink, lowered the sound of the record player, came across and sat beside her. 'Told you what?'

'About all this ... this trip. The Amazon, all that.'

'But I did. I did.'

'No. Only that it was an idea, not that it was a fact, that you were leaving, going, gone.'

121

'Nothing was so sure. You know how long it takes, papers, permits, everything. I only got news all is okay this morning. Right?'

'Taken me unawares, that's all. How long for? About?'

He sat forward, knees apart, hands round his glass. 'I cannot tell. How can I tell? Is a long way. A big deal.'

She took a sip from her drink. 'Months?'

He shrugged, a large movement from a large man. 'Is possible. I cannot tell. I want to be there in the rains and in the dry, that is important.'

'And when does it rain in this bloody place?'

'About from July to December.'

'If you are going to follow this Amazonian Autostrada, or whatever it is, you'll be a long, long time.'

'It's called the Road of Bitterness. Is already two thousand kilometres long – so many people die making it, the forest comes back all the time. They fight to get to Peru, but they lose.'

'Why in the name of God is it worth going all that way to photograph a losing battle? And you could be lost there too, disease, Indians, yellow fever ... it's madness.'

'It's very exciting. I will start to look for Fordlandia ... you know this place?'

'Why should I?'

'Is built by the car man. Nineteen twenty-six. A big dream. The rubber was the dream. Fordlandia is now jungle again. Nothing remains.'

'Then why bother? Why go?'

Dubrovnik got up suddenly and started pacing. His usual occupation when he was forced to think. 'You put me down, Alice.'

'No. I don't. It's just a crazy idea.'

'Maybe I like crazy ideas.'

'Maybe you do.'

'Is what I am, a man of visions, of crazy ideas! So was Darwin, Michaelangelo, Vasco da Gama ... all was crazy ...'

'Modesty is not your strongest point.'

He turned suddenly and stood before her, legs astride, hands by his sides. 'And so you laugh a little at me? Idiot Dubrovnik? All I can do is cook for you and fuck you well ... that's it? You say so?'

'Didn't say anything of the kind. And don't shout.'

122

'I shout because you make me unhappy. Why do this? I am a man. I want to move. I want the adventure, to see things new, to try things new. I have this fantastic idea for the Road of Bitterness and you laugh.'

'I haven't laughed once. I'm far too wretched for that. What's going to happen to me? Have you thought of that? What do I do? Start off on my road? And where will I go? Can you tell me?'

The anger left him, he came and sat beside her gently, took one hand and placed it on his knee, leant across and kissed her on the lips. 'Alice, oh Alice! I love you. But you know, this you always know, it cannot be for always, we cannot be always together. I have children, and I love them. I have also a wife I do not love, but is Catholic, and she will never, not ever, let me go. This, always, Alice, we have known ... one day I must go back. It will be my duty and my decision to do so, but before that I must fulfil myself as a man in my work. You understand me?'

'You have always said that here, Los Angeles, America, whatever you like, was the only place for your creative work. You told me this, you were so certain.'

'I was wrong. They were very nice, sure. Pat me on the back, "Great job, kid", all that kind of thing, but they don't want my kind of movie ... I am only another foreigner trying to gate-crash ... you say this?'

'You can.'

'Well I do. They do not understand my work, or how I work, or what I want to work at ... it is too good for them. They want entertainment for TV, to sell things, not documentaries.'

'*Midnight Airport* was a success, wasn't it? You got an award for *The Big Divide* ... it's only a matter of patience, of waiting.'

'I waited too long already. *Airport* was about Jews fleeing Russia, *Divide* was about Germans who could not flee Germany ... art stuff. No one wants to see them. Even on television. They don't sell Brand A or Brand B.'

'So what is the point of trailing thousands of miles to make a film in Brazil about a town that no longer exists! Who the hell wants to see that?'

Dubrovnik sat back in his corner, his glass held on his knee. 'I do,' he said.

Alice ran her hands through her hair. 'I'm still damp ... have you got anything I could rub it dry with? A teacloth, anything.'

'I give you a shirt, that okay?'

'One of Hugo's?'

Dubrovnik was opening drawers in a chest across the studio. 'I am sorry for the jeans. I said so. I forgot.' He found a cotton tee-shirt and came towards her. 'You can use this. It is clean.'

'Did Hugo leave anything else behind him here? Books, papers, anything?'

'No. Nothing. He never came with things like that. He had just a few bits of old clothing to ...'

'I know. You told me.' She started rubbing her head with the tee-shirt vigorously. 'Odd thing is,' she said, coming up for air and parting, pressing, the heavy hair about her head away from her face. 'Odd thing is that yesterday, I can't think why, I suddenly had a thought and went to have a look at the mass of papers and things I've collected. His journals, notes, rough drafts for things, two unpublished manuscripts. A room of stuff.' She threw the tee-shirt on to a table, fluffed the hair around her head with busy fingers.

'And what?' said Dubrovnik, pouring himself another scotch.

'Well, it's silly I suppose. But everything is there, as far as I can see, except for his journal of 1979.'

'Is not here, Alice, I would know for sure.'

'And all the months up until the day he died in May '80 are missing from *that* journal. 1980 is half empty. Dead. Ripped out. Gone.'

'Why? Why he tear out all those pages? Leave half a book?'

'I don't know why. I wondered if you did. That's all.' She got up, untied the belt of the dressing gown. 'I'm dry now, almost, I'll go and try to brush a bit of life into my hair. I can't brush any life into me, not this evening.' She paused at the door to the small bedroom where she had left her clothes. 'Alice-sit-by-the-fire. That's me ... God! What a mess I've made of my life. What time are we due at Sybil's, seven thirty?'

Dubrovnik was standing in the centre of the studio, dwarfed by beams and timbers, the large bed, a giant poster by Capiello of a dancing Mistinguett. He had his head down, the glass pressed against his lips.

'Yah. Yah. We have time,' he said.

Alice laughed, shook her head. 'Not much, my dear, not much. God damn Brazil.'

'You want me to kill the music?' shouted the White Rat.

Jonathan leant forward, cupping his ear with one hand. 'What?'

'You want me to kill the music?' said the White Rat, turning the car radio down to a whisper.

'Ah. Well, yes. If you don't mind. It makes it a little easier to talk back here.'

'I don't mind. Just that some people reely love music. Stevie Wonder. Great artist. Great musician. You know Stevie Wonder, lady?' He was looking at Lea in his driving mirror.

'Yes. Yes I do. But it was a bit loud this time, Wayne. Thank you.'

'You're welcome. Music's company. But I guess with you two in the car I already got that, right? Cars is lonesome sometimes. Drivin', drivin' ...'

'They must be,' said Jonathan. 'I give you the address we're going to?'

The White Rat looked at the empty seat beside him, picked up a small book. 'I looked it up in this city plan. Off Sunset, north, up Benedict Canyon, seventh on the left. Right?'

'Superb.'

'Oh hell. It wasn't so much.'

'It's marvellous. Tropicana Drive. Is north of Sunset what you call okay?'

'It's okay. South's better. South always is here. But you just made Beverly Hills. Tropicana Drive is exactlee on the border of the city limit. Know that?'

'So we are within the pale?' said Lea.

Wayne reflected in silence for some moments. 'What the hell is that?'

'I mean, it's a good neighbourhood? Chic? Classy?'

'Oh sure. Classy. Just. Right on the city limit though. Whoever you're goin' to have a gig with just about made it right, mixed neighbourhood of course. Lots of Jews. But definitely no blacks. I reckon you could say it was Caucasian – and lots of Jews got theirselves a new name with the nose job.'

125

'And beyond that?' said Jonathan. 'Beyond the city limits. Desert?'

The White Rat snorted. 'Sheet, man! Desert! Is Bel Air beyond. Beautiful, gracious-living Bel Air. Now that is *real* class. I mean that is just the most in this area. You got a house in Bel Air you is either an Ayrab prince or you grabbed yourself a load, no matter which way. It's lotsa, lotsa money, Bel Air. You've arrived!'

'Very tribal,' said Lea. 'Everyone lives in ghettos here.'

'Hey! They ain't *all* Jews!' said the White Rat. 'Some is quite normal people. Just ordinary. Like me.'

'And where do you live, Wayne? I never asked,' said Jonathan. 'With your sister?'

'No ... I go to my sister when you go west ... I got a pad in Mar Vista District and that ain't class. That is not one little bit classy. Sheet no! But the woman I rent from don't mind my hours. She works in some club nights. Suits her.'

He swung off Sunset into Benedict Canyon, leaving the blaze and shimmer of neon and the glittering traffic. The canyon wound up gently; few lights, houses dim in the dusky night, no one walking. He started counting aloud. 'Fifth and sixth turning ... should be the next. You said seven along on the left?'

'I did. Tropicana Drive.'

'Is here,' said the White Rat and swung into a suburban street lined with tall palms. 'Somewheres here. Which one you want, you reckon? The Old Virginian homestead, the Arabian Nights, or the Settlers' Cabin? All is real classy. They *rate*.'

The Arabian Nights house was floodlit.

'I think it's that, with all the lights,' said Jonathan. 'Can you see the number?'

'Call it out for me. I got no head for figures, notes yes, sharps and flats, not figures, 'cept on a dollar bill.'

'6745 ... Arabian Nights it is. Dear God!'

'Well anyways,' said the White Rat, 'it ain't in no bears-cage.'

Sybil Witt's house might have been lifted, with the small area of land on which it stood, intact from North Africa. White, square, flat roofed, a slight dome on top like a flattened breast, slender moorish arches, mosaic panels, blue tiles, blue shutters, a blue door.

In the centre of the sandy yard, among artistically arranged

126

rocks, cacti and stubby palms, a ceramic fountain dribbled into a circular tiled basin afloat with white and pink plastic waterlilies. The entire yard was brilliantly floodlit, illuminating the two houses which stood, four arms' length apart from it, on either side. On the left a tall colonial mansion; portico, pillars, manicured lawn, shabby magnolia supported by wires to keep it erect. On the other side a log-cabin in a shroud of shrubs, dominated by two valiant, dying spruce.

'The Ideal Homes Exhibition?' said Lea.

'Want me back to collect you eleven thirty, okay?' said the White Rat.

'That's right, Wayne. We'll be on time, I promise.'

The White Rat shrugged. 'With all this light I don't reckon on gettin' mugged. I gotta jingle I'm workin' on, I'll be happy. Have a nice time.' He started to open his door, then shut it, turned in his seat, one arm along the back of the seat beside him.

'Hey! I just realized. This is our last trip out. You know that?'

'I know that Wayne. You gave me the happy news.'

'It's terrible. I liked drivin' you. You talk to me so nice. Real nice. Call me Wayne. Sheet, man! No one ever calls me that. No one says nothing to me really. Not thank you or goodbye. You know, when they told me at the office this morning you was off the list as from this job tonight, I felt real depressed. I really did.'

'I did too, Wayne. I was a bit surprised myself.'

'And for me to have to tell you the news, I mean that's sick. Whyn't Cristal do it? Why leave it so damned impersonal?'

'I don't know ... but we must get to dinner, we'll be late.'

The White Rat opened his door and started to help Lea from the car. 'A real schmucky deal. Real low, tacky deal. Okay. See you around eleven thirty, have a nice time, and don't worry about me if the party's wild ... I got my jingle to keep me occupied.'

'A real schmucky deal,' said Jonathan as they walked up the pebbled path between fat cacti and spiky palms.

Lea slid her arm through his, her head rested for an instant on his shoulder. 'Schmucky,' she said. 'Like the rest of this place.'

When the White Rat had told him that he had been 'struck off the list as from the end of tonight's job', Jonathan, white with anger, had gone up to his bran-mash room and called Cristal Productions.

A few discreet purrs, not more than three, a light, cheerful, over-bright, female voice.

'Cristal Productions Incorporated, good morning! May I help you?'

'This is Jonathan Pool. May I speak to Mr Shapiro, please?'

'I will connect you with Mr Shapiro's secretary. Please hold.'

A clicking, a hiss, another female voice, impersonal, irritated. 'Who is this? To whom am I speaking?'

'Jonathan Pool, might I speak to Mr Shapiro. It's important.'

A pause. A rustling, a sudden dull thump somewhere at the end of the line. 'Jonathan Pool,' the impersonal voice repeated distinctly. 'Mr Shapiro is in conference right now and cannot be disturbed. I'm sorry.' The tenor of the voice suggested that the conversation was about to be terminated instantly.

Jonathan spoke quickly. 'That is Mr Shapiro's secretary?'

'This is she.' Irritation growing.

'Ellen?'

A pause. A hint of unease crept into the impersonal voice, almost giving it life. 'This is Ellen Luftgarten, I am Mr Shapiro's secretary and I've told you already that he is in conference ...'

'Ellen dear,' said Jonathan, 'I really don't think that I need to speak with Mr Shapiro. I am perfectly certain that you can help me; I am only sorry that I am reduced to speaking to you through the medium of a telephone. And not through a bowl of orange cotton marigolds.'

'I don't understand what you say. Who is this? Will you repeat that? What is it you want to know?'

'I understand from my driver, who has been hired by your firm, that I am no longer "on the list" as from this evening, Friday. My car is being withdrawn. Is this correct?'

'It is correct.'

'But the car was available to me under my contractual rights for the duration of my stay in Los Angeles, that ends on Sunday night. Today is only Friday. Can you give me a reason why I have had two days cancelled arbitrarily?'

A thread of hysteria in the now staccato voice. 'I can not. I have orders that a car will be made available to you, to take you to the airport on Sunday evening, at eight p.m. precisely at your hotel for the ten o'clock flight. I do not have any other orders.'

'I take it then that Mr Shapiro will have no further need of my services? Is that correct?'

'Correct.'

'He doesn't want to see me again before Sunday?'

'Mr Pool,' said the voice, which had suddenly gained courage and was reading at dictation speed, or as if it had suffered a mild stroke, 'Mr Shapiro does not want to see you again. *Ever.*'

'Well, that's pretty clear.'

'I hope so, and now goodbye . . .'

'There is one thing, Ellen my angel, do you have any idea of what has happened to my script of *The Familiars?*'

'I do not. I'm sorry. I have no recollection of anything which we hold as *The Familiars.*'

'*Voodoo Death?* That anything you can recognize?'

The voice surged up with confidence. '*Voodoo Death.* Yes. We do recall such a subject. The project has been dropped. We have no plans at Cristal Productions for the production of *Voodoo Death*, now or in the coming future.'

'You are very kind.'

'You're welcome, and now . . .'

He cut in quickly. 'Ellen, sweet child, if I thought that Mr Shapiro could write anything other than a reluctant cheque, I would say that he was right there beside you scribbling this dialogue just a few inches from your pretty little hatchet face, but since I am certain that he could not put pen to paper I must assume – mustn't I? – that you are the one who is giving me the thumbs-down and making me, in consequence, the happiest man in all Los Angeles. Apart from that hellish tautology just now, you'd make a pretty good script-writer yourself. Just ponder on that thought, and give him my warmest thanks for what must be your very wise decision. And tell him, in passing, that he will be hearing from my agents and from my lawyers, most determined people, and have a very, very, nice day, Ellen dear. You've got a great future in the CIA. Unless, of course, you *are* the CIA?'

He hung up. Stared at the bran-mash fabric walls of his room, at the dead television set, at the bowl of red apples. 'Compliments of

129

the Management', which were already beginning to wrinkle like old women's elbows, and then he started to laugh.

He was still laughing when he reached the over-ornate lobby below where the White Rat, in his orange suit and some degree of anxiety, was sitting on the extreme edge of a crimson Knoll settee.

Ellen Luftgarten replaced her receiver with a crash of fury in her office at Cristal Productions, her brow lightly beaded with a mist of sweat. She laid a consoling, if unsteady, hand on the white-knuckled fist of Mr Andy Shapiro who teetered, dangerously, at the side of her desk.

'That man is a nut!' she said in a conspiratorial voice. 'He is completely crazy! More, he is, well, Mr Shapiro, I feel certain he is a *psychopath*! He talked real dirty to me. Innuendo! What *is* this with the CIA? What is he after? How did he know that my name was *Ellen!*' Her voice had risen several octaves. 'Tell me that! How did he know *my name*? My own, private, personal name! Mr Shapiro!' Her voice came down the scale from 'panic' and stayed steady at 'concern'. 'Mr Shapiro! Are you all right? What is it? You look so wild! Are you ill? Mr Shapiro ...'

Mr Shapiro slowly slumped to his knees, his head fell a little to one side, rested on his shoulder, and then with infinite grace he slid beneath her desk, eyes staring, a frill of foamy bubbles round his ashen lips.

'Oh shit!' said Ellen Luftgarten. 'He's croaked.'

In the white-plastered hall, moorish bird-cages hanging from the ceiling like a host of stalactites, Sybil Witt embraced Jonathan and Lea with warmth.

'Now, listen, just listen,' she said. 'Do not think for one moment that you will be eating cous-cous cross-legged on the floor, nor will you be required to wrench apart a roasted sheep with your bare hands, nor indeed,' she said, slipping her arms through theirs and leading them under a high tiled archway towards an enormous white room, 'will you be offered a candy jar of nuts. I'm off the nuts for a while. Monotony got hold of the game, quite apart from the fact that no one ever bothered to tell me that if nuts is all you are going to eat you gotta go around with a Water Pik strapped to your back. Whatever this decor may give you to believe, you will eat quite normally, at a table, with knives and forks, I hope, and the champagne is chilling as I speak ... Juan!' she yelled at a closed white door across the vast space of the room. 'Bring the vino, will you?'

She stood before them, trim in a white shirt, blue jeans, tightly curled chestnut hair, her brown face unmade up, freckled, amused. 'Have I changed since we met at Alice's last Monday? Tell me now, before the rest arrive, I have to know. Gospel truth, please.'

'Alarmingly,' said Jonathan.

'Alarmingly! Holy cow. What's so alarming!'

'No, no, I meant unrecognizably.'

'Then for God's sake say what you mean. You scared me half to death.'

'I do have to confess, though, that I rather miss the hedgehog look.'

'Still there. Under this. But it gets hellish depressing in the mornings when you look at yourself and say, "Sybil Witt, you have gone too far, and you are getting old, and you've got to use your Water Pik." You just give in, pull on a wig, and smile at the world. "Smile and the whole world loves you, cry and you cry alone" ... know that old thing?'

'I know it,' said Lea. 'It's true.'

'Sure as hell is, honey. And your Aunt Sybil knows too ... now listen. Comment! Say something about this palazzo ... get that out of your system. It is not mine, I have absolutely nothing to do with it apart from paying the yearly rent to an elderly gentleman who is living in Athens with a soldier who's into tutus ... It's the casbah, right? Hedy Lamarr, Boyer and Bergman ... and it is all genuwine.'

Lea looked about the room: white on white, scattered rugs on a blue-tiled floor, a giant half-circular settee, a fire blazing, beaten-brass tables, bare white walls except for one perfect Tabriz carpet, and several bird-cages here and there which, to her relief, contained nothing more distressing than pairs of paper doves.

'Well ...' said Lea. 'It's a bit amazing. Rather fine in its way.'

'In its way, I give you that. You are *so* British! The tact overwhelms,' said Sybil, handing them both a glass of champagne from an offered tray held by an aged Mexican in a white jacket with a cigarette stub stuck to his lower lip. 'Oh Juan! Hell take it, darling! That stub has been there since lunchtime ...'

131

He shrugged, smiled, set the tray on a brass table.

'If he doesn't smoke serving the drink, he'll leave the butt in some unremembered place and we all go up in flames. He's done it twice already. Listen, if you want vodka, gin, whisky, anything ... the regular booze, just say. You don't *have* to have this.'

'Champagne,' said Lea, settling into one of the enormous white chairs, 'to celebrate.'

'Celebrate? Celebrate what?'

'I got the sack this morning,' said Jonathan. 'Cristal Productions. They dropped my project.'

Sybil took a handful of peanuts from a dish. 'Ain't the only thing that dropped at Cristal today, honey.'

'What else did?'

'Andy Shapiro did. Dead.'

Jonathan choked.

'Lea! Hit him! On the back! No! Real hard ... oh God! I thought you'd *know* ... it was on the radio. I'm *so* sorry. Really.'

Jonathan wiped his eyes and mouth, recovered himself, brushed his Dom Perignon-soaked knees. 'I think I spewed some of your wine on the floor. Sorry.'

'It's tiled. No problem. You all right?'

'Overcome. I'm probably the killer! Oh God! What a thought. Lea!'

'You think?' said Sybil refilling his glass. 'Well if you are, you have done this stinkin' town a service. He was a really not-nice fellow. You know? The old school. Hire and fire. Greedy, mean, out of touch.'

'I met him.'

'You know something? Something terrible. He had a younger brother lived here, went to live in Vienna, had four kids, a nice job, the Nazis came. He applied to come back to the USA, had relatives here. Could be supported, you know the deal. Remember? Andy Shapiro was the relative. He refused to sign the affidavit. He said how could he be certain his brother could support himself?'

'And?' said Lea.

'Aw Lea, sweet, come on. There wasn't any "and". Finish, finito, oblivion.'

'Oh God!' said Lea. 'And his wife was so proud, Jonathan told me, of someone who sent food parcels to what she called "Auswich". I couldn't believe it.'

'Hard to,' said Sybil. 'You imagine them handing everyone a tin of cling-peaches on the way to the gas chambers? *That's* this town. Too far away. No comprehension of what happens anywhere but in this place. Anyway, you lost the boss.'

'It doesn't worry me,' said Jonathan. 'It really doesn't. I just hope that his secretary Ellen goes the same road, and soonest. Oh! God Almighty! Los Angeles has started to brush off on me, and I've only been here a week.'

'It has a habit of doing that,' said Sybil. 'It either brushes off on you, or it brushes you off. Either way is dangerous to your health and sanity. But he was on the way out anyway, Shapiro, he was out of touch, lost. The new mafia have taken over the movies now. It's not movies any more, television. The bosses are younger, tougher, concerned with the ratings, they don't have heads like people; they have computers. Everything is time-slotted, no one cares about anything except how many aspirin they sell, or automobiles, or how much shampoo.' She got up and started towards the wide arch to meet Alice and Dubrovnik who were coming across the huge room. 'It's Detergent Entertainment. Alice! Dubrovnik! The party starts ... how great you could come.'

'Terrible traffic,' said Alice. 'We are a bit late.'

'Not a second late. Champagne? Or a regular drink, it's all here? We are celebrating, Jonathan just got his project dropped by Cristal Productions!'

'We just heard, on the car radio. He's dead, Shapiro? Is right?' said Dubrovnik.

'Is right,' said Jonathan.

'Oh my dear,' said Alice, sitting on the wide arm of his chair. 'How bloody for you. Your first big deal ...'

'I'm happy as hell.'

Alice took a glass of champagne as Dubrovnik moved towards the fire.

'You know,' he said, 'is real clammy outside. Is raining a little.' He rubbed his hands together briskly, stretched an arm behind him to the heat. 'Real cold. You get like in the song ... "Hate California, it's cold and it's damp", you know?' He dropped the crushed Polaroid into the heart of the fire as Sybil crossed to him with bowls in her hands.

'Carrot sticks ... or hot cookies? Real hot. Mexican ... and there is an avocado dip right there on the table. Alice! How do you do it? You look good enough to eat, I mean, but really! Dubrovnik, you are monopolizing the fire, you want a carrot stick? No? A hot cookie?'

'Well, I suppose that if they have dropped the project, there's no reason for you to hang around, is there?' said Alice.

'No. Not really. It hasn't quite hit home yet. Almost.'

She used her finger as a swizzle stick to remove the bubbles in her wine. 'Why don't you stay on a little then? Or have you got to get back to Europe?'

'No. Not really. Haven't thought.'

Dubrovnik wandered across to the Tabriz carpet. 'You know, Sybil? This is good. Valuable.'

'Full of moths,' said Sybil. 'You like it?'

'It's beautiful.'

'Wish I could give it to you. If it was mine I would.'

'The colours are so soft.'

'Faded.'

'In centuries of sunlight, I think.'

'I think you really ought to make a trip now that you're here. It's dotty to come all the way to California and just see Wilshire Boulevard; there is more to it than that,' said Alice.

'I'm staying on a little. I'm not going back on Sunday. No real point in rushing. And there are loose ends ...'

'Loose ends?'

'Ummm. To tie up. Lawyers, agents. So on.'

'Oh well ... if you are staying, that's fine. Take a trip to San Francisco. You simply have to see that, it's the most European city in America.'

'I haven't really thought about much yet. Lea, you want to see San Francisco?'

Lea had joined Dubrovnik and Sybil across the room. 'I want to see what?'

'San Francisco?'

'It's beautiful ... and fun. Yes, sure,' she called.

'I've got the car,' said Alice quietly, tracing a finger down the seam in the back of his jacket. 'I can always park the children for a day or two, with a little warning. A couple of nights. Something like that. We could go up to Carmel, Big Sur ... it's ravishing.'

Lea came slowly back towards the fireplace.

'As you are passing a full tray of delicious drink,' said Jonathan, 'could you bear to bring me one, please?'

'Jonathan. You'll be pissed out of your mind. This is your third,' said Lea.

She handed him the full glass, removed the empty one. Across the room Sybil laughed.

'You are too much! Whoever heard of a peacock with a wooden leg!'

'My second, I think. I lost half a glass choking. Right, Sybil?'

She turned and came back across the room. 'Dubrovnik swears that there is a peacock in that carpet with a wooden leg, I mean, his imagination is *quelquechose*! Sure, Jonathan, you lost half a glass.'

'Can I get pissed? Lea says I am.'

'I don't mind, honey. I'll get worried when you start wearing the lampshades.'

'I won't. Promise. I'm free! Tiddly-tiddly-dee!'

'An airship? Or a balloon?' said Lea.

'Ummm. An airship! I want to be an airship. Zoom, zoom. You told me balloons were just full of ... hot air. Remember?'

'I do. So you are an airship full of Dom Perignon.'

'*What* a flight it's going to be!'

'What are you both talking about?' Alice slid from the arm of the chair on to the seat behind Jonathan, leant over his shoulder. Position of possession established.

'Helium Perignon,' said Jonathan.

'I *imagine* it's a private joke? A bit rude in company,' said Alice.

'No. No, it's not private. Anyone can hear it, eh Lea? Only Lea is being a bit bossy this evening, and Lea knows, don't you, what happens to bossy women and me?'

'Oh I do. They end up in Devon, right?' said Lea gravely. 'With a herd of ...'

'Shetland ponies!'

'I think you are both out of your minds,' said Sybil.

'It's going to be, no it *is*, a wonderful party!' said Jonathan.

Sybil slumped on to the settee. 'Parties. It's the only thing we do

135

in this dump. Have parties. Every night. Same faces, same food, same rented butler, same rented maids, same conversation, it is so God-awful. But what else to do here, I ask you? If you can get into one of those "quaint" European-style restaurants you risk food poisoning and instant deafness from the noise, or else are bored to death by the people you didn't ask to the party you didn't give that evening, and when you drive home you could be mugged by a carload of junkies. I mean it is all so damned civilized! Of course you can stay home and try bleeping out the commercials on the TV, but there is a limit to the fun in that. Dubrovnik is *so* lucky! Going to Brazil, he tells me, into the jungle. Death at every step from Indians and boa constrictors. I mean, it's *varied*, you do admit that? You want another drink, my brave explorer, before one of my half-witted and adorable Mexicans says dinner is ready? Or burnt.'

Dubrovnik bent down and kissed her head. 'I never kissed nylon hair before. Is great.'

'You dumb Slovak! It's *real* hair ...'

Alice made a determined effort to pursue her theme. 'I'm trying to persuade Jon to stay on a little, see the place,' she said.

'You should,' said Sybil. 'Lots to see. Right at hand. Grauman's Chinese Theater, the La Brea tar pits, Disneyland! Wow!'

'I meant a trip. San Francisco. Fisherman's Wharf, Chinatown ... Hugo adored it all.' She was deliberately leaving Lea out of this conversation. Aware of an enemy, aware that the enemy was aware.

'When are you going to Brazil?' said Jonathan.

Dubrovnik shrugged, hands in pockets. 'Sometime. Soon anyway. I cannot say for sure. I want to be there for the rain time, and for the summer, the dry period. It is documentary I do.'

Alice straightened Jonathan's collar; he moved forward slightly. 'You lose *your* job, and Dubrovnik just gets the permits to do *his*. Fate. But there are always second chances, aren't there? Or don't you believe in second chances, Jon?'

'Hadn't given it much thought really.'

'Oh, I think that you should. Life would be too dreadful if one only ever had a single chance at anything.' She looked calmly, directly, at Lea. 'Mind you,' she said, pressing her chin into Jonathan's shoulder with overt familiarity, 'I don't think that one can recapture youth. That's time lost. But it can still be fun to plan things. It isn't too late to do that, is it? Do you remember what an impetuous fellow you were?'

Jonathan looked at his glass. 'Was I so impetuous? Don't recall.'

'Spur of the moment things. Adventures! Of *course* you remember.'

Lea got up and walked slowly towards a bird-cage at the far end of the room, singing softly under her breath.

'There's nothing in there to see, sweetie. You think I maybe keep a raven in there?' Sybil had risen and joined her at the cage.

Lea pushed it gently with a finger. It swung slowly backwards and forwards; the two paper doves, wings raised, remained steady, beak to beak, wired to their perch. 'Cooing doves,' said Lea. 'You know they are really bloody creatures. Did you?'

'No. I didn't. Why?'

'Well, they aren't sweet and gentle at all. They smother their young, fight to the death, and ...' she paused, looking through the swinging bars at Alice, '... peck each other's eyes out.'

Sybil followed her look. 'That where it is at the moment?'

'That's where it is.'

'Jonathan?'

'*I'm* keeping him.'

'You do,' said Sybil. 'He doesn't come in batches of a dozen. Alice is my friend, I love her dearly ... however, give it a moment. I'll go break it up ... the perfect hostess, you'll see.' She raised her voice deliberately. 'Dubrovnik! What are you doing? Praying?'

Dubrovnik was kneeling on the floor with a thick coffee-table book before him, his hands clasped in ecstasy. 'You know this book, Sybil? *That Green Hell?* Is amazing. I never saw before. Is all about where I will go. The Amazon ... look at this. Amazing!'

'It's been in the house since I started renting. I prefer "The Merv Griffin Show"...' She walked over to Alice and Jonathan.

'My dears, we are awaiting a guest, not dinner. One Nettles. Usually so punctual but tonight a little late. If he's not here in ten minutes we start, or everything will be ruined.'

'Where is he, Geoffrey?' said Alice.

'You know he won't answer to Geoffrey. He's gone to a small, very in-teem cocktail bash that the Dean of Beekmann College is

137

throwing for him. A personal "thank you for all you have done to try and teach my slobs a little of Roman literature and letters". I guess they'll give him a present, don't you? They usually do. An ink-well or a ceegar-box or some damned thiag, so, Jonathan mine, if you want a quick refill now is the time to get it. We eat in ten minutes, Nettles or no Nettles.' Broken it, she thought. Given him a chance to move. Up to him now.

She caught Lea watching her, raised her eyebrows, went and knelt on the floor with Dubrovnik who was still going through his book. Lea joined them.

'Always very impetuous,' said Alice. 'If you have chosen to forget your madcap past, I am here to remind you. I remember exceptionally well. It was so much fun. Do you remember I once told you that I only really laughed with you? You were the only person who made me, truly and honestly, laugh. Isn't that odd?' She lay back in the chair, the empty glass in her hand, smiling. 'Jon! Of course you remember, 'course you do. I know that you do.' She flicked the rim of her glass with a fingernail; a fine crystal ring eddied round them, faded and was gone. 'Avignon? Forgotten?'

Jonathan edged to the extreme limit of the chair-seat, turned, looked at her.

Smiling still, the finger which had flicked the glass trailed across parted lips, her eyes were bright, shadowed, he could see, far away at the back, with unease and doubt, hair a wild disorder of gold against the white cushions. Still desirable. Still Alice. Alice of Avignon, even. But no one I really know. I don't know this woman. Worse. I don't want her.

'A long time ago,' he said. 'Such a long time ago.'

'Oh! Come on now! Not that long ago. Not millions of years ago ...'

'Yes it was. In my calendar anyway. I can't remember so far back.' He touched her arm lightly, took the empty glass, rose, looked down at her. 'Much too late now. A refill? I'm getting one for myself?'

'Kinder than kind,' she said; watched him leave.

Rejection. There we go again. Rejection. This time pleasantly done; a gentlemanly way to do it, not brutal like Hugo ... sweet rejection from dull, always-waiting, adoring, Jonathan. What the

138

hell has he found in one single week in this town? Lea; nice, boring Lea. Just what he needs. A sort of jelly-baby love-affair. But where did I go wrong? Where have I always gone wrong? I fell in love with only one man, Hugo, and then failed him. Still wanting him; still loving him. But not he. He didn't want me either. Christ! I've been a failure all the way through. The laughing, golden girl, desired by many, taken by few. Lost him to wriggling black girls with Afro hairstyles and parked chewing-gum. Ethnic, he said. Savage, real, so exciting, violent and primitive.

Ethnic my foot.

He just wanted a different kind of sex. And got it. And left me out. I couldn't hope to deal with them. Ethnic! Sweet heaven! Nothing but lust and common or garden carnality. I was no longer interesting sexually. That's all. Nothing more. Used up.

She swung herself gracefully into the seat of the chair, rearranged her hair, rearranged her face, so that when Jonathan reached her with out-hold glass she was smiling. 'Lovely. One does rather need it. I mean, what a party. Five people in a room the size of an aircraft carrier! Hollywood evenings: one gets used to them in the end.'

'Nettles will lift things.' said Jonathan.

'I've been thinking,' said Alice, pulling a strand of hair behind her ear. 'Which usually means that the party is a disaster and one has time to consider, that everything which went wrong with Hugo ever since the day we hit this wretched town didn't *really* happen to Hugo Arlington at all. Do you follow?'

'Not really, no.'

'It happened to Arthur Sean Sproule, not the glittering fake which he wore like cheap jewels. It was Arthur Sean Sproule who went to bits here, couldn't "carry his corn", know what I mean? It wasn't Hugo Arlington who failed, because he didn't, in all honesty, exist. It was the weaker man who tried to camouflage himself with all the glitter and glamour, all those fucking clever bits of writing, but it all came to pieces in Los Angeles. Sproule, the man inside, couldn't handle things here. If there ever *had* been a real Hugo Arlington, the elegant, fastidious, so certain of himself, he might have done things better. Los Angeles, all the "tricks and treats", none of those would have thrown him at all. And the strange thing is that I have only just come to realize it here, in this

139

extraordinary room. What I married and in fact what I got, was Mr Sproule, with all his faults. Not Mr Arlington with all his virtues.'

'Very complex,' said Jonathan, who had remained standing. 'And a strange time to find out.'

'Well ...' Alice raised her glass, pushed the heavy hair behind her shoulders, 'we all of us find out ... a bit too late. Don't we?' She turned as Sybil hurried past with a cry of welcome as Nettles arrived in the tall archway, slim, elegant, haggard as a hanging judge.

'Dinner is saved! We can eat at last! Oh Nettles, we have so missed you,' said Sybil, leading him towards the small group of four by the fire. 'A little drink before we eat? Anything?'

Nettles raised an imploring hand. 'I am awash, my dear Sybil, with some hellish wine-cup, and almost killed by a surfeit of kindness. The Dean and his lady, Mrs Pilkinton, who implored that I should call her Milly, which I could not bring myself to do, have given me the most perfect, "personalized", farewell party you can imagine. There were various members of the Faculty and their wives and everyone made speeches of the utmost gravity and lethal boredom in a perfectly hideous room in a concrete-and-plastic hotel and I am half dead with it all. The kindness ... the warmth ... After all, we did have the official farewell dinner at the end of term ... but this was "personal". And awful.'

'Sit down,' said Sybil, putting a glass of scotch into his hand. 'Drink this and then we'll go eat. Dinner will hold a few minutes. What we all want to know is, did you get a present? A scroll of honour? An engraved cigar-box or ink-well ... something?'

Nettles sipped the drink, closed his eyes. 'It is all so appalling. Yes. There was a presentation.'

'What is it?' said Lea.

Nettles opened his eyes and looked at her. 'You'll *have* to pack it.'

'What is it? Gold, silver, what? Wood or paper?'

'Brass.'

'Brass?' said Jonathan. 'A toasting fork?'

'A most accurate model, I am assured, of Grant's tomb. Circa 1886.'

There was a moment of silence.

'I suppose,' said Jonathan, 'that there is a classical connotation somewhere?'

Nettles nodded tiredly. 'They seemed convinced of it. I have never seen Grant's tomb. Next time perhaps ... next time around?' He looked up, grinned suddenly, and finished his whisky.

Dubrovnik put his arm round Alice's waist and followed Sybil out to the hall and the dining room. Nettles managed to get off the settee and walked between Lea and Jonathan.

'Isn't it funny,' he said, 'how many things can happen in a perfectly ordinary day?'

Dubrovnik lay on his back in the dark, Alice heavy in sleep, on his outstretched arm. I never noticed those damned jeans. I never go to the cupboard. Well, not many times. I cleared all his things, all his stuff. But not those. Not that Polaroid. Now *what* was that? Something I don't know about. I know about the rest, dragged him back here often enough. But Polaroid pictures. Like that. Where? His? Did he buy it ... are there more? Did he take them himself? There is no camera here; no sign, he never said anything to me.

Carefully, he raised himself, slid his arm from beneath Alice's body, turned on his side.

What to do? Etty Baker. Maybe Etty Baker would know? If she'll tell, but no. She wouldn't tell even if she knew, and I suppose she didn't know, because whatever happened at Minty's in those days it sure as hell wasn't that. Minty would have stopped that pretty damn quick. 'Nothing under sixteen, chickadee,' she'd say. 'At sixteen you can make a choice. Not younger, no sir.'

Hugo Arlington. Your wife is in my bed, okay. But Christ! How you haunt. How you haunt. Go away, you bastard. Go away! She must never know about this terrible thing. She never will. You seek to destroy your family even from beyond the grave. Evil! Evil! Evil!

5

Conversations

Mouse sat upright in her chair, arms folded about her body, motionless apart from her feet which swung nervously a few inches above the worn carpet of her bedroom.

'I don't know. I really don't know,' she said aloud in English. 'It is not at all the behaviour of Irina Miratova, it is not at all. Is she ill? Perhaps I should telephone Doctor Frost . . . such a responsibility! House calls are so expensive in America, and his appearance might alarm her greatly. I'll wait.' She nodded her head in agreement. 'I'll wait until tea-time. She told me to awaken her then.'

'Come to me at tea-time, Mousie,' she had said.

So I shall wait. But it is a great worry.

For Irina Miratova to refuse her food for three days! To be coaxed, pleaded with, finally implored to take a dish of hot soup just to give her a little strength after all the vodka which she had consumed. That was the oddest of things, odder than the silence, for she was, by nature, generally exceedingly greedy. The fact that she spoke hardly at all was not, in itself, alarming. She was frequently silent now. But not to eat!

Of course she was a good Russian, and vodka was something to which she was well accustomed. She could, and often she had, drunk a man under her own table and been none the worse. Merrier even, and proud of it.

But this form of drinking was different. Steady, silent, joyless. All in the few days since her tea with Alexi Andreyev. Something serious must have taken place at that meeting. What could it have been?

142

Irina Miratova was not in the very least interested in anything which had happened to Mouse that afternoon, not the slightest glimmer of interest did she show, but that was really not unusual. She hardly ever showed interest in what Mouse did, and if bored by detail, yawned. But it was strange that on this occasion, an unexpected journey into town, a taxi, bargains to discuss, she had showed not the very least signs of curiosity or even awareness, but had simply sat silent in the taxi and stared ahead as Mouse recounted, with a degree of suppressed delight, how she had managed to secure six toilet rolls for the price of only four at a discount store. A bargain which she shyly hoped would bring at least a murmur of praise and which she would then be able to cap with the astonishing fact that she had found a liquor store where she had purchased three bottles of vodka, saving thirty cents on each. She had been elated by the great whitewashed letters scrawled across the windows. 'Slashing Reductions! All Stock Reduced! Save DOLLARS! Must Close!' Normally such an eye for thrift would have elicited at least a nod of approval from Irina Miratova.

But not that afternoon.

Mouse's breathless announcement went almost unnoticed. A slow, sliding look from pale grey eyes, hooded now with unaccustomed concern. Nothing verbal at all. What had gone wrong?

'Countess, dear,' said Mouse speaking in Russian so that the driver would not understand her. 'Are you quite well? Perfectly well? I am suddenly persuaded that you are not yourself at all.'

'I am perfectly well, Mouse, thank you.' Irina Miratova stabbed her silver-topped cane into the floor of the car, turned and looked away through the far windows.

'I have not vexed you? Please say if I have, I beg you?'

'You have not vexed me. Not you.'

Mouse nodded her head with relief, sat clutching the plastic bags of bottles and toilet rolls on her knees. 'If I have not vexed you, and if you are perfectly well, then it is because you wish to ponder on the conversation you will doubtless have had today with Alexi Andreyev, and I prattle away like the thoughtless creature that I am. I am, in all respects, quite unthinking.'

'And I,' said Irina Miratova in a strangely loud voice, 'am but a cog. *A cog.* I am nothing more.'

143

Mouse was quite bewildered. However, she refrained from making any comment because she didn't know what to say. And when they had reached the house and she had paid off the taxi, there was still a void of silence about them as she fumbled with the keys, for she was quite unable to phrase a question or offer a soothing remark. It was far above her head. Cog? What did that mean?

The evening was most depressing. The Countess had refused to eat, declined to speak almost at all, had said that she did not wish to listen to the radio, and finally went to her bed in a slightly tipsy manner (one could hardly say drunken, but a good deal of vodka had been consumed all the same), in complete silence.

And she hardly murmured at all while Mouse removed her corset, the snake-rolled hair-stuffing, the black coat with the beaver collar and her well-darned black cashmere and put them away in the wardrobe with the speckled mirror. Thinking, hoping, that it was just The Mood and that tomorrow the Countess would be quite recovered, Mouse left her in the high bed, the vodka close to hand, and pattered off to lock up the house and prepare for nightfall.

But The Mood persisted to such an extent that within three days all the vodka which she had so prudently bought from the liquor store was gone, and she was forced to drive into the local shopping precinct for replenishments. It was there that, aware that her mistress had eaten nothing but one boiled egg which she said made her feel ill, she discovered some packet soups and a little chicken wing and breast in a paper platter wrapped in cling-foil, which she had purchased for half price because the date of expiry had passed, and hastened home with a singing heart, her head filled with ideas for some delicious dish – perhaps chicken and rice? – which she was perfectly certain that her mistress would find acceptable.

She did not.

It had not even been regarded; merely waved distastefully away, so that Mouse mournfully ate her little treat by herself in the shadowy kitchen, keeping one eye on a simmering saucepan of packet tomato soup.

It had been a wretched three days: four in fact, and she found that the normal pattern of life was seriously altered and bothersome. Irina Miratova rose late, was helped into her bundle of woollens, assisted down the wide staircase, murmuring softly, 'Dust! Dust! Dust!', and eased painfully into a high-backed chair in the big room, facing the windows which looked out towards the grey Pacific. She sat there without speaking, except to reply occasionally, in a perfectly civil manner, to any sensible question which Mouse cared to ask her. She ignored what she considered trivial ones.

Mouse knew, very well indeed, that although her mistress might appear to the casual onlooker to be doing nothing more interesting than staring blankly at a dull sea, she was in fact looking far beyond that, towards their native land, for she had said often enough that beyond the pale horizon lay the infamous islands of Japan, but that beyond them, and a little to the north, was Russia.

'Oh, Countess!' Mouse had said one day many years before, 'it makes it seem so near! If we were to walk, in a straight line mark you, right across the sea, across those deceitful islands, where should we arrive? Can you say, Countess?'

The Countess (who was not certain) said with authority, 'Vladivostok!' And therefore, ever after, Russia had seemed nearer to California, and afforded them both comfort in difficult times.

'Across the sea is Japan. *After* Japan is Vladivostok!' Mouse was strengthened.

And so she knew exactly why her mistress sat staring daily to the west.

And then one morning, grudgingly accepting the dish of soup, to the great delight and consternation of Mouse, she demanded some crackers, which she crushed into the chemical brew and made of it a mush, which she supped eagerly, grumbling inaudibly. It was the grumbling, more than the crackers, which set Mouse's heart a-flutter. Irina Miratova was emerging from her deep Russian Gloom, like a bear from its long winter sleep, and she was convinced that soon she would be quite herself again, thinner perhaps, but the Countess Miratova of old.

And she would be alive because Mouse had had the imagination to purchase a few packets of soup and tend her with loving care.

Sitting in her room alone, arms folded about the small body as if hugging it for warmth and the affection which she had so desperately lacked for years, Mouse remembered that this was not

145

the first Russian Gloom into which Miratova had sunk so deeply: that had happened a long time ago, had been profound, and straining when Senator McCarthy had reduced their guest-list drastically and the house to a silent place.

No one laughed often in those days. The teas, for which the house had been so famous, ceased altogether. The samovar grew tarnished beneath its cloth cover, the guests fled to the east, either to New York, or, some said, even Europe. In the middle of it all, perhaps due to stress, Miratov had fallen dead while shaving, and shortly after his funeral, which Miratova considered had cost her far more than was necessary, three men in long overcoats and grey felt hats arrived one day from the FBI.

Useless for Mouse to say that her mistress was in deep mourning for a much loved husband (she excused herself the lie by crossing her fingers under her pinafore and swore to confess that evening to her icon, an event which was as unlikely as her riding a camel, for she had long ago renounced religion and only paid lip-service now and again to an ill-defined Saviour), but she insisted that they should remove their hats and lower their voices. Which they did.

She never knew the reason for this visit, and was never told of it later, but she did hear, through the closed double-doors of the big room, an outraged and impassioned speech from Irina Miratova about being driven from her class and from her country by the 'swinish Bolsheviks' (a phrase which caused Mouse to double up with suppressed glee), that she had taken an oath of allegiance to the Star Spangled Banner, that America had offered her sanctuary at a desperate period in her life, and that she would never, at any time, offer hospitality to, or knowingly harbour a traitor to, that country, in her own home or anywhere else for that matter, even be they members of her own flesh and blood!

It was strong, histrionic stuff, and went on for some time, and whatever she said seemed to have a soothing effect on the gentlemen from the FBI because, after she had dutifully recognized one or two names on a long list provided, they gave up and left, hats in hand, and were never heard of again.

'I named names on the lists only of those I knew were safely out of the country,' Miratova said later. 'I know those tricks. They seemed unaware that I have had close experience of the GPU.'

But the house remained calm, silent, dusty; for finally the two

146

daily women had to go for lack of funds and the house reverted to Mouse and her mistress. There were fewer and fewer parties to which she was invited, no one was sure who anyone was, politically, and her monthly meetings with her 'messengers' were managed with the greatest care possible. Anyway, she had nothing very much to offer them. During the years of McCarthy her 'messenger' was a slight, pale, fair-haired girl, who knitted all the time and read her own poetry ... aloud. It was perfectly dreadful stuff, quite unremarkable. But then so was the situation. An elderly, one could almost say old, woman sitting on a bench on the sea-front with a plain, over-eager girl with a red nose, a permanent cold and a knitting bag. No one could remark on that.

No one did.

And so they managed together, frugally, cautiously, and finally, with the end of McCarthy, triumphantly.

But it was the end of the days of splendour; they had gone beyond recall.

Mouse leant back in her chair, legs idly swinging, smiling softly at the remembrance of things past. So far away! So long ago! How one had had to fight to exist, to survive. And these last few terrible days at last appeared to be ending. At tea-time, as instructed, she would take up Miratova's glass of lemon tea and see how she was.

If she had sunk back into apathy and gloom, then Mouse would call Doctor Frost, no matter what the cost; a Russian Mood could, after all, sometimes be physical rather than mental, and Miratova, when all was said and done, was in almost constant pain and no longer young. She was really very old. Much older than I am, thought Mouse, for I remember exactly when *I* was born. I remember the year. Nineteen hundred. The start of this disagreeable century. She looked at the tin alarm clock by her bed. It was exactly a quarter to three. She had an hour and a half to herself. What to do? What luxury!

Her pine wardrobe was much smaller than that of the Countess and contained many fewer garments. The beige suit, and the blue for formal occasions, three hats of no particular shape or style save for the one which she had redecorated for that last interesting journey into town by taxi; a long flannel house-coat and a heavy woollen coat for the colder days. She had owned it, she thought, since just before the war, but could no longer be certain. Its hem

147

had been lowered and raised so often that she had finally given in, and left it where it was. Her eyesight was failing, so that made close stitching impossible, and her spectacles were almost as old as herself.

But behind this drab collection there lay beauty.

A dark green taffeta dress which years ago someone had given her because it had a cigarette burn in one of the many flounces which ran round the rustling skirt. A little piece clipped from an inside piece of selvage, which of course didn't show, and gummed to the back of the hole, made the dress as new as ever, and she had been much complimented, in the early days, when she appeared in it at the evening soirées which the Countess had once, long since, given.

But on days such as this, with the grey light pressing hard against the narrow window, when depressions and fears yammered about her like clamouring beggars causing her ill-defined panic and distress, or when she had the time to herself, she would come up to her room, lock herself in, and play her own invented game.

It was very simple. Required no great effort, just the taffeta dress and two chairs, three if anyone was to 'call'. But they seldom did; she found that inventing a third person was tiring and, often, distracting.

So there were just two chairs, one on either side of the dead fireplace; for Mama and Papa.

Today, changing from her rusty black dress with the removable collar and cuffs into the green taffeta, she decided that, perhaps just today, she'd invent a visitor. And because it was such a drepressing day, and had been such a worrying week, she decided to reinvent Hugo Arlington to join their group; he always cheered them up so well. And as she arranged her only necklace of ivory beads (a long-ago gift from Sybil Witt), she considered her conversation, for as there would be no one present – all her guests were long dead – she would have to do all the talking.

She'd listen, of course, politely to anything that anyone had to say and remember the little jokes, the odd turns of phrase, with which they had once delighted her. If she could remember them. Memory was becoming a problem.

Of course, she reasoned, buttoning the long green sleeves, she could always invent, or reinvent to be accurate, her sisters Olga and

Nadia, but because they had been older, and alas! far, far, prettier than she, she usually found it convenient to keep them uninvented, somewhere in the shadows of her mind, lest they become too troublesome with the visitor. She wanted no trouble with Hugo Arlington. He was most desirable to young and impressionable girls, and she was, today anyway, quite determined to have him all to herself. Apart from anything else she knew him better than the others; for the others had never met him, of course. Never met. She fiddled with the last difficult button on the left sleeve. They were dead long before Hugo Arlington even saw the first crack of light, or uttered his first cry. Dead. All dead.

'I suppose,' she said aloud. 'I *suppose* that they died?'

The harsh bite of the frost, the curious way that it melted so slowly as she lay, face to iron earth, hardly daring to breathe, under the glacial myrtle bush. She was too afraid to call out, even in a whisper, to her father. They were somewhere on her left, she knew. Grigori, who was guiding them through the thick forest, had instructed them in a low voice to spread out and take cover, and as the sun rose, a scarlet disc burning through black trees, silvering the icy bark of the birches, they had crept away from each other on hands and knees into the scrub. Poland, Grigori told them, was across the field.

The field lay pinky white in the frost and rising sun. It terrified her by its width, by the sheer nakedness of its length which they would have to cross in order to reach safety in the woods beyond. And then she had heard him leave stealthily. She knew the sound of his heavy breathing, the rattle of phlegm in his chest. He had gone to contact the other guide who would take them over the border. She lay quite still. Once she called out very softly, 'Papa?' and he had whispered, 'Hush!' Then silence.

She had heard the sudden crackle of twigs, the brushing of ice-heavy leaves, Nadia murmur something, her father start to protest, Grigori mutter angrily, and in the wild confusion of words and cracking sticks she heard the shouts, the shots, her mother cry out in shrill alarm, a black crow flap away, low, across the white iced field. And suddenly she knew that she was alone. That she would never see them again.

*

149

'So I suppose that they died then? For so many years I have *supposed*. I have prayed so often, dear Saviour, that you made it as quick as it seemed. But I shall never know for certain, I'll never know.'

In the sudden hush she had inched even deeper under her myrtle bush as booted legs stamped, inches from her small body. She lay for a long time, eyes closed; heard the shouting, sudden bursts of laughter, the clattering rumble of a cart being brought up, and covered her ears instinctively with her hands at the first heavy thud of something hitting the plank floor of the cart. What? A body? Mama? Papa? Olga or Nadia? There was no other sound, no woman's voice, for although she covered her ears she still half listened in her dread. And then men laughing coarsely, talking, spitting. The groan and wrenching of the cart as it swung about, the clumbering of the horses, snorting with effort, the jingle-jangle of the metal harness-bits, the swish and sweep of bushes bent and roughly pushed aside, and Grigori's voice. 'One missing! We've lost one!'

Betrayed. Papa had said that they often did that, the guides, especially if they had been well paid before to lead them, as Grigori had been. 'You don't have any need to fear, little Miss,' he had said when they set out, hand on her head so gently. 'It is the White Army sector where we go. No stinking Bolshevik will be near ... We'll have no trouble ...'

No trouble.

After the cart had trundled into the distance the silence fell about her like a cloth, a silence so infinite, so long, that she was almost dead with fear, and the strange burning cold of the ice which even penetrated the two thick skirts and the heavy coat Mama had made them wear, a tiny icon sewn into the lining.

As the sun rose higher, crows cawing, flapping above her head, she sensed that she was quite alone in the woods, but dared not move for fear that perhaps, just perhaps, they had left one man behind to watch and wait. An old trick. He'd pick her off like a hare.

It was not until dusk, crippled with cold, bowed down by sodden clothing, her mouth dry in spite of the constant licking of iced leaves nearest to her to slake her thirst, body wet through with the melted

150

ice on which she had lain so long, that she cautiously started to ease herself away from the sheltering myrtle and make her way in the gathering gloom down the side of the long white meadow, keeping close to the shelter of the wood which framed it, and then, at the far end, when the wood became thicket and scrub, she pushed through taut strands of vicious wire, ripping her hands, wrestling in fear and mounting terror.

There were male voices far away, somewhere to her left, lending panic to her efforts. She tore herself through the wire, hurrying half bent beneath the frozen trees and frosted bushes until she reached a rutted track which led, in time, to a small country road. It was dark now.

Ahead a shielded lantern bobbing, a woman's coarse voice calling, a male voice in reply, the sudden squealing and grunting of a pig, the woman crying out, scolding, angry.

In Polish.

And then she began to weep, and ran towards the bobbing light.

'Mama! You will be most interested to know that, today, we have a visitor! A visitor from England! Is not that exciting? He is a famous writer and most highly considered there, and so for that reason we shall be obliged to speak in English. Oh, I know that will pose no problem for you Mama, for you speak it with a fluency which has been greatly admired, and of course you have often been there yourself. But Papa! Now, Papa, you will *have* to try your very best. I shall ask our visitor to speak most carefully and slowly, so that you should have little trouble in understanding him. He has a voice of mellowness and beauty, which will delight you, and we shall, of course, entertain him as he is accustomed to being entertained and for that reason we shall use a tea-pot and *not* the samovar! Papa! You frown! Fie! What poor manners! You will see, we shall drink tea from the finest bone china. The same, I am assured, as that used by the Czarina in her own sitting room at Tsarskoe Selo, in the Violet Room, and we shall drink Lipton's Darjeeling, a rare tea of great flavour and distinction, and as a most particular treat we shall offer him McFarlane and Lang's own shortbread which, I know, Papa, is a particular favourite of yours. Only this time, on this especial occasion, I would beg that you do *not* dip it in your tea. This

151

is much frowned upon in good circles in England. Our visitor will appreciate our delicacy and taste. We shall show him that we are not Russian vulgarians, which is too often the case I fear, and although shortbread is not, strictly speaking, an English confection but a Scottish one, I am certain that he will not be in the least put out. Except that we must remember to call it *Scots*. Not *Scottish*. That also is frowned upon, I am told.'

Mouse moved from chair to chair during this monologue, her arm resting lightly on one, and then on the other, as she spoke and listened to her parents, head to one side, a small bird, eyes bright, sometimes folding her arms before her. She had brushed her sparse hair neatly, bound it round with a velvet ribbon which she had saved from a box of chocolates someone had thrust upon her many Christmases ago in a last-minute flurry of forgetfulness.

'Now then! Are we ready for our guest? Papa, you promise me that you will not doze off? Mama, you will be quite enchanted, he is wondrously handsome and very witty. He is here! I know! I know his tread upon the stair!' And then she turned towards the locked door, her hands to her lips, to contain the slightest cry of pleasure which might have escaped them.

'Mr Arlington!' she said, offering her hand. 'How exceedingly good of you to grace this modest house. Mama. Mama, may I introduce Mr Hugo Arlington, the writer, of London ... and this is my Papa. I fear that Papa is rather naughty ... ah! yes! you are, dear man, for you will *not* speak English, and he speaks it perfectly well, you know, he also reads it fluently. Are you perhaps acquainted with the *Illustrated London News*, Mr Arlington? He reads *that* exceptionally well. From cover to cover. Mama, of course, speaks it fluently. Oh Mama! You are *too* modest I fear. What will Mr Arlington think of me if I make false claims! Mama has spent three Seasons in London and also in the country, in some of the very prettiest places you can imagine, and she rides most beautifully. In this country of ours we are born and bred with horses, you might say. Ah! Now I have shocked Papa, but nevertheless, it is so. Mr Arlington, pray sit. This chair? Or perhaps this one, not so near the fire? I recall that the last time you graced our company you said that you preferred to stand, just to wander about quite freely as you spoke, am I correct? I think so. You said that a chair made you feel that you were imprisoned. Is that not droll, Mama? A chair to be like a prison? But you are a writer, and a writer must be free to move and express himself as he wishes, so please do. Tea will be ready in a jiffy, the kettle has not quite come to the boil, and that is very important to a good infusion, it is so? Ah! I am glad that I was right. No, Papa! Mr Arlington does not write *novels*! He writes serious books, nothing as frivolous as a novel, and he has other virtues unguessed at yet! He sings quite beautifully and he also plays the pianoforte. Now!' She suddenly raised a teasing finger, 'Here is an astonishing thing! He also takes photographs! He makes no boast of this, I know, but nonetheless it is so. You did not know that I was aware of your little secret, Mr Arlington, did you? Whatever next! Well, do you recall the time that you came to burn some papers in the big furnace below? Manuscripts, I think that you said they were? Do you remember? Well, that day you left your little camera behind in that dismal cellar, just lying in a cardboard box ... quite forgotten, and ...' she removed her hand from behind her taffeta back, '... here it is! Quite intact. As you left it. Am I not the cleverest creature you have ever met? It was perfectly simple of course, the place was so wretchedly dark, the camera is black, and you were in quite a spin that day I recall, quite a spin ... so easy to overlook. But directly you were finished down there I hurried to see if all was well. This house is all of wood, you see; the furnace had not been used for so long, and I was a teeny bit afraid that ... well ... a spark? Something? But I raked about in the ashes ... there was nothing left glowing ... you had burned *everything* quite up. I was just being prudent. The Countess gets into such a fuss if I venture into the cellar, she is afraid that I will do myself some kind of mischief in the dark! Or fall through the stairs. Such nonsense! And she thinks that I am afraid of darkness! Of all things! Darkness has been my companion for far too long, I could not fear it now. But, I prattle on! Here we are, your camera safe and sound. I was so delighted, for I determined that I should give it to you the very next time that you returned. But you never came back. Never again ...' She placed the Polaroid camera on a small table between the two chairs. 'You would be very curious, Papa, it is a kind of magic. One presses a button and click! there is the photograph already printed! And in colour ... in colour ... clear as day, real as anything ... in colour!'

153

She stood perfectly still, looking at the empty chairs before her, arms folded, a smile dying. In the sudden silence of the room the tin clock struck the half-hour.

'They are all dead,' she said. 'All dead, and I am alone. Playing a foolish game. But the game is quite over ... the dead do not respond.' She pulled the velvet ribbon from her head, rolled it into a tight coil, threw it into the seat of an empty chair. 'Talking to them doesn't bring them back.'

She walked over to the narrow window, tugging at the tight buttons of her sleeve, trying to reach the zip at her back, surprised that she could feel tears dribble down her face, curl into the corners of her mouth. She wiped her nose with the back of her hand, disengaged her arms from the dress so that the sleeves and bodice fell before her like a sagging apron.

'They never reply, you know, never. Dead is *dead*.'

She leant against the window, pressed her face against the cold glass. The sea was leadened, the light failing. Her glasses misting.

Somewhere, far beyond the nervous ticking of the clock, she heard the distant flapping of a crow's wings, a stick snap, a woman cry in sudden fear.

She stayed quite still, face against the window, looking into the gathering gloom through blurring eyes towards the thin silver thread on the horizon beyond which, she knew, lay Vladivostok.

Santa Monica Beach

'One gets infinite pleasure from walking along a soaking winter beach. In wet shoes ... don't you think? Aesthetic? Something of that sort,' said Jonathan.

Nettles looked down at his own feet. 'Are yours frightfully wet?'

'Sodden.'

'Well ... tell you what. Let's take them off. Far more comfortable.'

'Barefoot? In January? Freezing?'

'Oh, come now ... don't be so wet.'

'But I am! You can see ... Look, soaked through.'

'Well take them off,' said Nettles, sitting down on the sand and unlacing his. 'There is simply no point in squelching about in wet shoes. Catch a cold.'

'How far are we intending to march? All right if I ask?'

'Oh ...' Nettles removed one shoe, peeled off a sock. 'Yes. *I'm* wet too. *Quite* wet. Boring. Shoes today aren't what they were. March, did you say? Oh, not far. Those houses down there. All right?'

'All right. Mine are off. Look,' said Jonathan.

'So they are. Frightfully good shape, your feet; beautifully formed. Like those Italian medieval figures of the Christ, do you know? Bone or ivory.'

'Bone is what they feel like. Any idea how we carry these things? Shoes?'

'Stick your socks in them, tie them together with the laces, sling 'em round your neck. Simple. Like this, see?'

They got up and started walking again, trousers rolled to the shins.

'I think this is a bloody awful place,' said Jonathan. '*Far* worse than Cooden Beach.'

'I never was there, I'm afraid, and I'm a little prejudiced I suppose because I have had the privilege of seeing this place in the summer. Very jolly. Bright, one might say. Lots of colours. All the young smoking pot and screaming about with beach balls. The Americans take their, what they call "Leesure", very seriously. All true Californian – bronzed, tight-skinned, amazingly fitted out with dentistry. It's so dreadfully sad that they age so badly, without character and with desert wrinkles. The golden skin creases like a turkey's throat. Too sad. And then they all trail off and retire to Florida, at sixty.'

'What's the building over there, in the middle, that brick tent?'

'Ah. The public conveniences. Approach them at your peril. The stench is appalling, the mugging worse, and they do quite terrifying things to each other in the stalls. They have half-doors, you see, so one is able to notice things all too clearly, even if one turns one's head and holds one's breath.'

On their right the strange, eroded, earth cliffs, the Pacific Coast Highway. Tall Florida palms standing high, motionless in the spumy air, like mops. To their left the sullen, flat, January sea and

155

ahead, fading into the drifting mists, a vague headland, a clutter of wooden buildings.

'*Far* worse than Cooden Beach,' said Jonathan.

The sea slid along the wide beach, scalloping the sand with little half-moons of foam.

'I do think that you are being disagreeable, Jonathan. Really I do. Here we are, walking along the edge of the Pacific Ocean, walking along the edge of the whole Western world you could say, and you compare it with an unloved watering place in southern England. *Very* narrow-minded. And don't even *touch* those!' he cried as Jonathan stooped to wrench a cluster of mussels from a half-sunken post.

'Why? The size of them! Amazing!'

'Instant death. Pollution. I regret to say that the Pacific, on this side, is the dumping ground of all the lavatories, and God knows what else, in Los Angeles, and if you consider, should you so wish to do such an unsavoury thing, the proud boast that Los Angeles covers two hundred square miles, you can, perhaps, imagine ... well ... I leave it to you, dear fellow.'

Jonathan threw the clutch of mussels out towards the ebbing sea, scattering a tight covey of little black-and-white birds which scuttled on stick-thin legs backwards and forwards to the nudging water.

'That's exactly what I mean. It's bloody awful. But I am quite enjoying it. *Really.*'

'One would find it difficult to trace clues to that impression,' said Nettles.

Jonathan laughed suddenly, punched him lightly on the arm. They walked on in silence.

'She came to you when she was ten, that's so?'

'That's so.'

'Hell of an adjustment.'

Nettles looked across at him sharply. 'Tremendous. But, I hope that you have seen, we managed pretty well.'

'I have. Yes. Wouldn't have used the word "managed", though. Isn't quite the right word, is it?'

'Isn't it? What would you suggest instead? Coped? Struggled through? Made out? What?'

'I'd use a terribly banal word, I suppose. None of those. Loved?'
Nettles laughed, his breath drifting away on the still air. 'God!
Isn't it awful. A word so charged with magic, with so many glorious
meanings and interpretations, with such a diversity of possibilities
is, and you are perfectly correct, all at once banal. Over-use, I
suppose. But yes. Yes indeed, you'd be right to use that word. We
loved each other almost from the very first. I say "almost" because
our *very* first meeting, alone together, man and child all unaware,
wasn't pleasant. Under the circumstances. Bloody, as a matter of
fact. It is not the easiest thing in the world to do to go to see a child
whom you know only as a child, vaguely, amusedly, affectionately,
and explain to her that her parents are dead and that she is on her
own in the world.'
'You did that?'
'No one else. No real family strangely enough, any that mattered.
And both parents were orphans. I was godfather, ergo, my duty. I
could not fail in it, or fail her, or her parents, and it is not the kind
of thing one leaves to a kind and understanding headmistress,
however understanding.'
'Christ. What a hellish thing.'
'Oh it was. It was.'
'I was actually thinking of you.'
'So was I.'
'But you "managed"?'
'Somehow. Difficult at first. For us both. A good deal of re-
adjustment here and there. One's private life was considerably
altered, of course, and for the better. You see, the curious thing is
that in spite of my advanced and, I liked to think, sophisticated,
age, I had never really loved anyone or been loved by anyone. Not
unusual, of course, but unpleasant. Those banal words, love, loved.
Goodness me! But somehow they were not a part of my experience.
She changed all that. Sometimes the demands which she in-
advertently made on me were quite enormous. Terrifying, on
occasion. But I found that I could handle it because I knew that she
needed me. I'd never been needed before. It was a curiously pleasant
sensation. Still is. To my astonishment I discovered that I had made
the classical error of confusing sex with love. I sought sex constantly. Anywhere, with anyone, in the mistaken, and desperate,

hope that it would one day bring me love. Of course it never did. I am bitterly ashamed to have to admit to you, striding along this empty beach on the edge of the world into what appears to be a thick fog, that I had a predilection for the companionship, shall we say, of some pretty rum people. Guardsmen, bricklayers, policemen ... an amazing number of policemen in my life, isn't that strange? and what one knew, in my shady life, as Rough Trade. Naturally they brought no love at all. Sometimes we only met once – furtive, ugly, almost silent meetings which ended, for me, in abject shame and misery. Horror, regret, all the banal words you can imagine. I think, in fact I know, that when Lea was suddenly thrust into my life by the unexpected and brutal killing of her parents under a blazing petrol-tanker somewhere near Coventry, I had reached the point of such self-hatred, was so suffused with a burned-out loathing of myself, that I decided to pack it in. I had collected, over a period of time, a very jolly collection of pills which I planned to swallow with a bottle of scotch. Hadn't the guts, you see, to do it sober. And when I say that they were "jolly" I really only mean that they were colourful. Hundreds and thousands we used to call them as children, a mixed bag of stuff I'd hoarded. Of course the jokey thing is that I have a shrewd feeling that had I done such a thing I'd have vomited, nothing more. A most awful let-down having to face another day with a reproachful nurse and a stomach pump ... I'm told the best way is to spread them all out in a sandwich, crushed up if they are pills, or emptied out if they are capsules. Depends on your brew. It does seem a little idiotic to make oneself a deadly sandwich and solemnly eat it all up with a glass of whisky. Easiest way is a razor to your wrists in a warm bath, I'm told, but somehow, after the war, I rather dislike shedding blood. Particularly my own.'

He stubbed his toe on a half-buried stone. 'Shit!' he said.

'I'm sorry,' said Jonathan.

'Doesn't hurt ... just a stone. Wasn't looking.'

'Not about that. The pills, so on.'

'Oh! You really needn't be. Absolutely no need at all. Everything changed in one extraordinary, dreadful, day. I was sent for to make the official identification. Can't remember quite how they got on to me, or how they did so quickly, but I went. It was a peculiar time. Time out of life. It didn't seem to be happening to me. It was as if

158

I was watching me doing something from behind a two-way mirror, do you know what I mean? Not a reflection of life, a falsity. It was quite unreal, so it didn't, at first, hurt as much as it might. It did later. I was able to identify Rooke's car, what remained of it; knew the number-plate, strangely. Odd how *that* stuck in my mind. But they wouldn't let me see them. Emmie or Rooke. Very nice, understanding, but firm. I identified his signet ring, crushed flat, half melted it seemed, and a bit of cloth. A piece of plaid from a suit which I knew he rather liked. It was harder with Emmie. Fragment of blue wool, a bit of metal which could have been a brooch or a clip. Really nothing. Anyway I couldn't positively identify anything, but I did recall that she had a tiny scar just above her right eyebrow, not enormous, rather attractive actually, a childhood fall . . . something. I don't now remember, and the policeman or policewoman or whoever it was, I can't be sure, said, "Oh, I'm sorry sir, but there is no face." '

They walked in silence. Nettles cleared his throat. 'So you see it was quite difficult. Really very hard indeed. Finally they produced a bit of a bracelet . . . well . . . a few stones. But I recognized them, they'd bought it in Jaipur or somewhere. I knew it well. A few stones, that's all.'

'Nothing to say. Is there?' said Jonathan.

'Nothing,' said Nettles. 'Nothing needed, it's all over and done with now. Years ago, and Lea, by the way, doesn't know any of this part, so just hold your tongue, will you, about that?'

'Of course.'

'I'd met her father, Rooke, in 1945. Joined my division in the East Indies, a bad time, a civil war going on, grenades at breakfast, that sort of thing, terrorist stuff. He was very young, glowingly good-looking, not the greatest intellect I suppose, usual well-bred public school product. Good at games, well mannered, keen. Anyway I fiddled things about so that he became ADC to our rather common, but pleasant, General. Worked out very well. He was excellent at the job, and brave. Perfectly splendid.'

'And Lea's mother?'

'Oh. Emmie? Amazingly beautiful. Half Dutch, half Javanese, spoke English perfectly. Her family had been wiped out by the Japanese, and she'd been locked in a tiny windowless cupboard for

159

over a year by them as a punishment for stealing spare parts and petrol and so on for trucks and cars some of the young people had hidden in the jungle in preparation for the Liberation. Madness, really. They rounded them all up. But she was wonderfully brave, very determined.'

'Like Lea.'

'Like Lea indeed. Extraordinary resemblance between them. Same odd humour, too ... anyway we needed interpreters badly, she volunteered and became Rooke's assistant on our frightful divisional newspaper. Worked wonderfully well. Two of the most beautiful creatures I think that I have ever met, or ever will.'

'And they got married?'

Nettles scuffed wet sand ahead of him. 'Yes. Got married. I had a hand in that, as you might guess. She was reluctant – black babies, throwbacks, that sort of thing. He was so besotted I really don't think he would have minded if she'd produced a packet of Liquorice Allsorts at the birth. You follow what I mean?'

'Goodness yes.'

'So she was heavily persuaded by me to take the risk. Of course she was as dotty about him as he was about her. Their first child was ravishing. Died early from some kind of problem babies can get, I don't know. Cot death or something ... and they waited a bit and then ...' he turned towards Jonathan, arms outstretched, '... we got Lea. I *do* think that we were wonderfully fortunate, don't you?'

'Wonderfully.'

'She's woefully stubborn. I suppose you have discovered that in a few days? And she has, or had, the worst taste in men that I have ever encountered in a woman. Really ghastly.'

'Thanks,' said Jonathan. 'You are more than kind.'

'Oh Lor'! Well, naturally I didn't mean you. I mean if I had, I wouldn't have said what I did. Would I? Follow?'

'In a rather muddled way, yes.'

'Oh no. No, you're all right. As long as *she* thinks so. It'll be the first sensible thing she has done, emotionally I mean, in her life. Really, some of the others were quite intolerable ... I don't know why women do that kind of thing.'

Jonathan saw that they had reached the clustered houses along the edge of the beach. 'This is our limit, isn't it? The shacks? Lights

160

are going on, so it's getting a bit late. Should we start back?'

Nettles sighed. 'No spirit. No guts. Really, Jonathan. And these "shacks", as you call them, would cost you your fortune should you wish to purchase one.'

'Nothing could induce me. They look like those railway carriages on the shingle at Pevensey ... I've told her that I love her, by the way. I mean she knows. Whether she believes me is, of course, another matter.'

'Oh, she believes you, I think,' said Nettles doing an about-turn and starting to walk back towards the pier. 'Been singing round the house for two days ... and the preparation for lunch this morning! God! You'd think that every plate was to be set before emperors.'

'As long as you know the situation,' said Jonathan. 'You have to know that.'

'Doesn't make much difference to me now. Lea has lived her own life for some time now, I don't literally wait for her to spoon-feed me. We have different places of abode, see each other, oh ... once a week sometimes. Sometimes just telephone. But the marvellous thing is that I know she is there, and she knows that I am there. And if something troubles her she comes to me. Sometimes it *is* a bit inconvenient. I could be worrying away at, say, *The Marriage of Peleus and Thetis*, and she crashes in, sobbing, about another blazered Flash Harry who has let her down. But one copes, one copes. Of course she has far outgrown my advice, so she does exactly what she thinks is best. It often *isn't*, however. I just hope that you'll stick. It *would* be so relaxing, and although you are not exactly in the first flush of youth, so to speak, I would venture to say, should you have asked me, that you are very suitable. You'll bang her about a bit when she gets tiresome. She needs it, and she likes it as a matter of fact. Useful. She can become incredibly bossy ... my fault in the very early years. I let her have her way a bit too much, perhaps.'

'It is perfectly extraordinary,' said Jonathan, 'walking along a winter beach as we are, the lights springing up, the mist coming down, gulls planing about, to be talking about her to you. Loving her as I do, remembering her, even now, with little surges of pleasure which knot my guts, do you know what I mean? Christ, I'm saying it badly ...'

161

'No, no, no ... I know exactly what you mean. Even I, without carnality, experience those surges. Quite sudden, sometimes unexpected, and often, if I didn't know what they were and who had engendered them, I'd go to a clinic for a check-up. Madness.'

'I love her so bloody much.'

'And what of Alice Arlington?' said Nettles, vaguely looking towards the lights of racing traffic along the Pacific Highway.

'What of her?' said Jonathan.

'We met, if you remember, for the first time at her house, four days ago. She said that you had known each other for a thousand years. I merely asked.'

'Oh, I've known her ages. And that tiresome husband.'

'Wrote some good stuff. Arlington.'

'Some. Yes. He patronized the arse off me, so perhaps that's why I didn't like him much. I know that my dislike should not extend to the man's works, but it does.'

'Yes, he could be exceedingly patronizing. I suppose one should not speak ill of the dead.'

'He would not have had the same scruples. I suppose that Alice said that I had been in love with her for years and years. A hopeless love? She rather enjoyed the idea of a faithful, yearning, adoring swain.'

'Oh, something of the sort. Nothing much, an implication only.'

'If I know Alice it was more than an implication ... and she was right. I loved her for a very long time, hopelessly, idiotically. Went pop! that night.'

'Pop? Do I take it that you mean the night we all dined there?'

'You do. The instant I saw Lea. Poor Alice became poor. She lost her swain, she lost the devoted, slavering spaniel, who sat ready to obey her every whim ... "Good boy! Come for walkies ... Fetch your ball-ie ... Catch! Guard! Seek!" I ran about doing everything I possibly could to please her, and Hugo was charming. Sometimes I thought he might pat me on the head – for excellent behaviour.'

'Alice know? About your feeling, as they say, for Lea?'

'I think that she does ... last night at Sybil Witt's supper. She's suddenly found herself alone here, west of Sunset as she calls it, because the lover-chap, what's his name?'

'Boris Kragujevac. Dubrovnik for short.'

'Him, well he's apparently off to Brazil or somewhere, as you gathered. She'll be on her own, so she decided to call her devoted spaniel to heel. But I didn't catch! seek! or guard! I had waited too long, just too long. And I'm afraid she knew.'

A wind swirled the sea-mist up and away along the beach, dimming the brick tent, spinning a length of sodden yellow ribbon across their path like a bilious snake.

'A yellow ribbon! Goodness, how quickly it's all forgotten,' said Nettles sadly.

'So she knows. I don't very much care anyway,' said Jonathan. 'I know where I am now, and who I want, and I'm going to get her, by fair means or foul.'

'It'll be a great relief to me,' said Nettles. 'Great relief.'

'It'll be a great relief to me to get back to Europe. To leave this place. I know I've only been here a few days, that it is *not* America, but I really don't care for it, you know. Really not. There is an infinite sense of sadness, a sense of loss, of missing out. You were perfectly right just now when you said that we were walking along the edge of the Western world. We are. One is aware of it all the time, and I am absolutely terrified that I might fall off or, much worse even, be forced to stay here in this twilight existence as a permanent refugee. Like the rest of them.'

'Not much longer now,' said Nettles briskly. 'In a week or so you'll probably look back on this time with enormous nostalgia. Lea says that she will. She likes it here, strangely enough. Mind you, three weeks' holiday is hardly time to form an opinion ... neither is a short week, like you. I've had a year – vastly interesting. At my time of life one grabs the chances, you know. This is one I wouldn't have missed for anything. The Americans are the most generous people on earth, but I do wish that I hadn't collected such a mass of junk I can't bear to leave behind. An iron skillet, for God's sake!'

'Grant's tomb.'

'Oh God! Yes. That too. Such *kindness*. I say, I think that perhaps we'd better put on our shoes and socks, wet as they are. We are almost at the pier, you know, and the hazards of walking barefoot along it, or the promenade, are simply frightful. Gobs of spit and masticated chewing-gum. Rather have wet feet, wouldn't you?'

'Much.'

They sat together, back to back, on the trodden sand.

'No easy matter,' said Jonathan, struggling with a sanded foot and a sodden sock.

'I'm sorry that I've talked so much,' said Nettles. 'Bored you witless I shouldn't wonder. Habit. Lecturing. You should have stopped me.'

'Not for anything. Thank you. Thank you, really.'

'Can't get my socks on. I'll just wear shoes. If we get back to the house safely it'll be perfect timing for a cup of tea. And remember, never a word about her parents' deaths to Lea, you promise me?'

'I promise,' said Jonathan.

Torcello Avenue, Venice

Dubrovnik kicked a tin can hard across the yard. It hit the side of the wrecked car with a 'clunk'.

Etty Baker came out on to the porch wearing a thick knitted pullover sagging round her hips.

'You do that?' she said.

'Yeah. Tin can.'

'You take goddamned liberties with people's property. Catch your death, you walk about like that with no coat.' She turned and went into the house.

Dubrovnik followed her up the four wooden steps, across the porch, into the dingy hallway.

'You come for your things? Shirts? Is all ready.'

'I brought a couple of others, can you take them?'

'Oh shit,' she sighed. 'It's Saturday ... I got to be slaving all the week?'

'No hurry.'

'It's cold, right? Real nasty. This my eldest, Sabrina.' She indicated a girl sitting by the window, head bent low, hands plaiting strands of coarse black hair. 'Sabrina! We got a visitor. You say somethin'? Nice, okay?'

'Hi,' said Sabrina, without looking up.

She was, Dubrovnik thought, about sixteen. Fat pouting lips

164

shining with crimson lip-salve, silver shoes, a tight skirt, tee-shirt with 'Screw Pigs' across heavy breasts.

'She making her hair all plaits, with beads and things,' said Etty.

'Reggae,' said Sabrina.

'Whatever it is it ain't going to get a wash.'

Sabrina sighed, 'So what?'

'You lose your job, you look like a dirty girl.'

'Who cares?'

'Your father'll give you a whippin' ...'

'Let him.' Sabrina laughed, head low, fingers ferreting among beads and hair.

'I brought something,' said Dubrovnik, holding out a wrapped bottle.

Etty took it, sat down at the table which had taken the place of the folding ironing board. 'You wanna sit? Move that goddamned cat off.' She unwrapped the bottle. Held it high to the light from the window. 'Ain't that just the prettiest colour you ever did see? Clear gin. Beefeater. You so good; want a glass?'

'Sure. It's tea-time. Right?'

'Is gin time,' said Etty. Found two dusty glasses on the sideboard with hearts and spades printed on them. 'Just a touch, right?' She unscrewed the bottle and poured them each a small measure. 'What you brought. Shirts? You want them real quick?'

'No, no hurry. There's a pair of pants.'

'Pants?'

'Jeans.' He unwrapped the small bundle, threw them to her.

'They too small for you? These yours?'

'The Duke's. I just found them.'

She held them for a moment, stroked the cloth. 'They his okay. Designer jeans. Real classy. These cost. You found them?'

'In a closet. At the Loft. I didn't know.'

Etty put her hand in each pocket.

'I did that already. There is nothing,' said Dubrovnik.

'Well. Sometimes people leave things. In pockets.'

'He did.'

'Did? The Duke? What he leave then?' She was smiling in-differently, sipping her gin, the jeans tumbled before her on the table.

'Ten dollars.'

'He had the smallest waist, longest legs, that Duke.'

'You got someone they fit? No good for me. Keep them, you would like to?'

'Sure. I know someone.' She touched the jeans with a curious gesture, half affectionate, half cautious. 'Touchin' them. So strange. Like he's close by. Like he could walk in that door.' She withdrew her hand. 'Is all gone. The wild nights. Minty's. You see Minty's now? A Vietnam place, all with lanterns and dragons.'

'Etty, you ever know if Duke had a camera?'

She looked up at him slowly, eyes half closed, raised her glass, sipped her gin, smiled, head to one side. 'I never see no camera. Never did see the Duke but bare-assed.'

'A Polaroid? I'm thinking to myself maybe that he had one.'

Etty shook her head slowly. 'I never did see. Why you ask?'

Dubrovnik looked across the room at Sabrina worrying her hair. Etty caught the look, said suddenly, 'Sabrina. You scat now.'

'I'm doin' my plaits. You see me? Real clear?'

'I see you. Do 'em some other place, you scat gal or I make you hurry.'

'My beads! My mirror! Don't mess up my beads for chrissakes.'

'I mess you all up, you don't get out of here, so help me. Scat!'

When Sabrina had left the room, slamming the door hard behind her, Etty turned to Dubrovnik.

'So. What you want to say you didn't want to say in front of my Sabrina?'

'In these pockets. I find ten dollars, right?'

'You say so.'

'There was a photograph. In the back pocket.'

Etty raised her glass. 'So?'

'It was very bad. A not-nice photograph, you know? Two children. Black children.'

Etty looked vaguely around her cluttered room, her eyes came slowly back to him. 'What so bad? You goin' to tell me?'

'They were little. Maybe nine years old ... ten. Naked. Tied on a bed.'

'You think he made this picture?'

'I don't know. That's why I ask you about a camera, you see.'

166

'I never saw no camera. Never at Minty's. Not ever there.'

'I wondered.' Dubrovnik shrugged, finished his gin.

Etty fisted a hand, rubbed her nose hard. 'One day he said to Minty, and I recall clear, he said, "One day, Minty, I going to do something real bad. So bad these kids here will stomp me to death."' She drained her glass, put it on the table. 'I ain't never forgot. He was crazy. Death crazy. No good in that man's soul, no good.'

'Sometimes he was fine,' said Dubrovnik. 'I remember sometimes when he was okay. My fault for bringing him to Minty's in the first place. He wanted to look around . . .'

'Caught his fancy, I reckon. Hoomiliation, eh? And now what you think? He into kiddie-porn or something, that it?'

'Maybe he bought it? Hollywood Boulevard is full of places for that. Maybe he just bought himself some photographs.'

'They was nine or ten, you say? The kids?'

'About.'

Etty got up, screwed the top onto the gin bottle, picked up the jeans and threw them into a chair. 'Shit,' she said. 'I never saw no camera. He never said.'

'He maybe had a place of his own. Did he ever tell you? Like a room? A long way from his home?'

'He never did say.'

'Because they can't find his diary for a whole year. 1979 . . . and almost half of '80 . . . all the pages torn out. Maybe he had a secret place, a room somewhere.'

'We didn't do so much yakkin', you understand? At Minty's it was action. Not jest talking. Oh, sure, sometimes, before the coke really got to him, before the drink got to the coke, sometimes, now and agin, we'd talk . . . a while. No great deal, I don't remember no room, no private place he ever said about. I only knows your place, and when to give you a call come collect. Remember? Minty would say, "Get Mr Boris right smart . . . this gone on too long." So we'd call you up on Whitecrest. Those days, remember?'

'I remember, said Dubrovnik, thumping his knee with the flat of his hand. 'Most times I blame myself.'

'Is a fool born every day, so they say,' said Etty. 'Too late now to fret.'

167

'I'm going away for a while. Maybe six months, eight, I can't be so sure yet,' said Dubrovnik.

Etty sat in a chair at the end of the table. 'I *got* to remember to sit. I stand so long, I got feet problems. Where you goin'?'

'Brazil.'

Etty was pleating a small corner of the tablecloth. 'I don't exactly recall this Brazil,' she said.

'South. Way south.'

'Like after Mexico . . . ?'

'Like after Mexico. Well after.'

'And the widder. Your friend. She goin' on this trip?'

'She has children like you do, Etty. Schools, so on. No, she stays here.'

Etty pressed the flat of her hand over the creases she had made in the cloth. 'So she stays. Is lonesome. And the Loft on Whitecrest? You closin' up that pretty big room? Be all ripped out if you do, afore you get back. Leave it empty they just strip it bare.'

'I think maybe I'll rent it. A man I know in New York. Painter. He will care for it. You think I should tell him you will wash his shirts like you did for me?'

'I ain't no washer-woman. I do for you because I like you. Right? I don't wash for no strangers. I got kids. I got, when he home from San Diego, a man. Hallelujah!' She got up, pushed the hair from her forehead, stared into the darkening light of the day.

'I got enough,' she said.

'I was asking only.'

'I was saying only,' she said. 'Was real sweet of you bringing that bottle. A real sweet idee. Ain't so many of those floating about this place . . .'

Dubrovnik got to his feet, tucked his shirt into the belt of his pants. 'I better get going. It is almost dark.'

'Yep, you git, afore dark. This ain't the best neighbourhood to be alone come the dark.'

The door opened, Sabrina put her head round. 'Hey? It's too dark now to see in that room. I come in here? You finished?'

'You come. We finished. Sweet Christ!' said Etty looking at her daughter. 'Your head is just terrible!' What you doin' this reggae-thing for? You look plumb crazy . . .'

168

Sabrina carried her box of beads, the comb, the mirror back to the seat in the window where she had been originally. 'It's only half done. I can't see . . .'

'You look like you was covered in rats'-tails is what,' said Etty. 'Rats'-tails.' She suddenly put her hand to her face, turned slowly to Dubrovnik. 'Rats! I remember something. Something Duke said sometimes. He had a friend . . . you know her? Very good friend he said. Wasn't rats . . . somethin' like that. You know anyone called Mouse?'

6

Sunday at Alice's

Pale sunlight glimmered through the smog, suffusing the kitchen with soft light, translucent as watered milk. Alice weighed out spaghetti, snapped the bundle into manageable lengths, rummaged in the table drawer for a can opener; Clemency watching her, leaning in the doorway.

'Do you remember where the can opener is? It always lived in this drawer and now it can't be found. At least, by me.'

Clemency eased away from the door, wandered into the kitchen, opened a drawer under the sink: laid the opener on the table.

'Don't you simply *loathe* Sundays?' she said.

'Loathe them,' said Alice, opening a can of tomatoes.

'I don't know why we have to have them.'

'Day of rest. People work hard all week. Some people want to go to Church ... lie in bed with the Sunday paper. They're useful.'

'I get so depressed on Sunday. It feels as if everything was closed up and locked away, one can't reach people.'

'Well, that's a bit silly, darling. You still can. Pick up a telephone.'

'Some people go out of town on Sunday. To the mountains, sometimes to the ocean.'

'Well we can't today because Sybil is coming for lunch, sorry.'

'It's all right. Is that what you are doing? Cooking lunch?'

'I am *preparing* to cook lunch. Spaghetti and tomato sauce, ice cream after, that do?'

'It has to, I suppose,' said Clemency with a tight smile. 'It's all you can cook.'

One day I'll brain her, thought Alice. I'll take a bottle and hit her.

170

Instead she said, 'I'm quite good at *boeuf stroganoff* ... you said so yourself.'

'And boiled eggs. Do you know why all the eggs in America are white? Never brown?'

'No. I don't.' She poured the tomatoes into a pan, set them aside. 'Why?'

'So that they can be candled.'

'So that they can be what? Candled? I never heard the word.'

'I thought you wouldn't have. Alan Spinner Junior told me. It's so that the Jews can hold a candle behind them to see if they are fertilized or not.'

'I see. A lighted candle?'

'Of course. It shows up everything in the egg, I mean if there was anything funny.'

'I'm very grateful for the information.'

A sudden blast of music from Hope's room was turned down instantly.

'What's Hope doing? Apart from playing records?'

'Nothing. She hates Sundays too. She's read the comic section already. Now she's fiddling with her ladybird bracelet. It's too large.'

'Clem darling. You could give me a hand if you liked. Wash up the coffee cups from breakfast? And check we have clean knives and forks – we'll be four.'

Clemency sighed, took down an apron, turned on taps, clattered china. 'You remember, last week, I told you what I thought about ... you know ... Jonathan Pool?'

Alice set out salt, sugar, dried basil, garlic, chopped onion. 'I can't hear you. The water's running.'

Clemency twisted taps. 'About Jonathan Pool; I said.'

'What about him?'

'Well, you remember after your party-thing that evening. Last week. In my room?'

'Oh yes. Yes I do. Darling, you are in my way, duck, I want the strainer.'

'I'll get it.' Clemency reached up, handed her the strainer.

'What about Jonathan Pool?'

'I've changed my mind.'

'I see. Where the hell is the pepper-mill?'

171

'You're not listening to a *word* I say.'

'I am, Clem, I really am. I am also trying to get some kind of a lunch prepared so that when Sybil arrives I'm not stuck in this bloody kitchen all the time.'

'Well, it's only that I took your advice. He's too old for me.'

'Ah ha. You think he is? Very good-looking ... and that super voice? I'll dry the cups, hand them to me.'

'Well, if he's going to be fifty or something grisly when I'm only twenty, or whatever you said. It seems silly. Alan Spinner Junior agrees. I asked him.'

'You like Alan Spinner Junior?'

Clemency shrugged. A shoulder strap of the apron slid down her arm, she pulled it back. 'Okayish. He's not brash. Also he thinks my name is terribly romantic.'

'A very good point, I'd say, in his favour.'

'That's what I thought. It shows a certain amount of taste, don't you think?'

'Perfect.'

'He's sixteen, going on seventeen.'

'You'll have things in common, won't you?'

'I was absolutely dreading that you'd say he was "more suitable".'

'Were you now. Give me the saucers, just rinse them under the cold tap.'

'It's the sort of maddening remark that grown-ups make. Patronising.'

'No, I'm certain that you know your own mind.'

'Oh I do. But I get so furious, you know? Being patronised like that. His father is in General Motors.'

'How *interesting*! General Motors! What an exhilarating thing to be a part of. A place full of imagination, or the chances to show imagination. What exactly does he *do* in General Motors, do you know?' With a mild score behind her she stacked cups and saucers in a pile, took them to the cupboard above the work-top.

'I really didn't ask. Something quite important, I'd say. High up anyway. I mean he never flies Economy, or anything like that, and they have cable TV and, what's more, a chauffeur. White. *Not* a black.'

'That counts.'

'Enormously. They've also been to Europe three times. Once to Paris, once to Rome and once to Heidelberg. Alan's elder brother, Robbie, is in the army there.'

'Well travelled, I'd say. Sophisticated.'

'But of course,' said Clemency, wiping out the sink and squeezing the cloth dry before throwing it on the draining-board. 'He *is* American. So it couldn't be for long. My going out with him. We are just friends ...'

'You can always bring him here, darling. Any time. Just let me know.'

Clemency removed the apron, rearranged her pleated skirt, hung the apron on a hook behind the door. 'This is not quite suitable. This house. They live where we did before Daddy ...' She stopped. Restarted. 'They have a house on Crescent. *Quite* lovely. Beverly Hills. Remember? If we still lived in our old house he'd be just about in walking distance. But here, well ...' She shrugged Brentwood into oblivion with the slightest of gestures. 'It's really not suitable. I mean, we only have that terrible, long room. And our bedrooms. That wouldn't be quite proper, would it? And the *place*, well. I mean it's awful.'

'All that I can afford. Sorry darling.' Alice went into the dining area, pulled open a drawer under the table with controlled fury. Laid out four table mats, arranged the pottery Mexican candle holders. 'Did you check the four knives and forks, Clem? And four dessert spoons ... no! eight ... We have ice cream after.'

I detest Sundays too, my loathsome little daughter. But you'd never guess, would you? I don't let it show, try not to anyhow. There isn't very much of me in you, my little dove; you are all Daddy. Have you the least idea how much *I* hate this bloody house? How I hate the murky light. Having to live by electric lamps all day every day, even in the middle of bloody summer? Do you think I like that crummy yard out back? That black tree? The coarse grass, the lack of air. Do you think that I really give a tuppenny bugger about spaghetti sauce or your damned pistachio-flavoured ice cream? Think *I* don't miss the house we had? The cool, clear rooms, the humming birds in the canna lilies, the pool. Being able to get away

173

from you for a while? Do you really think, can it be possible? that I have no soul of my own, Miss Sproule? *You* have no goddamned soul, Miss Sproule; and that's exactly who you are. Clemency Sproule. You carry within that slender body of yours a billion ugly genes. The Sproules are marching through you in hobnailed boots with their shillelaghs, and you haven't the least idea! You are an appalling throwback to some grubbing, treacherous, peasant past overlaid with elegant Arlington false enamel. You are a fraud, my child. Somewhere deep inside you there is an Irish crone preparing to set off a bomb: peat fires, peat bogs, potatoes, pottery pipes, potheen, Hail Mary Full of Grace The Lord Is With *Me*. There is one great consolation to all this pent-up fury and dislike, my unsweet child, and that is that I dislike you almost as much as you dislike me, only I try not to let mine show; yours blazes like neon.

'Clem? Darling? I'm going to pull up my bed, put on a face. Be an angel and try to remember the knives and the forks *and* the dessert spoons for the spaghetti . . . I've put the mats out. We'll need glasses. I've got a couple of bottles of wine, and the spoons are for the spaghetti, remember. Do this for me?'

'Okay,' said Clemency, with the enthusiasm of someone agreeing to be lowered head first in a bucket down a well.

'What are you banging things around for?' said Hope, drifting in. 'I could hear you slinging knives about like they were spears or something.'

'I have to lay the table for lunch. Sybil Twitt is coming. Remember.'

'Goodee. Maybe she'll be able to fix this ladybug bracelet . . . I can't.'

'Lady*bird*,' said Clemency taking a tray of cutlery into the long room.

'It's "bug" in America. But everything about America bugs you. I know.'

'You know *so* much.'

'Where's Mom?'

'Mother is in her room. Putting on her face.'

Hope filled a paper cup from the Lake Arrowhead water-container, drank, threw it into the trash bin. 'Wouldn't it be nice

174

if we had a cat? A dear little cat. Or maybe a dog. I wouldn't mind a dog, would you?'

'They make messes,' said Clemency, coming back into the clutter of the kitchen.

'It'd be more homey, though, right? This place just isn't like a home.'

Clemency set two glasses on the tray, a bowl of ready-to-use Parmesan, a carton of 'farm-fresh cream'. 'We won't be here long enough for it to be a home. We'll go a-wandering again. You see.'

'Where to? Where will we wander?' said Hope sticking her finger into the pan of tomatoes. 'Jeeze! is this sour! Jimminy-jim-jam ...'

'It's not cooked yet. Don't stick your finger in things. It's not hygienic. She'll have a fit if she sees you do that.'

'Who,' said Hope, 'is *she?*'

'The cat's mother,' said Clemency and took the tray to the dining-table.

Alice smoothed the bottom sheet, tucked in the edges, dragged up the top sheet, pulled the cheap candlewick cover over the bed, sat at her dressing-table, brushed the hair back from her face, piled it on top of her head, turned left and right, regarding her own profile with care. Signs of a downward pull to the mouth? Eyes creased, just a little, at the corners? Throat showing tendons? Age?

This messy little room; this ugly, dark house, the whole stinking place. Whose fault, I ask myself. Trace it back to the beginning ... if you can bear to. 1978. London. Hugo's American publisher. Alvin J. Plumb.

Smooth, seal-sleek, plump, over-manicured. A man who had dragged himself to power over the uncountable corpses of his rivals without so much as snagging a fingernail. Soft-speaking, steel-eyed, adoring, even worshipping, his Author.

As well he might. For Hugo had made Plumb Inc. a modest fortune over the years.

Alvin J. Plumb. Long feet in handmade shoes, suits by Huntsman, suites at the Savoy, haircuts at Trumper's, scents by Givenchy or Floris, depending on mood, taking his snuff with the elegance and disdain of a Regency fop which he so well resembled; his American accent, whatever it once had been, carefully smothered by a *faux* Eton English, only occasionally betrayed by a careless vowel.

He disliked speaking of Money, Sales, Percentages or Profit, the word Agent never crossed his lips, nor did one ever cross his path if he could possibly help it. He had long ago decided that these things smacked of Trade, and a Tradesman was not what he wished to be. It was obvious, to those very few who knew him well, that he had made desperate, but never despairing, efforts to eradicate his New Jersey background, plus the parents who had struggled, on a modest teaching salary, to assist him in his ascent to glory. The feat was astonishing – and could have been impressive, had he chosen his cuff-links with more care. As it was, his Lanvin shirts and Huntsman's jackets sagged at the cuff with cartwheels of gold, silver, platinum, onyx or jade. As Hugo had once said, Alvin's Achilles' heel was, paradoxically, on his wrist.

But he was lethally persuasive.

'You have been in England too long, Hugo my dear fellow. They have grown "used" to you, and you know very well that that is *fatal* in England. It is time to move on, to go elsewhere and astonish; seek a new setting for the jewel of a writer that you are; find a new dimension. England is perfect for the predictable: the unpredictable worries them, they dislike it intensely, it alarms them. The ornate, the baroque, the brilliant, the gold and the silver make them uncomfortable. They really prefer everything to be subdued, quiet, smothered in layers of dark-oak varnish. Do you follow me? And here you offer me, my wondrous writer, a quite astonishing outline and you ask my opinion. This outline which I hold in my hand, *The Golden Immigrants*, is, in a word, breathtaking! You *must* write it, and you must write it immediately. Go and do it, Hugo! I implore you!

'Pack up your family and go away with them to where this extraordinary phenomenon took place. Los Angeles. California. Live there, become part of it, smell it, sense, hear, touch it. Search out the ageing witnesses to that amazing epoch. Some still survive in Homes; drab apartments, modest villas. Question, revive memories,and I promise you that you will be astonished by –shall I say? – the artefacts which will tumble into your hands while you dig in the desert soil. It is quite extraordinary to know that in the

176

early forties, just as the world was reeling into carnage, much of the brilliance which had been European culture was supping its corn-flakes and living in rented houses in that hideous place.

'Driven out by the war, by apathy, by ideals, by the lure of riches, by a thousand things, there they all were, your Golden Immigrants, in one small, one could almost say remote, area, as far away from Europe as they could possibly get: Brecht, Weill,the Manns, Auden and Isherwood, Feuchtwanger, Stravinsky, countless others ... Remember also the *other* "creators". Who worked for the cinema and who so influenced the entire world! One thinks of Garbo first, of course ... but there was also Nazimova! Did you know that Elinor Glynn even worked there once? And Dietrich, the Hitchcocks, the Laughtons, Lubitsch, Chaplin. One's head reels. All Europe exported its magic and lustre to that frightful suburb on the edge of the Pacific. For a time it bloomed like a desert flower after rain, and then, as suddenly, it died. For when the war was won it fragmented; the drift back began, the decade was over. *Write it!*

'Now, I have most useful introductions that I shall give you. There is an extraordinary woman, whom I adore, Irina Miratova, who still lives there and knew it all intimately. Her *salon* was considered the most elegant and erudite. Her "teas" were famous! Not to be invited was Social Disaster! She still sits there; alone with her memories. Go and awaken her! Consider it, Hugo. A year to research; more if you wish. A year to write; longer if you have to. It is something you must not resist. England is no place for you today. It no longer needs the work you offer, it much prefers the Lower Orders; sombre stories of North Country Life, or the drear banalities of suburbia. English writers today, in the main, have had no classical education what-soever; thus their vocabulary is appallingly limited, and their characters speak in an ugly tribal language. They have spotty backs, varicose veins and coarse hands. It is drear, sear, real and *wretched*. Envy, anger, class hatred, resentment, malice and for-nication. Magic is not in demand, elegance is suspect. So come to America, where you have always been more appreciated than in your own country. It might amuse you to know that long before England knew who Beatrix Potter was *we* were reading her with devotion and awe! America is not as backward and new as she sometimes might appear, so come to her! She awaits you with open arms ...' – he paused to smooth a perfect lapel – '... and an irresistible advance! Go West, young man! Every one of *your* Golden Immigrants had to do that, why not you?'

And so we came West. We came to this servant-girls' paradise. And found it to be exactly, and precisely, that.
God rot Alvin J. Plumb.

Her hands slipped gently down her face. A caressing. She let them rest in her lap. Her hair, released, cascaded about her shoulders. She tossed it back, stretched her throat, took a lipstick, lined her lips, pressed them together.
All right. It was all, almost, marvellously all right: at first. Like the dawn of a perfect picnic-day morning.
No hint of the storm ahead.
A pleasant house. White, cool, Spanish (Hispanic influence, the agent had said), above the city, which wavered in a haze of heat, smog and bleary sun below. A swimming pool of sumptuous size, with a Japanese gardener who cleaned it, set out the pool-side chairs and tables, and, when he had time to spare, planted Californian ivy on every inch of crumbled land. To prevent erosion, he said.
Unaware, as I was, that the erosion would not start on his modest plot but within the house. Not within the earth, but within our lives. Mine. Hugo's. Ours.
And there was Jupiter: laughing, willing, roaring up to join us every morning in her bright pink Chevvy. Jupiter, who adored the girls, 'Oh! they so *cute*!', who cooked up corn-bread, spare-ribs and anything else we wanted. Singing joyful hymns. Oh Christ! At first it was all perfect.
The parties which never ceased. A different place each evening. New people, faces made familiar by television or the cinema or the press. All mainstream stuff: and we were part of it. The guests of honour.
'Who was there, Mama? Tell ... did you see ...'
'Robert Redford came, and Paul Newman and his pretty wife were there ...'
'Robert Redford!'
'Wowie!'

178

'And there were agents, people you wouldn't know; some you should *never* know ...'

'Don't you feel it throb?' asked an intense woman of fifty, roped in Mexican beads and lumps of turquoise. 'Feel the pulse? Isn't it just the greatest, most ongoing place you have ever known? So alive, vital. Don't you feel the whole place trembling with creativity?'

Well, frankly, no. Not really. But it felt good on three martinis and an empty stomach. And the San Andreas Fault just below.

Pulsing creativity. That was the impression. Hard to tell, at first, in those early months, that the whole damned set-up was as false as the people themselves. Nothing but a walk through the Fairy Grotto. Plaster and cardboard and rented gnomes: plus dwarfs.

But we didn't know that right away. I didn't, anyway. Saw the dwarfs but thought that they were a little larger than life, because everything around them was. And the brunches. The dreadful brunches that Peter Clivden gave in that dank house up a danker canyon. His teeth slipping when he laughed, the neatly knotted silk ascot at his wrinkled throat, his blazer bright with someone else's regimental buttons, the aproned maids scuttling about like black beetles bearing silver dishes of, what he called, 'tid bits'. Tit bits was what they were: vile little things of watery olives and imported cheese. But 'tit' was out. That was rude. And at the plastic-upholstered bar his truck driver pouring drinks like Niagara. Oh, sweet Heaven! Just to remember how easily we were impressed then. How quickly Hugo took to the waters and swam. And drank. Like a fish.

I suppose that the main thing we salvaged from the whole clutch of those early days was Irina Miratova. A divine saviour at the hideous brunches. Tall, calm, solid, serene and funny. Sometimes.

'She's a spy, darlings, I warn you!' Clivden had hissed. 'Don't mention anything you don't want Moscow to know tomorrow!' and he had covered his mouth while he laughed, to prevent one seeing a collapsing set of teeth.

The frenzy had lasted until they had used us up. It took a month or two. 'After three weeks,' Sybil Witt had said, 'you quit and go East. If you don't they'll start asking you when you are going back to Europe. If you stay on they'll get bored with you, and be shit scared you're in competition and want someone's job.'

179

'Hugo is researching a book. He isn't in competition.'

'He's pretty. So are you. Competition in this town isn't just business: it's bed. Watch out.'

But we settled down. Oh, tell me that we settled down? What happened to us all? Trips to the beach, to the mountains, out on someone's yacht to Catalina, journeys up to Big Sur, San Francisco, Las Vegas ... days at Irina's crazy house, Hugo with notebooks and recorders, researching, reading, working. Drifting away from me, unaware. Perhaps we were both unaware. I filled in the days, with a sense of guilt that I should be doing such a thing. Filling in a day. Getting rid of a day. Killing time. Killing bloody days of my time. My own *life*. Lunches 'girls only', at La Scala or the Polo Lounge. Days which suddenly seemed to stretch on for ever, like taut elastic which, when released from tension, snapped back and numbed my fingers. Numbness grew. Eternal sun, smog, the same voices, the same faces. Boredom, boredom, less and less of Hugo. Less and less of my golden boy, who had found other places in which to play; places I couldn't go, where he, frankly, didn't want me to go. Places with strange people, where the drinks flowed and everyone knew that coke didn't come in a bottle labelled 'Coca Cola'. Gradually, oh so gradually, I began to lose him. The white Maserati, his idiotic white velvet cap, fair hair streaming in the wind, his laughter rising, his restlessness increasing, his work lessening. Corruption biting in like verdigris.

'Hugo. You're on coke.'

'Everyone's on coke. So what?'

'You'll get hooked.'

'I am hooked. It raises one's comprehension to a higher level. Increases my perception.'

'You talk like a bloody teenager.'

'You talk like a nag. A fucking scold. Know what they did with scolds in days gone by? Stuck their heads in an iron helmet.'

'It's all going wrong. Stop, please. My dearest love, stop.'

'It's been going wrong for a while. You didn't notice.'

'I noticed.'

She brushed her hair until it shone like corn-stalks, pulled on a pair of jeans, buttoned herself into a crisp, clean shirt only half aware, and not really caring now, that it had once belonged to him, rolled up the sleeves, slung a belt through the belt loops of the jeans, pushed feet into heel-trodden espadrilles.

Somewhere in the house David Bowie at low pitch; a sudden cry of pleasure from Hope, the slamming of a door; the house was suddenly still, silent. She stood before the pulled-up bed, the cheap candlewick cover.

'I noticed. I'm not made of metal.'

She had reached for him, touched him; expert hands caressing, lips whispering, he had moved away, as if she was soliciting: stood across the big white room, naked, tall, his back to her.

'I can't,' he had said.

'Can't.'

'Don't try. Don't try. It's gone.'

She sat up in the great bed, breasts absurdly covered by crossed arms in sudden, acute embarrassment. 'What has gone? What?'

'I can't do it with you. I don't want it. Nothing happens.'

'Nothing happens?' A parrot cry of incomprehension.

'Fuck nothing. You can see. Look! I don't have to spell it out, do I? You can *see*. You don't want me to go any further, do you? Do you?'

'*Yes!* Spell it out for Christ's sake! What's wrong? What's happened to us?'

He stood still, a silhouette against the early morning light. 'I don't want you.'

She had slid down into the bed, head against the quilted headboard.

'And don't cry about it. I can't take weeping women, you know that. It's happened, it's done. I can't pretend. One can't pretend sex. A man can't. Easier for a woman ... they writhe about and groan and never have an orgasm and no one is the wiser. But not a man. So leave it. Leave me alone. Don't humiliate ourselves any more than we have.'

She took a box of mascara, pencilled her lashes, squinting into the spotty mirror above the wash-bowl.

And that was that.

*

181

'Is there someone else?' she had said without originality. Odd, how in desperate situations one speaks in the banalities of a bad script. 'If there is someone else I can cope ... I'd *try* to cope that is. But if it's just sniffing bloody white powder ...'

'It's not just sniffing bloody white powder. But I like the heights. I like getting dizzy, okay?' He had pulled on a dressing gown. 'And for good measure I'll let you into a secret, want me to? Nigger ladies.' As he went to the bathroom he had called back to her hunched figure in the wide bed. 'They smell good. Sweet, rich, moist. Like plumcake, with a hint of garlic. Nigger ladies do.'

She closed the mascara box. The fall of the House of Arlington. All fall down.

And I wept all over poor Dubrovnik.

Boris Kragujevac. Where did we all first meet? At Irina's. In that crazy wooden palace on the cliffs.

'All my refugees!' she had said, arms wide in welcome. 'Kragujevac is brilliant. Do not shake your head in mock modesty, Boris. Brilliant! He makes quite extraordinary films. He has a passionate political conscience which he translates to the screen with fury. This great, quiet man ... Hugo? Your cup is quite empty, let me refill it ...'

And he was quiet, and gentle as only really strong men can be: those brilliant eyes, observing, missing nothing. A little shabby; clothes of no consequence to him. Hugo and he, side by side in that vast, ugly room, looked so incredibly strange. The great body in a shaggy jacket, worn jeans, scuffed boots. Hugo slender, whippy as a willow wand: elegant, white, lithe. It was pretty obvious that he adored Irina; liked Hugo, and was very aware, behind the dark lashes of those extraordinary eyes, of me. And Hugo brought him home for Christmas. Home! God! But we did our best. 'For the children.' An enormous tree, red, yellow, blue and white flashing lights, wreaths of glittering tinsel, gifts in a hundred different wrappings, red and white shining baubles, frost-sprayed, the tree standing in the California sun kidding none of us. Except perhaps Jupiter, who wept with pleasure.

'Kragujevac is coming to spend the day with us. I asked him. So don't complain.'

'I haven't complained. Won't.'

'The children will like him. He's alone in some murky Loft down at the ocean. We must share our good fortune, don't you think?'

Good fortune? That had gone long ago. But the children did like the man, and called him Dubrovnik, and he was wise and kind and funny with them, and they laughed. The only honest laughter of the day.

In the evening. Oh Christ, the evening. The careful manipulation of the evening; of playing a game, a careful, watchful game, with Hugo.

'My wife, you know, gentle though she may appear to you to be at first meeting, is, if the truth be known, quite viciously cruel.'

'Not in the *least* bit cruel. I'm adorable! Easy, understanding. Don't believe him.'

'Do believe him! She is convinced that when I grow up I shall have a ... silicone nose! Now what do you make of that remark, Dubrovnik, eh? Cruel?'

'Hugo darling! Not true! Perhaps a little too strong ... your brandy?'

'Piss off. Answer me, Dubrovnik. That is a cruel remark or not? You think that she is right, or that she is wrong?'

Dubrovnik had looked slowly from one of us to the other, Hugo standing before the fire, I sitting calmly; controlled, smiling a fixed adoring smile. My amusing husband.

'Hugo. I will reply, so? Will you *ever* grow up?'

'Ah ha! You think that I won't? Very clever. Eternal Peter Pan ... she is my little Tinkerbell ... tinkle! tinkle! tinkle! a dancing light warning me of danger? So. I'll never grow up you think? Then I shall never have a silicone nose.'

'I do not say you will *not* grow up. I ask you if you think that you will?'

'How can I tell? Did you know that, in fact, my wife is a General's daughter! Comes from a long, long line of soldiers. Very strong-minded. Pukka and correct, doesn't approve of me at all. Do you? Strict *disciplinarians*.' Suddenly he had giggled like an idiot youth, fair hair tumbled across his brow, hand unsteady with the over-charged brandy glass, raised it slowly and drank. Watching me.

*

183

'Mom! Mommie!' Hope called from the corridor. 'Think she's here. Sybil's here. A car's just turned into the driveway.'

'*Strict disciplinarians*,' Hugo had said. 'With no silicone noses!'
'You must take care, Hugo. Los Angeles is easy. I know. But be watchful. You get arrested maybe. If you have that stuff around. If they search you, you go to prison. Not so good for your wife, for the children, not so good for you too. Big reputation? Right?'
'They won't catch me! Know what I'd do? What I'd do if they chased me? The Drug Squad, whatever it is ... know what I'd do? I tell you, my old Slavic friend, I would slam that Maserati of mine right into a truck! Wham! Bang! Explode! Do it quick. No second thoughts. That's the thing, Dubrovnik! *No second thoughts*. Out like a light. Explode! Deliberate explosion of one silicone nose! That's how I'll go.'
In silence, a silence I hear now, he went to the drink table. Dubrovnik looked at me, I can see his eyes. He made a move towards me with his hand. Of comfort. Just as Hugo turned back towards us, a bottle in his hand. 'Explosion! Then you'd be free of me, Alice! What a relief that would be! Tinkle! tinkle! tinkle!'

'Mommie!' Hope pushed open the bedroom door. 'You coming? It's Syb ... she's here, right here.'
Alice straightened up from the wash-bowl over which she had bent, head bowed.
'Mom! Mommie? You all right? Is something wrong? You okay?'
'I'm fine. Really fine. The ... plug-hole thing. Got blocked. I was fiddling.'
'Well. She's arrived, Sybil, she's brought a huge package of junk for you, she says.'
'I'm on my way, right this minute, darling,' said Alice.

'Well what's wrong with the bracelet? It's cute. It's as cute as anything I've seen,' said Sybil, pushing her dish of ice cream aside.
Hope swung her wrist. 'See? Too large. I know what to do, if you could do it ...'
'Hoppy, I get to dance and sing but I'm no mechanic. Show me again.'

'See? There is a ladybug, then a daisy flower, then another ladybug and so on, all the way around. The one Daddy gave me was the same, and it was too large, but it was my most precious thing, and he kinda fixed it so it fitted real good. He cut one ladybug off, so there were just two daisy heads together, right? And that made it smaller. So it fitted.'

'My head reels with the complications! You want me to remove *one* ladybug and then join it all up again. With two daisy heads together? Right? I got it?'

'Absolutely. It's on elastic, so if I got some scissors . . .'

'Hoppy my dear, I have a heart of gold and fingers like bananas. I couldn't do it, it is just not my *métier*. Don't you have some beau who could fix it? Some real bright guy with good eyesight and nimble fingers?'

Hope shrugged. 'Well, maybe. I could ask Kenny Aller, he's always fixing his car . . .'

'Well you do that. Ask a real mechanic.'

'Irina gave me this one. Wasn't it just amazing? She found it in some store down in the Palisades, the *last* one! I was so thrilled. Of course it isn't quite the same as the real one, Daddy's one, but it's great to have it. He just made it very personal, you know?'

'Got you. I know.'

'Honestly,' said Clemency, stacking up the ice cream plates. 'The fuss you make about a tacky little plastic bracelet from Taiwan. Really. You'd think it was gold or something.'

'It is to me,' said Hope quickly. '*Gold*. So just you shut up.'

Alice came in from the kitchen with a tray of coffee: set it on the half-cleared table. 'Stop bickering, you two. Sunday tempers. Just stop. Hoppy, give Clem a hand with clearing, Sybil and I have work to do, so be sweet to me. Someone will fix your bracelet . . . if that's what the snarling is all about . . .'

'Ask your beau,' said Sybil, taking a cup of coffee and sitting in one of the crushed armchairs.

'He's seventeen. He's not my beau, for heaven's sake! Just a nice guy. He wears his hair like Elvis, y'know? All greasy.'

'Well get on with things,' said Alice.

'Clem said it was made in Taiwan. Like it didn't matter.'

'Get out, the pair of you, and don't slam doors . . .'

185

Sybil was sorting through costume-sketches spread on the coffee table. 'This is the one. Number six. I'm wild about it. You really do have the best eye, such a line, Alice Arlington ... I want it to be this one, and we can use the lace.'

'Must we?' Alice sat opposite her, coffee cup in hand, stirring idly.

'We must. I have this great feeling for lace. I want to come down that staircase but foaming! Lace everywhere ... you simply have to find a way to smother me in the stuff. It's right for the number and I'll look divine. Nothing is more flattering to an ageing face than a haze of beautiful lace, and I have loads, but loads, of it ... we *must* use it, honey.'

Alice picked up a handful which had tumbled to the floor. 'Where did you get it?'

'Garage sale. Sherman Oaks. Lying in a trunk, no one wanted it. I got the whole deal for five bucks, can you believe? I mean some of it is just glorious ... and the bridal veil ... I can't resist that ...'

'All different kinds. This bit is Brussels ...'

'Sherman Oaks! So strange, these garage sales, I never miss one if I can get there, I go all over, you know? It's fascinating that people, when they decide to retire to Miami or someplace, just leave the house and sell everything. They take nothing with them, no roots ... nothing of the past. They kind of reject the past deliberately and start out again all over, in retirement. Crazy. All this stuff came from the Old Country ... they just cut their past away with a razor blade. No memories. Therefore rootless.'

'Perhaps they feel happier like that: no responsibilities. The past has debts.'

Sybil pulled off her knitted woollen pom-pom hat, shook it, brushed it, set it back on her head. 'Maybe. I'd rather have the debts than no past. No roots, I should say.'

'But you have roots. God almighty, Syb! You have *all* America.'

'And all America is rootless, except for the Red Indians ... the rest of us are, one way and another, uprooted from someplace else. That's why I don't understand the deliberate severance, like in garage sales ... I've seen family photographs, old, brown, faded things, just left for someone to grab ... some fag interior decorator ... *they* swoop on them ... I mean, mothers and fathers, aunts and grandparents, whole family groups, just left lying in boxes, like junk ... a whole past rejected. Prague, Dublin, Vienna, Berlin ... right

186

on out to the heart of Russia. Abandoned for the delights of a condominium someplace in Florida or wherever the hell they retire to. It makes me so mad!'

'Perhaps people don't want to be reminded of that past.'

'Perhaps not.'

'America is for starting off again, right? A new world. A new deal, a new and a better life ... perhaps those sepia aunties and grandparents are haunting reminders of what was? And perhaps what *was* wasn't pleasant.'

'You could be right. You're so bright, Mrs Arlington ... I don't know, really I don't. All I do know is that I envy your bickering daughters more than they could ever imagine. They have inheritance, they have it instinctively, it makes them strong and secure, something we don't get here – at least, it isn't commonplace.'

'But you have it, don't you? You were born here, it's in your blood ...'

Sybil poured herself another cup of coffee, spooned sugar, stirred. 'In my blood. How the hell do I know what's in my blood? My grandparents arrived here, way back, from somewhere in Europe, Poland I guess, with four kids, my mam was one of them, and two tin trunks. They had no language that anyone could speak, and they couldn't speak English. They got stood in line on Ellis Island to be searched for ticks and TB and God knows what else, and when he was asked his name, my grandfather, kinda understanding but unable to reply, just pointed to the man in front of him, and so the immigration official wrote down *his* name for our use. With one nod of a head, and the stroke of a pen, we were *instantly* "Karovski" ... I don't know what our true name was, I never remembered to ask, they never bothered to say ... so I was born Irma Miriam "Karovski" ... a stolen name. I feel the lack of my real name way deep down. I want my roots.'

'You might hate them if you found them? Possible?'

'Possible. I'd just like the chance of making my own mind up.'

'And Sybil Witt? That name?'

'Oh that! Christ! Can you see Irma Miriam Karovski in lights?'

'Gertrude Lawrence wasn't all that glamorous a name, or Ethel Merman, but they didn't do so badly, did they?'

'I wanted something of my own. Chic-er. Know what I mean? I

187

thought "Sybil Witt" was so Noël Cowardy, get it? Good for my persona. Something to live up to. Is all.' She leant across the table and picked up the sketch of the dress she had chosen. 'I'm going to be a knock-out in this. You get the lace fixed ... remember it's a waltz number ... so the skirt has to be nice and wide, and frilly as hell. One, two, three, one, two, three ... "*Waltz me around again Willy, around, around, around. The music is dreamy, it's peaches and creamy, So don't let my feet touch the ground...*" One, two, three ... we start in a sweet way, you see? Very Victorian ... Edwardian? I don't remember, and then it gets wild ... and *I belt*. Ham Reiner has done a really swell arrangement ...'

Hope pushed open the kitchen door, a dishcloth in her hand. 'Was that you singing, Sybil? It was just great.'

'It was I, child ... One, two, three, one, two, three, "*I feel like a ship on an ocean of joy...*" '

'You don't sound like you at all when you sing.'

'Thanks loads.'

'It's so pretty ...' The door swung closed.

'It was a compliment, of course. But she gets the point strangely. I'm not "me" when I'm singing. I'm the "me" I want to be, and I stop wondering who the hell I really am.'

Alice collected the coffee cups, stood up. 'How long have we got? I mean for the dress? When is the Opening? I forget ...'

'Boston, March twenty-third, Philly after, New Haven and then New York, all being well, April twentieth. Six weeks there, then London, Paris, Copenhagen ...'

'Of course. Sorry ... I can't remember anything. I feel rather odd. Light headed, I don't know. Something.'

'What sort of something? Sunday Blues? More than that?'

'More than that. Like driftwood. Stuck high on the beach ... the tide pulling out. Me stranded.'

Sybil opened her canvas bag, found a cigarette, lit it. Alice carried cups to the kitchen.

'You are angels! Both of you ...' The door shut, cutting off the compliments.

Sybil hunched up, blew cigarette smoke into the fireplace, watched it drag away, swirl up, spread, fade.

Alice returned, the banging door announcing her. 'They're really very good – it's all done. I wish I wasn't such a bitch.'

'The sweetest-tempered mother I ever saw.'

'I try to be. The strain nearly kills me.'

'About driftwood,' said Sybil, 'and the tide going out. Explain.'

'Oh ...' Alice sat opposite her, legs spread. 'Oh, I don't know ... I *do* know, of course I know. Everyone leaving suddenly. End of the holidays ... You. Dubrovnik off to his Amazon. Nettles. Jonathan. No one left.'

'Jonathan was never a very great part of your life, was he? Or was he?'

'No. Not a great part. But always there. If I needed him.'

'A bastion?'

'I can't define a bastion. Maybe.'

'No love though? I mean on your part. You were never in love with him, right?'

Alice reached across and took her cigarette, drew on it, gave it back, shook her head. 'No. Never *in* love. I used him as insurance cover, no more ... Dubrovnik is something else.'

'He's as tie-down-able as a bison. You had no hopes of Dubrovnik, for God's sake?'

'In some mad way I did, Syb. I did. I don't know why.'

'He is strictly a wanderer. I know. I've been married twice, I've been *Mrs* O'Conner and *Mrs* Ciapellino. Both times I was utterly convinced it was the Real Thing. It never was. Never. So I sing and I dance and they all think I'm happy as a grig. Which I am. Alone.'

'Alone is what terrifies me. I dread Alone.'

'You have the children.'

'Alone.'

'Come East. Come to New York. They'll eat you all up. Who wants this place? New York is alive, you get flights in daily from all over, fresh freight of new faces ... you *can't* be alone in New York.'

'The songs tell one differently.'

'Forget the songs. Come on East ... leave this dump. It was fun once. But now ...'

'I can't. Leave the shop? The children are settled, at last, in decent schools, I have work on hand, I can't leave, start all over again.'

'You could. Screw the schools. Who's most important? You or your children at this very moment?'

Alice pulled off an espadrille, tried to pull up the trodden heel-canvas. 'The children, I guess. Then the shop.'

'Westwood Village won't actually fall apart at the seams if you pull out, you know.'

'I'm just starting a customer-relationship ... it's important.'

'So is *Women's Wear Daily*. They already "found" you, right? A big spread, "A Touch of Tweed" or some such headline, I forget ...'

'"Touch of (Classic) Tweed" it was ... yes, that was nice. They weren't even bitchy.'

'In New York they'll gobble you all up. You see if I'm wrong. You'll be part of the crowd, the WWD crowd ... Andy Warhol, Bianca Jagger, Gloria Vanderbilt, all the little Furstenbergs, Calvin Klein ... the mainstream, the Beautiful People. Maybe they're a little indigestible as a steady diet, but you can choose the meals you take ... see what I mean?'

'They'd kill me. Competition. Would you say?'

'Go fight. You can do it!'

'Oh, Sybil-Satan! Get thee behind me ...'

'Think! The best table at Elaine's. Blowing kisses to Baryshnikov at Joe Allen's. It could all be yours.'

'And who would pick up the check?'

'I'd be there, I'd be den-mother. You could do all my robes for the show, not just this one ... I'm not immodest, honey, but I'm not unknown.' Sybil threw her cigarette into the dying fire and Alice burst into tears, hands covering her face.

'Hey!' said Sybil. 'That won't help. It never helps.'

'I feel so shitty. Helpless. You are so kind ... I mean, honestly ...' Alice smothered the tears which had streamed down her face, wiped her nose, sniffed, shook her head to bring the moment back into focus. 'I'll manage. Cope. Soldier's daughter, I am. But thank you, dearest Syb ...'

'God! I just hate you feeling like this. Driftwood. It's crazy. At your age! You have so much going for you, so much time, Alice. Come East. I couldn't live here! I only rent Mecca up on Tropicana Drive so I don't get to stay at lousy hotels while I'm taping a show ... but I couldn't *live* here, be a part of it.'

'You are wise. I am certain that you are right, but I can't leave. I'm breaking into something, doors are opening. I worked too bloody hard for that ... I can't junk it now.'

'Stubborn bitch.'

190

'Always was I suppose.'

'Maybe that's part of your charm? Alice the Fearless?'

'Except for being alone. You know, Syb. I never, in my wildest dreams, my worst nightmares, really thought that Hugo would die and leave me on my own. Never, never.'

Sybil stuffed a handful of yellowing lace into the bag she had brought.

'Well,' she said, 'he did.'

Afternoon

Irina had been dozing lightly in her chair by the window when the telephone rang, startling her awake. She heard Mouse crossing the hall, heard her speak in English, a small cry of pleasure, the receiver replaced. She sat waiting. Sunday. It could not possibly be anyone from the Bureau . . . not yet anyway. And no one, or almost no one, now telephoned her on a Sunday; it was a drab, silent day usually. What could this be, then?

Mouse came into the big room on cautious feet. 'Countess? Countess dear? Are you awake?'

'Do I look asleep?'

'I was fearful of disturbing you . . . you have been so sad. I thought perhaps that you were resting.'

'Resting? Why should I rest? I have been trapped in my bed for days, I do not require rest. Who was that?'

Mouse sat on a small stool near her mistress, hands clasped, eyes bright behind the glittery spectacles.

'A Sunday guest! Can you imagine! Boris Kragujevac has asked if he might come and take tea with us, this afternoon. He is not far away, almost here.'

'You said that he might? Without reference to me? Mouse, you are altogether a little too presumptuous.'

Mouse bowed her head. 'I am so sorry. Yes. I said that he might. Truthfully I felt that a visitor, and one that you like so well, would be welcome. Would cheer you.'

'Cheer me? Have I been *sobbing*, pray? *Moaning* in despair? Have

191

I been so ill-mannered as to allow my discomfort to show to that extent?'

'Countess dear, no. Of course you are never ill-mannered. What a thing to say! But you have been, shall I put it this way, you have been "absent", in a manner of speaking, for a few days ... I was so worried ... but now it seems that you have returned to us. That is all.'

'You make me sound as if I were awakening from hibernation, Mouse.'

The fact that she had used the affectionate name instead of her given name reassured Mouse that she had not committed any grave error, and that Kragujevac was welcome. So she relaxed.

'We can use the last of the real tea ... there is just enough for two brewings ... and I have a small box of cookies. But no sugar.'

'You have no lemon, I'll be bound.'

'Ah yes! I bought some lemons the last time at Thrifty's ... was not that a good thing?'

'Lemons,' said Irina leaning against the high back of her chair. 'Lemons in my father's garden in Yalta. We had trees ... the scent in spring was so heavy. I well recall.'

'I had never seen a lemon growing ... or an orange. How fortunate you were, Countess.'

'Things which, at your age, Mouse, you would hardly remember anyway. So you are not deprived.'

'Ah Countess! I remember things in the past too. But I was in Petersburg. We had no tropical trees in Petersburg. But I remember the night the great battleship *Aurora* bombarded the Winter Palace: it is a different memory, I agree, from lemon trees in Yalta ... but it is no less vivid to me. Countess. All the city seemed ablaze, we were very frightened ...'

'I was *never* frightened,' said Irina, looking out across the Pacific.

'You have always shown the highest degree of courage, Countess.'

'It is true,' said Irina. 'I can recall the big, sweet, scarlet melons we would take to the peasants in the fields at harvest time. The sky brilliant, cloudless, burning; the cool shadows in the ditches and the woods where they would go to take their rest. My father and I would carry the melons to them ... so refreshing. The creaking of the

192

cartwheels, the golden glory of the corn ... the Dnieper as wide, as slow, as a muddy sea. It was all peace, all happiness. So long ago. Too long ago. Near Kiev.'

Mouse got to her feet, she had heard this before. 'Countess dear? Will you wish to change? Your dress?'

Irina looked down at herself, smoothed her broad lap and heavy thighs. 'Why, pray? Kragujevac is an artist. He wears careless clothes. I have no desire to embarrass him by changing. We must make our guest, as always, completely at ease. I stay as I am. After all, he has seen me in this dress for the last five years. It will hardly come as a surprise to him.'

'Then I shall start the water, and set the cups.'

Dubrovnik's size made the large, ugly room appear smaller. His laughter brought it life. Mouse sat, as she always did, across the room, behind her tea-table, and watched with delight the Sunday guest sprawl comfortably, legs stuck out before him, strong hands holding his cup, eyes flashing with pleasure as he spoke both of the Amazon, and the extraordinary things which he hoped to see, and to photograph. His excitement even fired Irina, who leant forward in her chair to question, listen, and sometimes even to laugh. The change he brought to the solitary, lonely house was incredible, and Mouse was suffused with delight that Sunday had lost its sadness, and that her mistress seemed, for the time being anyway, happy, content, and almost back to her old form. The form which had been hers in the days of the *salon*; when the room buzzed with conversation, laughter, and was charged with plans and schemes for a probable future. For so long now, she thought, sipping her tea slowly to make it last, her eyes constantly darting between the guest and her mistress, there had been little hope of anything like a 'probable future'. She had felt, for some time, that life was a railway train slowly running towards a long dark tunnel, brakes applied, the steam sighing, the darkness approaching with every turn of the wheels.

With Dubrovnik's arrival the atmosphere had altered. She had, for the moment, lost sight of any tunnel, any feeling of a life trailing towards inevitable darkness. And death.

'And they cleared vast areas of jungle to build this place, Brasilia? And now it is all falling down? Madness!' said Irina, easing her back cautiously among her cushions.

'The cement cracks, the lagoons leak, the jungle will creep back among the huge, big buildings ... even the cathedral ... all will be gone. Man is ... what you call when he is so small ... so weak?' He measured man's size between forefinger and thumb.

'A word?' asked Irina. 'You mean what word would one apply to man?'

'Yah ... this is what I mean. You know?'

'Puny,' said Irina.

'Puny,' Dubrovnik repeated. 'Is so. In that place, man is, pony ...'

Mouse laughed suddenly, blushed, set down her cup quickly. 'Excuse me, please! I was so rude.'

'Indeed,' said Irina.

'What I say? Wrong? Pony?'

'*Puny*,' said Irina. 'Take no notice of Mouse, she is practically illiterate.'

'Well, man is pony, he is puny, makes no difference. Nature gets him finally.' He smiled across at Mouse to reassure her that he held no displeasure. She bowed her head, unable to hold the boldness of his strange blue eyes, brimming with contained delight.

'And Alice Arlington?' said Irina suddenly.

'Alice?'

'She will be sad, I think.'

Dubrovnik shook his head, looked about for somewhere to place his empty cup. Mouse was at his side, silently, instantly. 'Another cup?'

'No. Thank you. Is fine. Sure,' he crossed his legs, threaded his fingers under his chin, looked at the worn carpet, 'Sure, Alice. But she has her children ... she has her work. *I* must work! This is my, what you call it, my dream? I have to do ...'

'Of course,' said Irina. 'One has to do what one has to do, one cannot, *must* not, stifle creativity. It is greatly important. If one does, hah! then one dies. Eh?'

'I suppose. Ah yah, yah! That is *very* good, is right. *Very* right!'

'Like her husband, Hugo ... for weeks and weeks he sat at my feet like a small boy, begging me for stories, writing, making me speak into a machine ... books of notes he made. Incredible! For his book, you recall? *The Golden Immigrants*. Such an odd title. A little vulgar under the circumstances.'

'Was vulgar?'

'To consider Mann, Brecht, Lenya, Huxley and so on as immigrants...'

'They were not?'

Irina shrugged. 'It is a word I dislike. It was applied to myself when I arrived here, as it was to Tatiana Ivanova, this Mouse of mine.'

'He was most clever, Hugo.'

'Brilliant. But then ... Mouse, you may take my cup, I am finished.' As Mouse came to get it she continued, 'But then something terrible happened, the creativity began to fade in him. I could see it, like a sun setting; the pale clouds drawing up, the light lingering, dying, you follow me? He lost the passion for his work, he began to find other releases for the brilliance which he suppressed, as he moved towards, it is strange to say it but I will, as he moved towards his evening.'

'Is true. Yah. True.'

'You of course knew this. You were a good friend.'

'A bad friend.'

'Bad?'

'Yah ... you see, I did not stop this ... what you said ... this move towards "his evening".'

'I doubt if any of us could. Not Alice, certainly, not myself. We watched him go. Tragic, tragic ...'

'He was here many times I think?' said Dubrovnik.

Mouse was suddenly uncomfortably aware that he was addressing the remark to her, and not to the Countess. She kept her head lowered, rearranged the used cups on her tea-tray.

'He spent weeks and weeks here ... what delight it was for me!' said Irina. 'No little detail was too trivial. He demanded exhaustingly ... I was quite exhilarated, the past came back so vividly under his questioning. Dear, half-blind Huxley ... Lotte and her coarse, flat voice. "Did she sing for you?" he asked me. "Certainly ... in this room ... the voice of Lenya is still in this room," I told him. And it is so. If we had a machine which could register, or do I mean, recall? sound, gather the widening ripples, for they spread, you know? Like the ripples on a lake when one has thrown a stone, they grow wider and wider from the source of the disturbance ... if we

195

had such a machine, oh! the sounds which it could bring back to us, how glorious it would be!'

'But there would also be terrible sounds, is true? Not *only* pleasant ones?'

'It's true. Yes.'

'I think we do not want this machine. Eh, Mouse?'

Mouse tried not to look at him, folded a small napkin twice, in some confusion.

'What you think? Is so?'

'Answer, Mouse! Boris asks you a question.'

Mouse looked up, unease spreading through her small body; she crushed the folded napkin. 'It is true. Yes. Terrible sounds. Terrible words. I would not like it, Countess.' She had deliberately avoided Dubrovnik and addressed herself to Irina.

'Well . . . it is possible,' sighed Irina. 'One cannot only hear beauty in life. There were other sounds, of course.'

'Is more crying, we would hear. Is right? In all the world of sound, is more weeping than laughter. You think so? Is my philosophy I think.'

'I cannot answer, dear Boris . . . cannot answer. But we will not have this machine. I agree. It is best that silence remains. In silence one can imagine only, one is not disturbed, distressed. No, I do not want to hear the sound of weeping again . . . no, no.'

'Or guns. Cannons,' said Dubrovnik. 'Like faraway thunder.'

'Or guns,' said Irina. 'No.'

Mouse suddenly addressed herself to the room, not to either of the occupants, her head high, her eyes, behind the spheres of glass, over-bright. 'I think that there would be more laughter than tears and distress. I think there would be more beauty than ugliness. That is *my* philosophy.' She sat perfectly still, her hands folded on the little table. There was a moment's silence. Irina coughed discreetly, a smothered sound of disapproval.

'I beg your pardon,' said Mouse. 'It is what I think. Excuse me.'

Dubrovnik, she saw, was watching her with apparent unconcern. Her unease increased. She collected the cups, the plate of uneaten cookies, put them on the tray.

Irina said, 'Hugo was a brilliant creature, but too weak for the temptations of this appalling place. He fell from grace. Icarus tempting the sun.'

196

'It is a dangerous place. The standards are not so high. I am right?' said Dubrovnik.

Mouse rose, lifted the tray.

'Be careful!' said Irina. 'It is a heavy tray, let Boris assist you, otherwise you will drop the whole thing.'

Dubrovnik was on his feet, moving towards Mouse. 'I can help. Please.'

'No, no. It is quite all right, thank you.'

'She has bad hands. It is quite difficult for her to carry heavy things.'

'I am sorry. Please ...' said Dubrovnik and took the tray. 'Your hands? Why didn't I know long ago?'

'Because,' said Irina firmly, 'it happened long ago. She cut her hands when she was a girl. That is so Mouse, eh?'

Mouse, in an agony of embarrassment, placed her hands flat to her side. 'Long ago.'

'It was an accident you had? I am desolate,' said Dubrovnik.

'On wire. I cut my hands on some wire. But I am perfectly capable of carrying the tray, it is not heavy. And I can drive, too!'

'The china is all we have,' said Irina. 'Let Boris take it for you.' Her face was suddenly sallow with pain.

Mouse followed him out into the hallway. 'The kitchen is here. I would be grateful if you allowed me ...'

Dubrovnik cut her short. 'I take. What wire? When? Really so long?'

Mouse switched on the light in the kitchen, somewhere far away she heard a stick crack, a woman cry out in sudden fear.

'Yes. Many years ago. The Polish border. A funny place ... look, the tray will sit here, on the table. You are most kind.' She cleared a space among the scattered dishes which remained from their frugal luncheon and which she had not had time to clear and wash. 'I am sorry. This is a very untidy place. Excuse me. But, you see, Sunday is a quiet day, I am very lazy ...'

'It is a good room. A place to sit round the table. To talk and drink, I think. Is so?'

'Oh yes. In the old days we did that at this long table. We just sat round and talked. Like students! It was most pleasing. We had wine. And candles.'

197

'Did Hugo come to this table too?' He set the tray carefully down at the cleared corner.

'Hugo? Arlington? Oh yes. He wrote here sometimes ... I can see all his books and papers, the machine which the Countess spoke into, he would replay, is that what they say? Replay her words and write them down. Here, at this table. I made him tea. It was most interesting.'

'I am sure. And he was also a very good photographer I think?' Mouse stood still. 'Photographer? He wrote. Only wrote.'

Dubrovnik thrust his hands into his trouser pockets, rocked gently on his booted heels. 'No photographs? A perfect place. The shades of the Golden Immigrants! Tea at the kitchen table.'

'No. He wrote.'

'No camera?'

Mouse lifted the tea-pot, removed the lid, carried it to the sink across the room, ran water, rinsed the pot, poured tea leaves into a bucket at the side.

'No camera? Hugo?'

'No,' said Mouse. 'He had no camera. I never saw a camera. I'm sorry.'

The field before her was white with frost, a crow flapped slowly away into the rising sun.

She turned and smiled at Dubrovnik; replaced the tea-pot lid. 'He had no camera, I assure you. We must go back to the Countess, she will be quite fretful,' she said.

Evening

'I'm sorry,' said Jonathan, coming into the rectangular room, 'to, as it were, drop in on you.'

'Didn't drop in at all. You telephoned at least. I had warning,' said Alice. 'I do detest droppers-in, don't you? Maddening. Sit where you like, the place is a mess, like the rest of the house. Sybil has been here all day. We've been working on a design for a dress – for her new show.' She sat in one of the squashed armchairs, head back. 'Exhausted, my dear. How lovely to see you. Sunday evening is hellish. This is treats.'

198

'Thank you. I was going down to Santa Monica and the thought occurred to me that I might just, well, you know, come and see you.'

'Super that you did.' She rolled her head against the chair back. 'Santa Monica? *What* on earth are you trailing off to Santa Monica for on a Sunday evening?' She sat up suddenly, laughed, hand to her mouth. 'Foot in it,' she said. 'Of course. She's very ... handsome.'

'Thank you.'

'No need to thank me, my dear. Her looks are hardly your responsibility, eh?'

'Perfectly true. A reflex action. Automatic.'

'Dog-like? Pavlov's dog?'

'Leave it,' he said.

Alice got up, went to the tape deck, slid a cassette into the player. 'Drive you mad? Brahms?'

'No. Not in the least bit.'

'Good. He's soothing, I find. And music fills the gaps ... I thought that you'd lost all your perks when Shapiro went, not so? Car, driver, so on.'

'I did. Rehired him back on my own, privately.'

'That'll cost you.'

'Must have a car. And he makes me laugh.'

'Who? Your driver?'

'The White Rat. Yes.'

'Well, you must be a millionaire.'

'Screw it. Won't be for long.'

Alice got up again, found a squashed packet of cigarettes, lit one. 'When do you leave?'

'Altered the flight to Wednesday.'

'Paris? Lucky bugger.'

'London. Lea has to report back for duty on Monday.'

'*Lea* does? Goodness me! She work? An heiress at the least, I'd have said.'

'No. She works. Psychologist. Children.'

'I *am* impressed. My word. I'm amazed. I mean she doesn't look the kind of woman who would be clever, you know?'

'Well she is. How about that?'

'Filled with admiration. Do you all go back then? Noah's Ark stuff ... the animals went in two by two ... Only three of you, of course.'

199

'Yes. Only three. I think Nettles joins us. He has a few loose ends to tie up here, so have I. Lawyers banging about with the Shapiro business. If they settle things, I'll clear ... hardly Noah's Ark stuff.'

'Hardly. Oh well. Everything comes to an end, they say. Right?'

'Yes. Really, Alice, I came to apologize.'

She rose instantly, went across to the kitchen door. 'Apologize?' She pushed the door slightly with one foot. 'What in God's name for?'

'Sybil's supper. I was bloody rude.'

'Not in the least! Rude, you? Jon dear! I should apologize to you, if apologies were needed, which they aren't. I was a bit high. Dubrovnik filled me with scotch, I reacted, over-reacted, to his decision to go off and make his blasted movie. I was the one who was rude, a bit pushy. Frankly ...' she opened the door wider, '... I panicked. And I loathe Sybil's house anyway ... so don't apologize to me. Other way round.' She left him. From the kitchen a sound of high laughter, a squeal of pleasure. 'Wayne! You are too much! Too much!' The door closed quietly.

I hate *this* house. I hate this room. A coffin. How does she stick it? A long, low coffin, with the lid nailed down.

'White or red? Or scotch if you'd rather?' She was standing at the door, a bottle held by the neck, two glasses. 'And don't do any of that dainty middle-class stuff and say "Whatever is open" or I'll kill you!'

'White.'

'Very wise,' she said, opening the bottle with a corkscrew which she had stuck in her jeans pocket. 'Wise. After all, you may start dinner with fish. Does she cook? As well as heal disturbed children?'

'She cooks.'

'What a clever lady. I can't boil water.' She offered him a glass. 'Bit of cork bobbing about, I can't even open a bottle. Hugo would have killed me for that ... but it is not corked. Your health,' she said, raising her glass and sitting down again.

Brahms filled the silence between them on a mournful cello.

'Your driver, what's his name? The White Rat?'

'Wayne.'

'Looks exactly like the underside of a sole, know what I mean? Moist, white, almost transparent.'

'He works at nights.'

'Pretty evident. However, the girls are adoring him, stuffing him with beer and crackers. Anyone will do on a Sunday evening.'

Suddenly the kitchen door crashed open: Hope standing on one leg. 'Hey Mom ... Mother, excuse me. Can I go get your scissors? Wayne says he'll fix my bracelet. Can I?'

'Did you say Good evening to Jonathan? I mean he *is* present. In the room'.

Hope blushed scarlet. 'Oh. Sorry. Yep. Hi. I mean ... Hi, Jon. We did meet in the hall, right?'

'We did,' said Jonathan.

Hope shook his hand as if she was pumping water. 'Isn't it great? He's got his guitar in the car, he said ... and he knows "The Foggy Foggy Dew" and "We Shall Overcome" and everything ... can I get the scissors?'

'In the wickerwork basket. On top of my wardrobe. And put them back where they came from when you're through.'

'Jon? Jon, do you know the "Rolling Pin Song"?'

'No, Hoppy, I don't.'

'It's so funny! I'm going to teach Wayne.' She sang loudly, ' *"The frying pan said with mischievous glance, Good evening Miss Rolling Pin, Pray won't you dance ..."* '

'Is enough, Hope,' said Alice.

'Okey-dokey. But it's terrific.' She crashed out of the room shouting something to the kitchen group. The cello mourned softly.

'Never a dull moment,' said Jonathan.

'You'd be surprised. Christ.'

'It's just that I wanted to tell you about Lea, myself. Do you follow?'

'I follow. That was very generous. Thoughtful.'

'I know that you'll be privately thinking it's a bit boyish.'

'Quite wrong. I think it is charming and kind of you.'

'A middle-aged man, declaring his love.'

'What's wrong with that? As long as you are certain ...'

'Oh, I am.'

'Is she?'

'I think so. Yes.'

'Thinking is not enough. Is it?'

'I know. Better?'

'It sounds a little more secure, doesn't it? It's a bit late in life for us to make howlers.'

'Make them all the time, I'm afraid. One doesn't change. It seems to me that it is never too late to make an idiot of oneself. However, one lives in hope. I'd been doing that for far too long, hadn't I?'

'Living in hope? You mean hopes of me. That it? Indirectly?'

'Directly. Torch-carrier *par excellence*, was I.'

'Now no longer? Splendid. Past tense.'

'Yes. Past tense.'

'Torch extinguished by a clever lady psychologist. Who also cooks.'

'Sorry.'

'No need to be sorry. Really not. But I will confess that I shall miss that torch. It lit up some pretty frightening corners for me in the past, over some bloody moments. I have to thank you for that. From the heart.'

'Oh don't. Please don't.'

'You need a rest from all that carrying. Hand it over to someone else.'

'Anyone in mind?'

'Don't be lunatic. Who? Dubrovnik? Can you see him carrying a torch for anyone but himself? Anyway it wouldn't throw much light, would it, all the way from the Amazon or wherever he's trolling off to.'

'When does he go?'

Alice drained her glass, refilled it, offered the bottle to Jonathan. 'A sip more? A tear?'

'A sip, thanks.'

'He goes sometime. I don't know. Hasn't said. It's all got to be set up and so on; all he has are some vague permits. I should think a South American permit is about as useless as last year's Christmas card. They keep on changing bosses ... and of course the moment something happens to one of his benighted children, wherever they are, he's off like a rocket. Keening. I could willingly brain that damned wife of his. Oh! The Catholic mentality!'

'He'll never be free?'

'I honestly don't think that he wants to be – he quite enjoys the

202

situation.' Alice threw the butt of her cigarette into the fire. 'Makes him feel safer. I should have remarried directly after Hugo died, I suppose. Cold blooded, but I think it would have been sensible.'

'Dubrovnik?'

'Not a chance, I've explained. Anyway, I'm really pretty sick of that great creative-peasant mind. It's terribly limiting and not very profound.'

'And I didn't have enough to offer, did I?'

'Dearest Jon ... oh dearest Jon. What a sow you make me feel.'

'Brother and sister, that it?'

She nodded gently. 'It wouldn't have worked, Jon. You'd have throttled me within a six-month.'

'But at Sybil's the other evening you ...'

She raised a hand to halt him. 'I told you, I was a bit high that evening, panicked. I ran too fast ... I often do ... I was, what did they call it? pressing my suit rather too hard, and you weren't anxious to wear it. Follow? I was too late, as usual. But in any case, as you have always known, my dear, I'm still in love, I only ever will be in love, with that idiot bastard Hugo. Nothing to be done. He was the only one for me. Finish.'

'Look Mother! Look!' Hope crashed into the room, arm waving like a flail. 'It's fixed! Wayne fixed it! Isn't it great? My bracelet. See Jon? Ladybugs and daisies, and he fixed it so quick. This is better'n Christmas!'

Clemency came in from the kitchen with a slow, measured walk, hand outstretched. 'How lovely to see you, Jonathan! And on a Sunday! I mean, I know we met in the hall but I didn't know that you had brought magic with you.'

'Magic?'

'Wayne. He's *super*. Mended that tacky bit of plastic, so now we'll all get a bit of peace, and, if you don't very much mind, he's plunking away at his guitar ... Warming it, he said. We don't often have a real musician, do we, Mother? playing in the kitchen ... it's *quite* magic.'

'I'm glad. We have to leave soon though ...'

Hope gave a loud wail. 'Hey! Jon! Not before we teach him the "Rolling Pin Song" ... it's fun. You know how it ends? Clem, you stand here, we'll sing it ...'

'Don't be ridiculous,' said Clemency. 'Jonathan has better things to do ...'

'I'd simply love to hear it. Please ...'

'Well,' said Hope, clutching the bracelet to her wrist, 'the last bit goes ... um ... um, *"Dum dum dee dum dum. Why yes, she said shyly. But please hold me tight, 'Cause I don't want to do any rolling tonight!"* Isn't that just *wild* ...'

'It's enough, too,' said Alice.

'You really have to go? *Murder on the Orient Express* is on TV ... you wouldn't like to stay and watch that?'

'No, really. I have a dinner date.'

Hope crushed her heel into the carpet. 'Oh well. Anyway, he's fixed this – and that is stunning, amazing, wonderful! I'm just *never* going to take it off.'

'You'll have to to wash,' said Clemency. 'Filthy pig.'

'I will not! That's how I lost Daddy's one. I left it on the wash-bowl and it just went. It stays on ...'

'Listen,' said Alice. 'I'm delighted it's fixed, now just clear, and let Jon and me finish our conversation in peace. Please? Then he's got to drive to Santa Monica, so don't give whatever his name is any more beer.'

'He won't drink any beer, only milk. He's strictly teetotal,' said Hope. 'Anyway, Jon, thanks for a miracle. It's just amazing!' She slammed out of the room calling, 'Wayne! Wayne ... he says you have to leave soon, so if I just hummed the first ...'

The closing door shut off her question. Clemency put a small log on the dying fire. 'I'll go and keep an eye on things. It was simply *lovely* to see you, Jonathan. 'Night.' She walked studiedly across the room, turned at the door, smiled, raised her hand in a half-gesture of farewell, turned, went into the kitchen.

Jonathan laughed.

'Easy to laugh,' said Alice. 'Sometimes I thank God for them, sometimes I could kill the pair of them, beat their heads against a wall. Something.'

'You never would.'

'No. No, I never would. The story of my life. Loyal, loving wife and mother. Christ! Wouldn't it be simply wonderful to have nothing more pressing to worry about than a cheap plastic bracelet and a tired movie on the television? Wouldn't it just be ... the most? Simply "stunning", "amazing", "wonderful".'

'A miracle,' said Jonathan.

7

Monday, 26 January

'. . . So call in right now on 453-47766, your Friendly Dealer, the People Who Know What You Want At The Price You Want To Pay. On 453-47766, your Friendly Dealer!'

The water in the little saucepan came up to the boil.

'And now the weather.' The radio voice was unctuous, flat; Lea lowered two eggs carefully into the seething water, up-ended the egg-timer.

'Today there is a high of sixty-two in Manhattan Beach, Inglewood, right across to Glendale, with a low, low expected tonight of forty-two. Some hill fog across the San Fernando Valley. But last night's short rainfall has left clear skies all the way to Pasadena; the smog count is a low, low point five, and the weather will continue dry, warm for the season, and sunny. You are tuned to WXQZ.' Music filled Nettles's rented knotty-pine kitchen with the sound of throbbing violins which Lea switched off as she crossed to the door, tying her cotton dressing gown round her waist.

'Nettles? Are you running water? Can you hear? Your eggs are on the point of being ready. Coming?'

Somewhere above a shoe fell, hitting the board floor. 'Coming!' he called back.

Toast in the rack, coffee bubbling in the percolator with irregular 'plops' as the dark liquid hit the glass lid, steam wavering from the eggs. She opened the refrigerator door, took out the orange juice, filled a glass, set it on the antique knotty-pine table, peered at the egg-timer as the last of the coloured sand ran into the base. Always so surprising: how the last grains rushed through so fast after the slow start. She turned off the gas, lifted the eggs with a slotted spoon,

206

set them on a napkin-covered saucer, as Nettles arrived.

'All ready. Perfect timing.' She sat down and buttered toast.

'Oh, the agony before me,' said Nettles, pulling out a ladder-back chair and sitting opposite her. 'Why in the name of God don't they have egg-cups in America? Eating a boiled egg out of a cup is most irregular.'

'Must be used to it now. After a year.'

He was cracking the shells all over with the back of a spoon. 'I am. But that doesn't mean I have grown any less irritated. One burns one's fingers so.'

'You should have checked the inventory.'

'Too many other things to check. Never thought of bloody egg-cups. Who would?'

'*I* would.'

'Of course you would, my child. Never forget anything, do you. Beady eye for detail.'

Lea laughed suddenly, poured coffee. 'I nearly did. Last night. With Jonathan. Eggs all right?'

'So far as I can tell, perfect. Bloody hot. Agonizing.' He peeled shell into a small pile on the napkin, dropped the egg into a cup, started on the second one. 'What did you nearly forget? *I* forget. If you follow?'

'Nearly forgot my proposal. Making Jonathan propose, I mean.'

'Oh that. Ah yes. Very important. I'd rather taken it for granted that he had done so already.'

'So had he. Salt's here ... and pepper.'

'I'm quite scalded.' He peeled the second egg rapidly, dropped it into the cup, took the salt and some pepper; lifted his spoon. 'And now one commences. Goodness, what a business over a couple of eggs! I always liked, so much, tapping the top and then removing the little lid part, you know? The white under there is always the first taste of delight to come ... and then the moment when one thrusts in the spoon and the yolk spills out, so deep, so yellow, dribbling down the side of the egg-cup. Oh! what bliss. And sticking a slim piece of buttered bread into the very heart – a "soldier". Do you remember "soldiers"? How lovely they were. This is simply barbaric, mashing eggs together. A mush in a tea-cup. Quite revolting.'

'I was really rather surprised myself, as it happens. About forgetting that Jonathan hadn't proposed. I mean he'd said all the right things, you know. But he had not actually *said*, in so many words, that he wanted to marry me. I got quite a turn when I remembered. I was draining the peas.'

'Which is perhaps why they were cold. You must have been very shocked.'

'I was. You know? This is the last of the Dundee marmalade ... just as well we are leaving. No point in buying a whole new pot for a few days, is there?'

'None whatsoever. He did it quite charmingly, I thought. Jonathan.'

'Propose? Oh yes. Yes he did. He was rather astonished himself, I think. That he'd forgotten. He said he thought I'd taken it for granted that his intentions were honourable. I had, of course, deep down, but I wanted to hear him say so.'

Nettles scooped about inside the egg-messed tea-cup. 'I thought it was done with great elegance. I was quite touched,' he said.

Lea finished the orange juice, wiped her lips with the tips of her fingers. 'So odd. It was the very first proposal I ever had. No one asked me to actually go through to marriage with them before. That's why I rather forced things last night. You know? A woman wants to hear that phrase at least just once in her life. "Will you marry me?" Corny, I suppose. But I *am* getting on, I was rather concerned that I might never hear it.'

'Well, now you have.'

'Now I have. Although I was pretty certain really, it hit me like a sword-thrust just above the heart. All the soppy songs are true, you know. A heart *does* stand still. At a moment like that.'

I know, thought Nettles, setting his cup aside and reaching for toast, I know how it feels. *I* felt a sword-thrust, my dearest child. Through the heart. The thought of you leaving me, of belonging to someone else for the rest of your life, having someone quite other to share the worries and the doubts; although I want it for you, because you want it so, I don't want it for me. I'm getting on a bit myself. I fear loneliness too. Expected what has happened, of course, even rather hoped for it: for you. But now that it's come I feel an extraordinary sense of loss, inner desolation. Perfectly ridiculous.

208

'You are so like your mother, you know,' he said, spreading marmalade.

'But she didn't force a proposal, did she? You did that.'

'I pushed your father, yes ... she was very reluctant. Mad about him, with very good reason, but *I* had to force things. We had supper in some perfectly awful Chinese restaurant and I thought that if I didn't meddle a bit, bring things to a head, we'd be stuck there for ever. Frightful food. Of course it *was* in the middle of a civil war, nineteen forty-five, but even so ... I remember we had hot champagne. To celebrate.'

Lea laughed, took his cup and refilled it. 'Hot champagne? It couldn't be ...'

'Well, warm ... all they had.' He took the offered cup. 'Thank you. You know I shall miss this over-conscious little kitchen. I'm going to miss quite a lot of things. I've enjoyed it. But this room has great charm, I think.'

'It's so decorated. Knotty-pine fretwork everywhere, ticking wall-clock in a wormwood frame, that old coffee grinder, the rope of obligatory garlic, string of onions, dried herbs in a stone jar ... very Norman Rockwell.'

'I never dared to touch them. They must be years old, crumbling to dust.'

'Plastic,' said Lea ... 'Except the 'erbs. They drop the "H" here, don't they?'

'Good Elizabethan English. Like "fall" for autumn and "gotten" for our got. Your snobbery is showing.'

'No! Not at all! An observation only. I'm not a bit snobbish about America, it's too warm and kind – the kindest place I've ever been in. I think that's what I'll miss the most in England. The openness here, the interest, the amazing generosity, the in-built sense of classlessness.'

Nettles stirred sugar into his coffee, shook his head thoughtfully. 'Not really classless. It shows itself. From time to time. I found that. In college, other places. There are enormous divisions. And a quite frightening intolerance ... *that* surprised me. You saw it last night, a perfect example.'

'Last night?' Lea had risen and was stacking her plate and coffee cup; she stood still. 'When? Oh. Ah yes. Jonathan's driver. In the orange suit. Wayne.' She went across to the dish-washer, rattled it open.

'The White Rat,' said Nettles.

'Yes, that was scarey. But isolated, surely? Although Jonathan said not.'

Nettles shrugged. 'Common enough, I'm afraid. That machine will have to go on this morning. Full of last night's supper stuff ... have you room for these?' He raised his plate and coffee cup.

'Yes. Just. I'm afraid I led him on, the creep, I was fascinated, appalled. And enraged.'

When she had opened the front door, the White Rat was standing there, a cardboard box in his arms, Jonathan behind him, a fine rain falling.

'Presents!' said Jonathan. 'Wayne here insisted on carrying them across your garden.'

'Come in, it's raining, you'll both be soaked.'

'Where do I put this?' said the White Rat.

'Anywhere ... here ... this table.' Lea quickly moved a plastic fern and a telephone, made space for the carton.

'Two Mouton Cadet, imported, one Dimple Haig, two jars of asparagus, imported, one pot of pâté de foie gras. Fauchon, Paris, France,' said Jonathan.

'It weighs,' said the White Rat, setting it on the table.

'You are quite mad! Why the largesse? I've *got* dinner ready.'

'I thought perhaps a little touch of splendour. I felt extravagant.'

Wayne brushed his sleeves, adjusted his tie, ran nervous fingers through springy hair, coughed lightly.

'Ah yes!' Jonathan turned suddenly to Lea. 'Can Wayne use your telephone? To call his sister? I kept him waiting a bit, at Alice's. He's behind schedule.'

Lea's eyes narrowed slightly. 'Dear Alice, I hope she's terrifically well ... of course use the telephone, Wayne, it's right here, behind the fern ... can you reach it?'

'I got it. Thanks a lot. Margie worries if I'm late, scared of mugging, you know? At this time of night. The blacks are coming out ...'

'Well, you call her.' Lea picked up the two bottles of wine and went into the sitting room, Jonathan behind her.

'You really *are* potty. But thank you. Nettles will have a stroke, from sheer delight. He's getting a little weary of Napa Valley Pinot Noir ... or whatever it is. Why is whatsisname's sister scared of being mugged? She's at home, isn't she? Or not?'

'Not for herself she's worried. Him. A single bloke in a nice, shiny, new Ford ... alone on the freeway? The blacks do have a singularly disturbing habit of creeping up alongside you, in clapped-out old sedans, no lights or number-plate, and just start gentle harassing, nudging you into the side of the road, forcing you to stop.'

'And?' Lea stood one of the bottles of wine on the white marble mantelshelf.

'And then they beat you up, take the keys and piss off.'

'I see.'

'It's all over and done in minutes and no one lifts a finger.'

'Happened to you?'

'No. Not yet. But I know it does. Wayne's had it happen twice. He's got a little gun now. He seems a bit accident prone. Unless he's lying, which is possible.'

'A strange place. Shall I offer him a drink?'

'He doesn't drink. Very sober.'

'Well, a bottle of 7-Up? Can't hurt?'

'It's okay,' said Wayne, putting his head round the sitting room door. 'Margie was real glad I called. Thank you.'

'Nothing. Would you care for a glass of something? 7-Up? Or I've got Canada Dry?'

'Well ...' Wayne rubbed his hands down the seams of his pants, looked across at Jonathan. 'If I'm not interrupting?'

'Canada Dry?'

'Is fine. Thank you, mam.'

'Sit down,' said Lea, pouring his drink.

'I can't really stay. I parked right across the street, and it's late.'

'He deserves a drink,' said Jonathan. 'He's been force-fed cookies and milk by Alice's brats for the last hour or so, right?'

Wayne grinned anxiously, looked at his watch, rocked uneasily on his heels. 'Is right. Mending a bracelet and trying to play some kind of tune they knew in England ... quite a lilt.'

'Mending a bracelet?' Lea sat on the campaign-bed-settee. 'Diamonds and things?'

211

'No, Christ no! Was just some ol' plastic ladybugs on elastic. No big deal.'

'How clever.'

'I string a cello, the big bass, you know? So I can string a few ladybugs, right?'

'I suppose you can. Mr Pool's been telling me about the blacks. On the freeways.'

'He has? Everywhere you look is blacks. They come up from the ghettos like rats out of the sewers, that's what. If you'll forgive the expression, mam.'

'I take it that you don't much care for them, is that it?'

'In one, mam. They should all be shipped off back to wherever they came from.'

'That would take a very long time,' said Lea.

'Yeah. They breed like rats, too. Make everything dirty. They move into a neighbourhood, it's a ghetto in a week, and it stinks. There's places not so far from this very house you wouldn't dare to walk, they'd stone you, spit at you, carve you up, even. They're real mean. We should ship 'em all back to their jungles.'

'Do many people feel like this, Wayne? Or just you perhaps?'

The White Rat twisted his glass about in his hand, his knuckles butter yellow. 'Plenty feel like I do. Hate 'em. The blacks *and* the Jews. They rooined this land ... my grand-daddy said, way back, after the Civil War they just opened the flood gates to the trash of all the world. We was doing okay before that. Doing real good. We was clean, he said.'

'But wasn't the Civil War about abolishing slavery ... I mean letting the blacks go free?'

'Sure was,' said the White Rat, putting his glass on the coffee table. 'An' that was just about the craziest reason to start a war that there ever was. The Jews in New York was behind all that, the carpet-baggers.'

Lea leant forward, hands clasped loosely, eyes deceptively gentle. 'Are you a Christian, Wayne?'

He looked startled. 'Me? A Christian? Sure as hell am, mam.'

'Then you are a follower of Christ. Right? Jesus Christ. Get what I mean?'

'Jesus Christ?'

212

'The very same.'

'Know what those old Jews did to Him? Nailed Him up. And they ain't never forgotten. They don't like Christmas, they don't even call it that, they just say, "Have a Happy Holiday". You know the joke, "Cancel Easter: they found the body"? That's a Jewish joke. Don't you think that's disgusting? Real dirty? They just washed their hands of Him.'

'I think that was Pontius Pilate, actually.'

Wayne looked about the room anxiously. 'That Jesus got too uppity for them. Messed up the money-lenders, remember? You interfere with a Jew's money he'll get you right quick in the back. Everything in this town they own. Movies, the television, the banks and the stores. Everywhere there is a Jew behind. Old hook-nose with his diamond rings.'

Jonathan suddenly looked at his watch. 'Wayne, I think you'd better go ... before someone pinches your car ... be back here about ...' he looked across at Lea, '... about eleven thirty?' Lea nodded, hands still loosely folded. 'Ring the bell at the front gate when you arrive so I know you're here, okay? We don't want a mugging. Think of Margie.'

'Will do,' said Wayne. He looked down at Lea. 'And thanks for the refreshment, mam.'

'No trouble. Thank you for such a revealing conversation.'

'You're welcome. I like talking to you people from Europe. You got so many things to ask a person. Real interesting for me.'

'I'm sorry about the blacks, and the Jews. Difficult for you,' said Lea.

The White Rat grinned, head to one side. 'It's okay. We'll win, you know. One day.'

Lea rose and walked to the fire, avoiding the possibility of shaking his hand. 'How do you know, I wonder, that *we* aren't Jews in this house?' she said.

There was a silence. The White Rat's smile died slowly. 'I just know. You sense these things. I wouldn't lift a finger to help no Jew – only maybe to shut the doors of the ovens. Right?'

Lea closed her hands into tight fists behind her back. 'Jonathan? Be sweet and open the wine, will you ... Goodnight, it has been very instructive. Very.'

The White Rat was at the door. 'Like I said, no problem. Glad I put you wise to things, nice of you to ask. So ... eleven thirty, okay? And I ring the bell at the gate? Have a nice time, now. And thanks for the telephone.' He let himself out into the fine rain.

They heard the front door close quietly.

'God! God Almighty!' said Lea. She placed her hands on the mantelpiece, head bowed.

'I'm sorry. I've heard all that before, of course.'

'The hatred! The cold, unthinking *hatred*. I could have smashed him in the teeth.'

'All based on fear, resentment, sexual anxiety ... a lot of things ...'

'Oh shit!' said Lea, moving away from the fire, standing with her back to him. 'I *know* the reasons! But the bigotry, the narrowness, the unbelievable cruelty, the ignorance. Above *all*, the ignorance.'

'Good, clean-limbed boy from Oregon. Daddy was a lumberjack, simple family life. Then Wayne broke away, got fed up with saw-mills in Rock Valley, came down to the Big Time ...'

'The ignorance, the blind stupidity. Oh Christ!'

'Don't go on fuming away. It's here to stay, you know, nothing we can do about it, we are the foreigners. Not our problem.'

'Is that feeling general? It can't be, couldn't be.'

'I don't know how general it is in the Great Fly Over ... but it's not unusual in this town.'

'The Great Fly Over?'

'The heart of America. The bit you fly over between New York in the East and Los Angeles in the West. That's what it's called. It's the gut of America. I've never been there, neither have lots of Americans, but that's where the real pulse beats ...'

'Does a pulse beat in the gut?'

'Don't be so bloody literal. Where's Nettles? Out?'

Lea took the wine and went towards the kitchen. 'No. Up in his rooms, sorting things. He's accumulated so much junk in a year he could open a stall. He simply can't take it all with him.'

'A year is quite a while.'

'He hoards things. Bits of string, used envelopes, Jiffy bags. God! I just dread the thought of packing.' She pushed open the door. 'Help yourself to a drink, I'm going to be cooker-bound for a little. A leg of lamb, that do?'

214

'Terrific.'

'With "new" potatoes and "new" peas. Garden fresh, from the deepfreeze. God! I hope that Margie poisons her bloody little brother tonight.'

'I need him for two more days yet. He's all right under all that rubbish, you know, it's the way he's been brought up, taught to think.'

'German background, I imagine?'

'No, I regret to tell you, good Welsh stock. He told me with great pride. Very strictly brought up.'

'You amaze me. Parents have a hell of a lot to answer for.'

'No one,' said Jonathan, opening the bottle of scotch, 'knows that better than you, I'll wager. All your kids at Queen Alexandra's, right?'

'Absolutely. And it doesn't make it any easier to cope, hearing that filthy stuff spouted by a whey-faced little prick in one's own sitting room.' She went into the kitchen. 'If you want ice, come and get it. I forgot to put it out.'

Lea closed the dish-washer, set the switch to 'FULL WASH', waited for the bubble and humming, put the packet of washing-salt away.

'God! But he made me angry,' she said.

Nettles was still in his chair at the table tracing an abstract pattern with a spoon on the cloth. 'Oh my dear. It really isn't very unusual, you know. That hatred, his hatred. Look at Britain. Catholic against Protestant, whites against the Pakistanis. It's a worldwide manifestation. Hindu against Muslim, Greek against Turk ... and what about the wreckage of Iran at this moment? Sect against sect, tribe against tribe ... *all* in the name of God. Suspicion, hatred, jealousy, intolerance. It is not just the White Rat's prerogative. And he doesn't stand for *all* America. Yet, at least.'

Lea was leaning against the dresser, arms folded. 'Suppose you're right. Just gets my blood raging ... anyway . . anyway ...' she spread her arms before her, 'I *loved* the rest of the evening. All that stuff Jonathan carted in ... madness.'

'One could hardly call two excellent bottles of Mouton Cadet madness. I was simply delighted.'

215

'But the asparagus. What shall we do with that? Absurdly extra-vagant.'

'I really don't much care for it in bottles, do you?'

'Loathsome. They looked like terrible laboratory specimens. Something obscene, in pickle.'

'Graphic. We can put them with my sorting-out stuff. Someone might care for them.'

'Take them down to Irina with the rest of the things, why not? She'd love them.'

'And the tea, two pounds of Jackson's best ... we'll never use it, will we?'

'Never. And the books? Take the books?'

'And the skillet? Perhaps it's a bit heavy for them, but I really can't cart it all the way back to Fitzroy Square.'

'*I* can't even carry it with two hands ... what about Grant's tomb?'

Nettles shook his head, got up from his chair. 'What, indeed.'

'I can't see Irina throwing up her hands in delight when she sees that.' She took up the marmalade jar, licked her fingers.

'I think she might quite like the asparagus and the tea and the books ... I'll put them all together in a couple of boxes and we can take them over this afternoon. They can sort it out for themselves.'

'What time is Jonathan coming?' Lea screwed on the lid of the marmalade jar.

'After lunch ... three-ish.'

'You are sure, aren't you, that you don't mind me taking the car?' She closed the cupboard door over the worktop.

'Sure. Jonathan has never been to Irina's. He's curious to see the place before it tumbles into the sea ... no, you take it. Get your teeth looked at.'

'Tooth ... it's just that I don't want an abscess blowing up somewhere over the Atlantic, you know? An abscess is no laughing matter, especially on a long-haul flight.'

'Painful? You didn't say, my darling.'

'Lurking. I should have gone in London before I left. Such a rush.'

'Well, rush off now. I'm in good hands.'

'That bloody White Rat driving you. Intolerant half-wit. I worry ...' She took the napkin, shook the pieces of egg-shell into the trash-can under the sink.

Nettles straightened the tablecloth, brushed up some crumbs, replaced a bowl of fruit in the centre, hitched his trousers. 'I don't imagine that his intolerance will interfere with his driving. Don't fuss.'

Lea opened the front of the wall-clock, advanced the hands five minutes. 'This is slow, did you know? I'm not fussing, by the way. Seething. That's all.'

'Waste of energy.'

'I'll go up and dress. Lunch with Sybil Thingummy before the dentist ... at El Padrino. I'd better find something suitably Beverly Hills to wear, Pucci and Gucci, right?'

'Shouldn't have thought it would matter if you had gone there stark naked. It's so dark you have to take a torch to read the menu.'

'Well, I'll go anyway. And there's ham, lettuce, tomatoes in the ice box.'

Nettles came across to the door, hands on his hips. 'I know, sweet child, I know. I do wish that you'd get it into your head that I have lived here, quite alone, for a year and managed perfectly splendidly.'

Lea laughed. 'Omelettes. And chili beans on toast.'

'Very filling. Not as good as a pair of kippers, I agree, but filling.'

'And there's a bit of old Brie from last night.'

She leant towards him, kissed him lightly on the cheek. For an instant he held her, let her go.

'I'm a pretty good hand at a Bloody Mary, too. Full of vitamins.'

She turned away; he watched her cross the hall, start up the stairs. Bent his head. Thumped the wall under the ticking clock with a closed fist. Wretchedly.

Mouse was coming down the wide staircase with Irina's modest breakfast on a tin tray, which had just been rejected by a slow shake of the head, eyes closed with pain, when the telephone rang.

It stopped her with a start of fright.

She set the tray on the step on which she stood, then hurried down to the china-cat-cluttered table in the hall below.

'Countess Miratova's residence.'

'Is this she?'

'No. No, the Countess is unwell. She is in bed.'

'Who is this I am speaking with?' It was a woman's voice. Brisk, high-pitched.

217

'Her ... um ... her companion.'

'Miss Ivanova. Right?'

Mouse fingered the little icon on a chain at her neck.

'Yes. Yes, that's right. Can I help you. Who is it?'

'Tell me, what is the matter with her? She sick?'

'Yes. In great pain. With her back. She won't even accept the breakfast I ...'

The brisk voice cut in sharply. 'It is very important that I speak with her.'

'But it's not possible!'

'Listen, I have a personal message for her. Understand? Personal.'

'Are, excuse me for asking, but are you from the Bureau?'

There was a moment's silence, blankness; a hand had covered the mouthpiece at the other end.

The voice resumed, less urgently, more dismissively. 'I have to meet with her. I have something important to say.'

Mouse, was standing on tiptoes; a thing she often did when she was using the telephone and when she was frightened. The position was one of profound anxiety, she looked poised to flee. Suddenly she regained courage. She was in sole charge. There could be no help from the Countess. She stood back on her heels.

'It is *quite* impossible. She can hardly move a finger, her back is hurting her dreadfully, she couldn't meet you, or even speak to you. I'm sorry.'

A silence. The hand smothering the mouthpiece.

The voice again. 'Right. Can *you*?'

'I?' said Mouse in bewilderment. 'Do what?'

'Meet with me? I will give you the message and the ... uh ... the package which I have for her.'

'Where? I could meet you, yes. But where and when, please?'

'You know Venice? Right after the Santa Monica city limits. Take the Ocean Highway. Be there at ten o'clock, okay?'

'Be *where*? I don't know anywhere in Venice.'

The voice was stiff with impatience. 'Ten this morning. You have two hours.'

'I can't leave her alone in this house!'

'There's a parking lot right between Ozone and Dudley on Ocean Front, will you write that down?'

'I don't have a pencil.'

'It has a big mural right in-back of it. Wall of a restaurant. A wave, all blue and white, you can't miss it. It's the famous Hokusai wave, you know?'

'No.'

'Well, that's what it is. Blue and white. A wave. A sea wave. Okay? I'll meet you at the doorway of the restaurant, it's right on the corner, a one-storey building with a blue and white wave painted on it, and the restaurant is called Saigon ... *try* and remember?'

'But I won't know what you look like ...'

For the first time the voice showed a trace of pleasantness, if not kindness. 'I know *you*, Miss Ivanova. Just stand there. I'll find you.'

The line went dead.

Mouse replaced the receiver, trailed a finger across a dusty china cat, put her hands to her face with a leap of fear.

'I know you,' the voice had said. Who was it? How do they know me? I have never met anyone from the Bureau, that I know of ... what *else* do they know? What shall I do? Oh! Help me, someone help me! I'm too old, I don't know what to do. I can't leave this house. 'I know *you*,' the woman had said. Why? Who? Please someone help me. She's ill. Please help me. Please! I'm so afraid.

She had opened the front door cautiously, chain in place; he stood on the top step, the white car glimmering in the sun behind him, golden hair blowing in the wind. Blood on his face, his lip cut. Tieless.

'Irina's out. I saw her leave in a car,' he said.

'She's gone for a trip. They took her to Santa Barbara. A motor trip.'

'Can you help me? Please help me, Mouse. I'm so afraid.'

She removed the chain from the door, opened it wide; he came into the hall, his white suit crumpled, shoes covered in dust.

'What has happened! Mr Arlington ... what happened? You are bleeding.'

'Bleeding?'

'Your face. It's cut.'

He touched his face with a shaking hand. 'Help me, please. I am so afraid.'

Mouse clasped her hands tightly together. 'What can I do? Come in, come in ...'

'I am in desperate trouble, desperate. Please, Mouse. I've come to you.'

'I'll help, I'll try. You know that I will.'

Suddenly he turned on the step, reached back and took her by the wrist. 'Come. Come quickly!'

He dragged her down the steps, her glasses waggling, apron fluttering in a sharp wind from the sea. She cried out in muffled protest.

'No one must know. No one. They could send me to jail.'

Mouse tried to pull back.

'To prison! What has happened, what have you done? Tell me! My hand is hurting.'

At the back of the white car he stopped, let her go, swung open the boot with a quick, vicious throw: it sprang upwards.

'I could be sent to jail.' His eyes were glowing, pupils wide like those of a dog's caught in headlights.

'See?' He pulled her closer.

She looked into the open boot, opened her mouth to scream as his hand clamped across it, jerking her head roughly against his chest. He held her tightly until she stopped struggling. Her glasses fell to the gravel; then he let her go.

She stood perfectly still, arms at her sides, hair blowing in little spikes about her head, tears streaming down her face. He stooped, retrieved the glasses, handed them to her.

'I'm so afraid, Mouse. Please help me. Please.'

'What did you do?'

She put on the glasses, wiped her nose on the back of her hand. 'What happened? What did you do?' Her voice was as soft, as low, as that of a conspirator. 'What did you do?'

'I hit her with the car ... she ran out from a track somewhere. I didn't see her. The car hit her ... went bump. It just went bump. When I ran back she was lying there. She's dead.'

'Little. So little.'

'No one saw it. Help me to hide her, please?'

Mouse looked up at him slowly, hands to her mouth in disbelief. 'Hide her? We must take her to a hospital . . . a doctor.'

'She's *dead*. No one must know. I'd be sent to prison. There is Alice, my children . . . No one saw us. It was way off, up in the . . . up in the scrub . . . she just ran in front of me . . . there was no one else, no one saw. I waited, Mouse. I waited to see if there was anyone with her, but she was alone, so no one will know, no one could have seen . . . it was a lonely place.' He spoke in a rapid monotone.

'You killed her.'

'By accident. She was running loose. I don't know who she is, lots of kids like her . . . freeway trolls. No one knows. I must hide her.'

'Not here! No, no. Not here! Never, never. Not here!'

'Mouse, dear Mouse. I am your friend, remember, I am your good friend who loves you. Now I come to you in desperation, help me. Just for one day . . . I am pleading. Give me time to think what to do, just for a little while, please? Oh God, Mouse. I'm so afraid.'

Her voice regained strength. 'Bring her into the house quickly. I don't want to look, I don't want to see. Wrap her in the travelling rug, cover her up, don't let me see anything. Just come into the house, follow me, I'll show you where, but you must do it by yourself.' She turned quickly, half ran, half walked into the house, across the big hall, to a far door which she unlocked and swung wide, snapping on a light at the side which lit steps down to the furnace room.

She looked back as she heard him crossing the gravel driveway. There is nothing to be afraid of: nothing. He is simply carrying a bunched-up old travelling rug: nothing unusual at all. She took the key from the cellar door, put it in her apron pocket, looked up again as he reached the steps to the house and a thin black arm slid through a fold in the tartan rug, a lifeless hand dangling like a dead flower.

Mouse looked away, smothering a cry of anguish, hurried into the shadowy sitting room: stood bowed in grief.

A crack of sticks, the brushing of ice-heavy leaves, a distant cry of shrill alarm, the slow, rhythmic flapping of the wings of a crow across the wide white field.

'It's done,' he said, standing in the doorway. 'It's done.'

'What have you done?' She could not look at him.

221

'A trunk. There's a big cabin trunk there. Luggage, boxes.'

'You must take her away. You cannot leave her there. Soon, you promise me?'

'I promise.'

She gave him the key from her apron pocket. 'Lock the door. I will not.'

'I must clean my shoes. My face ...'

'In the kitchen. I'll get a clean towel.'

'They are only scratches ... nothing more. Just little scratches.'

'Go and lock the door, and bring me the key,' she said. 'Please, please, bring me the key.'

Beyond Ocean Front Walk and the ugly, squat buildings zig-zagged with fire escapes lay the beach, beyond that the sea: grey and flat like washing-up water in the early sunlight. A clatter of children rattled past her on skateboards, a black youth, slender as a stick, waltzed and spun on roller skates, naked to the waist, his legs in zebra-patterned tights, one hand clasped to his head-phone.

The Promenade was waking up to the new day: out on the sands two people jogged with slow deliberation, a group of Hell's Angels threw stones for a dog, opened cans of Pepsi Cola, wrestled good-naturedly, and a woman in shorts, high heels and a floral turban walked past, with a parrot on her shoulder, reading a Bible aloud to no one in particular.

The air smelt sweet, salt, with a strain of coffee brewing and something with which she was not familiar. Although, walking back towards the door of the restaurant on which the blue and white wave was painted, the unfamiliar odour suddenly presented her with a mental flash-picture of Hugo sitting at the kitchen table, a cigarette hanging on his lips, his fingers jabbing at a typewriter as Irina's recorded voice rumbled thoughtfully from the machine at his elbow.

'You ask of Schoenberg? A vibrant man, voluble, loving ... always quite at ease here, to be truthful. I always felt that he would have been happier perhaps in Paris ... or in Vienna ... anyway, in Europe ... some people, you know, do not transplant easily, he was not such a one ...'

The image died. She stood uneasily beside the closed wooden

door, the light breeze twisting and pulling at the dove's feather in her hat.

'My! Isn't this a gorgeous morning? Call me Holly.'

She was about twenty-four, red haired, pale, freckled face, tin-glasses, a nose like the snout of a shrew, wearing a faded green tracksuit and sneakers, a canvas hold-all over one shoulder. 'Shall we take a walk? Down to the ocean? Find a quiet bench in the sun?'

Mouse nodded, and they went together through the snaking skaters.

'Isn't this a wild place? Even at ten in the morning,' said Holly.

'I have very little time,' said Mouse. 'I must get back.'

'Too bad she's so sick. I'm real sorry.'

'Yes. Yesterday she was apparently quite well, but in the evening the pain began again.'

'Arthritis,isn't it?' said Holly swinging the canvas hold-all onto her other shoulder.

'Yes. Arthritis ... of the spine.'

'The weather has some effect, they say. Shall we sit there? We can watch the sea and all the sights.'

They crossed the boardwalk to the bench, avoiding a collision with two white youths on roller skates in skin-tight jumpsuits who wheeled and swung around them, squealing shrill obscenities.

'You said that you have a message?'

'Correct. We would have been happier to tell her ourselves, but since she's so sick ...' Holly opened the hold-all, took out a copy of *Cosmopolitan*, a packet of coloured pencils, a hard-cover children's book. She held it up. 'Know this? *Alice in Wonderland* ... it's for my niece, Heidi, and you know what? It is *all* black and white ... look ...' She riffled pages. 'So I have to colour them in. I mean you can't give a child a book with dull old black and white pictures, so Auntie will colour them. The stuff she has been giving us won't really do, you know. Not any more.'

'I *don't* know.'

'Well ... it's not any use. Right? Party tittle-tattle. It was fine, they say, in the old days, plenty going on, but now, well ... it's just useless. I mean for two hundred bucks a throw. They don't want it any more is what I am to say.'

'Who,' said Mouse, 'are *they*, please?'

223

Holly looked at her for a moment. 'Blue, do you suppose? For Alice's dress? I feel blue is right. They are phasing her out.'

'They?' said Mouse.

'That's who,' said Holly, choosing a blue pencil and starting to work on a page. '"They" is all you need to know.'

'I think that the Countess had a most satisfactory meeting, only a few days ago, in Beverly Hills. I went into town with her, she spoke warmly of Mr Andre—'

Holly cut in sharply, still working busily with her blue pencil. 'We don't use names. No names. And he's gone East. She won't see him again.'

'East? New York?'

'East,' said Holly. 'All the way East. Right across Europe.'

'But why? What happened? He was such an old friend.'

'I'm a messenger. That's all. I don't know *why* anything. All I was told to say was that the action is over. Party chatter and gossip is useless. There are more interesting things.'

'Interesting?'

'You heard of Silicon Valley? San Francisco?'

Mouse shook her head.

'Heard of microchips? You haven't ... well ... It would be a lot more use to us if she had. Parties are out, over. And all those European immigrants. And, let's face it, Miss Ivanova, she's old now ... she's had her time, we're grateful, but this is where we part.'

Mouse sat in silence looking out across the grey sea. A man sitting on the sand in front of them rolled forward slowly and began to stand on his head.

'Mind you,' said Holly, choosing a different pencil and starting to colour a tree, 'mind you, they will always keep an eye on her, so to speak. That's what they told me to say. But for now it's a wrap-up. It's been a long, long time, right? I reckon she'll be relieved. You tell her this?'

'I will tell her.'

'And,' said Holly, handing Mouse the copy of *Cosmopolitan*, 'this is for her. She might enjoy the pictures. But mind how you carry it, see? It's kinda full. A free gift sample inside, right? Don't let it fall out, that would be just terrible. And if you are leaving now, you wander away. Don't bother with me. I got plenty here to keep me

224

a busy lady. You just walk away. Remember, they'll have an eye on you. Just so everything is fine your end, okay? And watch the traffic ...' She chose a brown pencil, started to fill in a tree trunk. 'It's really rough at this time, on a Monday morning.'

Her head was low over her work.

Mouse held the magazine, smoothed the bright cover with gloved hands. Through the glossy paper she could feel a thin package.

'Good day,' she said, getting to her feet.

Holly did not look up, waved the brown pencil briefly. 'Have a nice ride home, now.'

Mouse walked slowly back to the parking lot in the sunlight. The woman in the turban with the parrot on her shoulder walked past, the Bible held close to her breast. Mouse noticed, without surprise, that the woman's arms were tattooed with hearts and anchors, and that she had a thick black moustache.

Lea swung Nettles's rented Buick through the ornate black and gold wrought-iron gates of the Beverly Wilshire Hotel, taking her place in line with the Rolls-Royces, Mercedes, Bentleys and Cadillacs, moving slowly, in the lunch-time rush, towards the marble steps and the imposing top-hatted black gentleman in a long scarlet coat who would have the cars parked, with shrill blasts from his whistle, and direct the occupants to their luncheons.

This time next week, she thought, inching past dusty tubs of ferns, chrysanthemums and a couple of Californian pears in full blossom, garlanded all about with a thousand winking fairy-lights as if the flowers which they bore were insufficient, this time next week I'll be back.

Queen Alexandra's. How strange. Weird. Among all this glitter. Unreal. Back to Auditory Sequential, Bodily Coordination, Audio Visual and the rest of my daily patter. To canteen meals on tin trays, white overalls, instant coffee in plastic mugs, the wide, uncomprehending eyes of my bewildered children, the laughter and crispness of nurses, the smell of floor polish and Dettol. A long, long way away from here. I have missed them. I miss them all. I want to go back. The day of the locust is really over now, I want to go back to "the other me". And Jonathan. Jonathan Pool.

She had drawn abreast of the top-hatted gentleman, who summoned an attendant with a blast from his silver whistle, screamed orders, bade her 'Have a nice day, now!' as she started up the steps banked high with poinsettia, geranium, palms and pink-and-white striped azaleas.

A silver-garnished Mexican saddle stood, rather improbably, at the entrance of El Padrino's which was piled with pyramids of more ferns and potted plants and attended by a vaguely harassed waiter holding a menu before him the size of a sail.

Yes indeedy. Miss Witt had arrived. She was at her table. Would she come along, please?

She stepped into apparent night. Followed him blindly past a long bar which, as her eyes grew accustomed to the gloom, she saw to be thronged by middle-aged men in blue or grey alpaca suits, pressing anxiously about it like ants around a sugar cube. On beyond crammed tables at which chattering women bobbed and pecked towards each other: hens at a corn bowl. All of them, for reasons best known to themselves, wearing dark glasses and gulping down martinis with the reckless frenzy and determination of a group suicide-pact. At the far end of the room, sitting hunched alone at an empty table in a small alcove, a cluster of dried gourds and corn-heads hanging above her, Sybil, a fat red candle burning before her in a circle of light, an opened bottle of wine.

'No. You were *not* late. I was early. God knows how! And I hate to sit alone in a crowd like this. But they gave me the best table, a bottle of vino, and a candle so we can read the menu. You need a big drink, right?'

And Jonathan. Oh! Jonathan Pool.

'Desperate for one. Vodka tonic, no ice.'

They ordered the drink, ordered their meal.

'Your tooth aching? Or merely weary?'

'No. Neither. Bemused.'

'As well you might be. Listen, Lea, to the sound of the hub of the world turning! Wildly sophisticated. They write the dialogue as they go along. Improvisation.'

At the nearest table a woman, immense dark glasses glinting, obese body shaking like Jello beneath a crimson chiffon caftan, rattled ice cubes in an empty glass, leant towards two eager companions.

226

'... and you want to know? Brooke Leger peaked in the 'seventies and it's been downhill ever since. She just went splat! Blew it! I should know. I'm her agent for godssakes; I couldn't give her away with a Hershey Bar!'

One of the companions, also in dark glasses, wearing a too-tight silk jersey top through which her nipples thrust like fingertips, nodded; drained her glass.

'You are so damned right, Patty. *Right*. Blew it! That "sneak" bombed in Boston, Tuesday like you never saw. The biggest hat-reacher since Mimi croaks in *Bohème*. And you know something Patty? I'm glad. I say it aloud. I'm glad! She was getting so damned Scarlett O'Hara she made me spit.'

The chiffon caftan rattled ice cubes angrily. 'Something else I know? Real goodie. The Küntz Bureau is dropping Keir Saxon. How does that grab you?'

'Keir Saxon! The rogue male?'

'Him. Found in a red-hot clinch with one of the teamsters, in his own trailer right out on the back-lot. Kissy-kissy stuff. *If* you get what I mean?'

The woman in silk jersey wailed, hand to mouth. 'I do *not* believe it!'

'I just heard, Judy.'

'Keir Saxon with a feller!'

'Well, you know. He *is* English ...' the woman rattled the glass hard.

'And they are dropping him, Saxon?'

'Judy. Listen to me. The Küntz Bureau is selling virility. What happens to their credibility?'

She looked irritatedly round the room.

'Well,' said Judy. 'What can you expect. *Europeans*. Oh God! And all the English are lushes or gay. They talk so damned pinch-assed. What can you expect?'

'I got a new client,' said the chiffon caftan. 'European. Ulla Binder from Berlin, Germany. A really great actress. We'll fix the accent and take care of the name. More Anglo-Saxon. She'll tear this town apart, I'm telling you, just tear it apart.' She looked around furiously.

'Where the fuck's that goddamned garçon?'

227

Lea spread a hand across her eyes, shook her head, stared up into the beamed ceiling.

Auditory Sequential, Audio Visual, Bodily Coordination, Visual Perceptual. My language. As strange to them as theirs is to me. But kinder.

She turned to Sybil, saw that she was smiling.

'I got proposed to last night. How's that for swank?'

'Ah! Great. I guess ... ummm ... I guess Jonathan P?'

'You guess right.'

Waiters surrounded them, set down platters, changed spoons and forks, fussed expertly, admonished them to 'have a nice time, now', melted away into the dark.

From the bar came a sudden burst of male laughter, a round of scattered applause.

Sybil observed her lunch with mild dismay. A half pineapple, sliced lengthways, piled with assorted fruit.

'So this is what it looks like. You know? I've often wondered. It's like one of Carmen Miranda's head-dresses; remember?'

'No.' Lea forked at a plate of cottage cheese and chopped chives. 'No. I don't remember. But it's wildly exotic.'

'So was Carmen Miranda. She too long ago for you, umm?'

'I don't remember, sorry. A singer, something?'

'No, sweet. Not something. A big star in the forties. Cuban ... Portuguese, I don't know. How I envy your ignorance. It means Youth!'

'I'm really not that young.'

'If you are too young for the forties, honey, you are young. Youthful anyway.'

She laid her spoon beside her plate of spilling fruits. 'So. You finally got a proposal? A week after meeting the gentleman. You twist his arm or something?'

'No. Nudged him. He'd forgotten. Looked rather startled when I suggested it, very tactfully.'

'Well, it's a startling thing to have to do. Propose. I mean, it's a definite declaration, don't you think? Binding. Agree?'

'Binding?' Lea looked suddenly worried, put down her fork, took a sip of her vodka and tonic. 'Yes. I suppose that it is. Binding ... well, it's binding until it's broken, isn't it?'

228

'Don't speak of breaking anything twelve hours after you got proposed to, for God's sake! I never got one single proposal in all my life, do you know that? The first gentleman I married just said, "How's about it, popsie?" which was the nearest he ever got to anything remotely romantic, and the second one said, "You wanna we should get hitched?"' Sybil picked up a fork, skewered a bottled cherry, chewed it. 'He didn't speaka da English so good. What *possessed* me, for Christ's sake? They were both disaster. No love no nickels. Oh well. Lust, sheer lust.'

'And there was never anyone else?'

'No. No. I had to shell out both times. I learned my lesson. I reckon though, that if someone had come up to me and knelt down, I'm wild about the kneeling part, and said, "Sybil Witt, would you do me the great honour of marrying me?" I'd have said "Yes" if he'd been Bluebeard. Know what I mean? It's a sign that your man has considered it carefully and made up his mind. He wants you. *Wants you.* That is just about the most important question a woman can get asked. It's inspiring.'

'Inspiring?'

'Which is more than I can say for Carmen Miranda's hat here.'

'A little daunting too, I suppose.'

'Daunting? How?'

'Well, as you said. It's binding, I suppose. I hadn't really thought of it in that light.'

'From now on perhaps you'd better.'

'Yes. I was thinking of your word "want". That has different connotations, doesn't it?'

'Well, not in my book. Just marriage.'

'It could be just physical?'

'Oh sure ... but that doesn't seem to me the way Jonathan meant it.'

'No. It was all gloriously right last night. Two bottles of wine, hands held, lots of laughter. I mean, such happiness. Amazing.'

'And?'

'And then this morning, driving into town, I got this terrible surge of panic.'

'What happened? The Cold Light of Dawn? Regrets?'

'No. Neither of those things. I just ... oh, bloody hell ...' She began pushing her glass about the table in little circles, one hand supporting her chin, hair falling across her face, brow furrowed in concentration.

Sybil watched her shrewdly for a moment. Broke the look. Prodded carelessly among her tumbled fruits.

'So what panicked you?'

'Well, I suddenly realized that there would have to be breakfast tables without him. Nettles. Do you know what I mean?'

'Geoffrey Nettles!'

'I'm using the breakfast table as a kind of symbol.'

'Thank the Lord!'

'And I realized this morning that after all these years together, I would miss him dreadfully. Miss his donnish little jokes about, oh ... boiled eggs, the news ... even the weather ... you see?'

'I would kill for less.'

'I'm explaining so badly. I had a sudden grab of fright.'

'Do you have breakfasts of this hideously cosy nature, as a matter of course?'

'No. Of course not! We live our own lives, go our own ways. Most of the time. But I realized that he'll have to go. After marriage.'

'Well, for God's sake! He couldn't hang around as a surrogate father-in-law, could he?'

'No, of course not! But then there's another thing. My job. My work. I love it. I am very good at it.'

'Jonathan has his work too.'

'That's the whole point.'

'Not a bad one I'd say.'

'He writes.'

'Some men embezzle, chase ladies, rob banks. You're lucky.'

'He writes, Sybil. For months sometimes. Even as long as a year. He told me.'

'So?'

'Well, when he gets the urge he just clams up and pisses off to his shack, or whatever it is, on a hill in Provence. He told me to expect that.'

'Fair. So what?'

'Well, what do *I* do during this gigantic pregnancy? What do I do while he wallows through his period of gestation? What do I do?

230

Pull a rug? Keep bees? What would I do sitting on some God-forsaken hill in Provence? Make jam? Pick posies of wild flowers for dried arrangements? He's already had one wife who did that kind of thing and she didn't last very long. He's really not keen on that sort of capering. But if I stayed on at the hospital, did *my* job, fulfilled *myself*, well, it wouldn't be marriage. Would it?'

'No. Not in my terms. But I'm old-fashioned, in spite of my dizzying stardom and careful make-up. You mean you'd rather be a career-lady than Jonathan's wife?'

'No I don't. But ...'

'There can't be a "but". No room for "but", Lea. Now listen. Just take a glance around this room, look at all the ladies who are lunching and munching. Together. Girls-time, career-ladies. No husband in sight, no husband they give a damn about, if they even have one someplace. Look at them all. Screaming over the third Martini, the second tequila, stuffing down the shrimp salad, the chilli con carne, depending on the calories they watch like Stock Exchange results. What do you suppose they've done this morning? A couple of deals? Made a few phone calls? These militant female agents, vice-president ladies of this company or that company? Had a massage, shopped at Lord and Taylor's with their credit cards, been to ballet class to keep their legs from atrophying under their desks, sold a book to C B C or N B C, fired or hired an actor. You want that? That kind of life? Arid, barren? Career-girl. Full stop.'

'God no! It wouldn't be like that. I work in a hospital. With children ...'

'Then you go work with children on a hill in Provence, while your husband slaves to keep you-all. Your *own* children, Lea.'

'And give it all up?'

'Those things you've mentioned. Snug little brekky-wekkies with Geoffrey Nettles, the hospital ... okay, that too. If Jonathan wants you, he *needs* you. You go with him, and be grateful you got asked. Just in time.'

Sybil pushed her overflowing platter away, poured herself a glass of wine. 'You asked me. I've told you. You got it sockko.'

'Sockko, all right.'

'You-all leave in a day or so, right? Enjoy what's left of this weird town, it's far too soon for doubts.'

231

'No doubts, truthfully. Worries...'

'They'll go as soon as you clap your eyes on him again. As long as you love him.'

'I love him.'

'Then God alone knows why I've wasted my breath on impassioned speeches! Well, I do in a way ... you scared me half to death for a second. Alice Arlington is my dearest friend, I'd cross deserts for her, but *she* is determined on Career. She'll end up like these creatures gobbling away around us. Sitting with the gals, chomping diet-food in dark glasses in a dark room, believing it's all she ever wanted. "Career" comforts the empty heart, Lea.'

A figure was suddenly beside their table. Sybil squinted into the gloom above her.

'Do I know you?' she said.

The figure leant down, the features of his face caught in the light of the table candle.

'Is Dubrovnik,' he said.

'You make a swell silhouette,' said Sybil. 'Grab a chair, or can't you stay?'

'For one moment.' He pulled up a chair, took Sybil's hand, kissed it, bowed to Lea. 'Can you believe? I am with my agent. Very famous, very powerful. He is going to find peoples who will give me much money. Is Mr Minsk, from New York, you know this man?'

'Manny Minsk! Sure I know him. You are in good hands, Dubrovnik dear, he'd screw money from the Sphinx.'

'This morning he came in. He goes to the opening of the new French movie.'

'He'd go to the opening of a refrigerator.'

'Is such a little money I must have. Enough only to do the, what you call, recce? For the locations in Brazil.'

'When will you go?' said Lea.

'Depends. Is depending on Mr Minsk. Soon I would like. I am restless in this place, in this town. I would like it to start. In Brazil.'

'You're just trading jungles, honey,' said Sybil.

'Everyone seems to be leaving,' said Lea. 'The party's over.'

'Except Alice,' said Sybil. 'She stays. Her choice. I tried to make her come East with me, but no way. The kids' schooling, the career ... Useless.'

232

Dubrovnik shrugged cheerfully, spread his arms wide as if to embrace the whole noisy room.

'Is a *sensible* woman, Alice, you know this? I think what she do is right.'

'I don't,' said Sybil. 'I just don't. This town is too local, too small, too far away from life. She'd have a lot more in New York, it's really alive there. And more fun socially. But as you know, she is so damned stubborn, she won't budge.'

Dubrovnik rubbed his chin anxiously, nodded, eyes veiled with discomfort. 'Well, what Alice says she will do, so she will do. She is very ... what you say?'

'*Very*,' said Sybil.

'And I worry much for her. This you must know. But what to do? She thinks only of Hugo, finally. He is between Alice and all the world. Always. I worry for her, also for the children. They are all close together, is right?'

'Sure they are. Alice has her life and you have yours. That's what you are saying, I think?'

'I am saying that. Yes. We are creative people. If you do not create, therefore you die finally. Is not this right?'

'Very right. Oh, very right. Of course you *can* "create" a family, a partnership, that's creation too. But you have to go off and "create" in Brazil, that's it?'

'Is so. But I worry to leave her. I worry all the time. Very much. Poor Alice ...'

'Never you mind,' said Sybil dryly. 'Never you mind, old chum. It'll pass, you'll see. It'll pass.'

'Bells,' whispered Irina to the empty room. 'Why do I hear bells?' She closed her eyes, lying on her back in the high wooden bed. The wan sun filtered through long, dusty lace curtains, throwing uneven patterns across the worn carpet, the heavy oak wardrobe, the back of a cracked leather buttoned chair.

Why do I hear bells? Ah no! Not elfin bells ... not sweet bells from childhood. Bells with sonorous tongues, solemn, deep, throbbing. The bell of St John. On the last day of Lent. I remember, oh, I remember! The single mournful sound; one stroke, to signal the Resurrection. Reverberating, wavering, across the city: calling us to worship the miracle. Summoning us; summoning by bells. Am I being summoned by bells. Hah! I who cannot even move; cannot even get to my commode. Helpless. The hideous, ultimate humiliation, the decaying of the body, the indignity, the squalor; to foul oneself helplessly. Go away, bells: I cannot heed you. I cannot heed you. I am old, I decay, I am cast aside. I rot.

Her hand clutched the bundle of dollar bills which Mouse had brought from her meeting with the shrew-nosed girl. Five hundred dollars. The pay-off: the price they give to, what was the saying? to phase one out. An old cog which can no longer function economically, function at all. It was not my fault. I still have my eyes, my ears, I watched and noticed; I sifted and collected, I gave them good measure. It was modest, but it was professional. It is not my fault that the times changed, the city altered, the demands grew greater. What are microchips to me!

In the house the telephone rang.

Irina opened sunken eyes. Stared at the ceiling. Waited. Closed her eyes.

Not *these* bells. I dislike these bells. Telephone bells bring worry and distress to this house. Dismissal. 'Phasing out'. Here is your fee, go away. But we shall keep an eye on you, just in case. In case of what? Ever since the Golden Man was killed in his beautiful car I have dreaded this bell. Why have they cast me aside? Tomorrow I may be well again. I am reliable; I can keep silent, I guard my secrets. I know when to hold my tongue.

Mouse cautiously put her head round the door, tiptoed towards the high bed.

'What is it?' said Irina, her eyes still closed. 'Tell me.'

'The English man, Mr Nettles ... it's not bad, not worrying. To remind us that he is coming to see us. That is all.'

'And you said?'

Mouse, who was exhausted from her journey to Venice and back, and who had tried desperately to make her mistress take nourishment other than the five strong vodkas on which she had insisted, shook her head wearily.

'I said to come, Countess. I could not be impolite. He has gifts for us.'

'I cannot see him. I am ill.'

234

'Of course. He knows. I told him.'

'I have not got my teeth in. I could not see him thus, and I will not put them back.'

'I understand. I will see him, just briefly ... he does not want to stay, only to leave some things.'

'What kind of things, pray?' Irina's voice was high, light, fretful.

'Oh ... oh I think things he has no room to take back to England. Books, I know. Tea ... we need tea you see ...'

'For a packet of tea we must be thrown into turmoil?'

'Not turmoil. He will go directly. I am certain. He is a most thinking, generous man.'

Irina raised the bundle of dollar bills in a trembling hand. 'We must put these away.' She opened her eyes for a moment, closed them quickly at the sight of Mouse's haggard face above her. 'Yesterday would have been a better time for this abundance. I was in great pain, but I behaved well. You noticed?'

'I noticed, Countess. No one could have guessed.'

'One has been trained not to show one's feelings publicly. Never to embarrass one's guest. That would not be proper. Although, to be sure, Mr Boris was *your* guest. Not mine ...'

'He came to see *you*, Countess! Not to see me.'

Irina kept her eyes closed, her hands on the dollars. 'Presumptuous, Mouse. You invited him, without my permission.'

'But you were pleased! You were pleased!'

'I was forced to be pleased. Forced to exert myself even in pain, and now you can see what it has done. Here I lie, here I lie ...'

'Countess! You cannot blame me! You cannot blame me ...'

Irina opened her eyes, grey as flints, hollow with pain. 'I can blame whomever I wish. I am ill. I will use the commode, give me the vodka.'

Mouse, her hands shaking with anger and distress, poured a generous measure from the bottle on the bedside table, gave it to her mistress who took it eagerly in both hands and swallowed the drink in one gulp. She lay back, exhausted by the effort, eyes shut, pale tongue licking slowly, caressingly, over thin lips, the glass tilted loosely in her hand.

'One feels the fire steal into one's belly. The pain eases. That's better.'

235

Mouse attempted to remove the glass, but the wrinkled hand held it tight.

'No! No! Let me be! I am ill-tempered, Mouse. Excuse me. I have no one but you in my pain ... no one else. I am ill-tempered. The commode?'

Mouse dragged the heavy chair-commode to the bed, lifted the wickerwork top. 'It is ready. Shall we try?'

'We'll try. Yes, must try.' Irina raised her glass. 'A little more, a little more. A teeny vodka for Irina.'

'Oh! you have had a great deal ...'

'I have a great deal of pain ... give it to me ... give it for courage.'

Mouse refilled the glass, watched her mistress drink, took the empty glass from the relaxing grip.

'Let us try, Countess ... let us try together.'

She pulled back the runkled sheets, tried to prise the dollars from the hand which still held them.

'No. No. I will keep them ...'

'You must use *both* hands, Countess, both hands. Let me put the money here, beside your bottle ... there. You see? It can come to no harm. Now we try. We must try ...'

Irina moved achingly into a half sitting position, head down, arms loose, let herself be half dragged, half pulled, to the edge of the bed, where Mouse took hold of her legs and swung them over the side.

Irina's calloused feet hung loose like a wax doll's, above the shabby carpet.

'Put them to the floor,' said Mouse. 'I will help you ...' With all her strength she eased the heavy body onto the commode.

Irina sat slumped, shaking her head, whimpering.

'So brave!' said Mouse, when she had got her breath back.

'I am a cog. Nothing but a cog. A useless cog.'

'No, no,' said Mouse, smoothing the rumpled bed, shaking pillows. 'No, no, Countess, you are very brave.'

'I fouled myself.'

'Because *I* was not here,' said Mouse. 'I went to Venice, for the money. I prayed that you would sleep ...'

'In my own filth.'

'Shhsh ... Soon tidy.'

236

'I cannot manage on my own.'

'Soon tidy. Everything was done ...'

'The mind remains, the body fails. God is cruel.'

'What a thing to say! Tomorrow you will feel quite well again, you will see.'

'God is cruel. He punishes with fire.'

'Shall we try to get back? The bed is ready. Come ... I'll help you ...'

Once there again, Irina lay still; uttering little fluting cries of distress, like a trapped bird. Mouse busied herself with the chamber pot, dragged the commode away, her glasses misting with effort, and the tears of weakness which rimmed her eyes.

'My money,' whispered Irina. 'Give it me. Give it back to me.'

'It is here, Countess. Beside you.'

'People are coming. Put it away. Hide it. Hide it away.'

Irina's speech was becoming slurred, words spilled from her toothless mouth in splutters of spittle.

'Where?' said Mouse. 'Where shall I hide it?' She picked up the packet of five hundred-dollar bills. 'Where?'

Irina's head rolled from side to side in irritation, her brow creased with anger. 'Hide it. The picture frame. In the picture. Dressing-table. There is a picture. In the back. You open it. Put it in the back. The dressing-table.'

The dressing-table was a clutter of china cats, ring holders, picture frames of varied shapes and sizes, pots of caked face-cream, empty scent bottles, scatters of spilled powder and hairpins.

'So many. So many here,' said Mouse weakly. 'There is a special one perhaps?'

Irina slapped the sheets with a veined hand. 'Miratov. Miratov my husband. Behind him. That one.'

Mouse looked among the frames with increasing anxiety. A pair of borzoi, a smiling young woman with a shotgun beneath a fir tree, a luncheon party in a garden. In a filigree brass frame standing almost in the centre, a young man in the uniform of the Corps des Pages; proud in his tight braided tunic, gleaming boots, white breeches, a plumed helmet on his knees.

'I have it,' said Mouse.

Irina's voice was fretful, impatient. 'Miratov! Miratov! Find Miratov!'

237

Mouse unfastened the brass clips of the faded watered-silk panel at the back, prised it open.

A scrap of charred suede fell among the dried face-creams, the figures 1979 impressed in gilt. Inside, flat against the back of Miratov's portrait, a half-scorched, heat-buckled, three-quarter-length Polaroid photograph of a small black girl. Thighs wrenched apart with cords, arms pulled above her head, secured to a hook by a man's tie. She was naked, apart from a scarlet ladybird bracelet on one wrist, her child breasts jutting forward, eyes wide with terror.

Mouse stood as stone.

Irina's voice came from an immense distance.

'Have you found him? Miratov? Answer me!'

Mouse spoke like a sleepwalker. 'So handsome. So young. So fine in his uniform ...'

Irina beat her hands furiously on the sheets, dribble trembling on her chin. 'Not *that*! Not *that*! It's wrong! *The wrong one!*' She started to weep, hiccupping, gulping for breath like a landed fish.

Mouse looked across the dressing-table, through the blur of lace, into the fading light.

He stood on the top step. The white car glimmering in the sun behind him, golden hair blowing in the wind. Blood on his face, his lip cut. Tieless.

'It wasn't true,' she said aloud. 'It wasn't true. You lied.'

'Help me Mouse. I am desperate. She was running loose: I don't know who she was.'

'Oh, you lied,' said Mouse. 'You *did* know who she was. You knew.' She looked at the photograph in her hand, turned slowly and walked to the bed.

Irina was sobbing, a fist crammed hard against her toothless mouth, eyes tightly shut.

'From the furnace?' said Mouse quietly. 'You found this in the furnace that day? You took this from the ashes?'

Irina's sobs grew less. She opened her eyes, removed the fist from against her mouth. 'From the ashes. From the ashes. Foolish creature! Foolish creature! The *wrong* frame, the *wrong* one.'

'Why did you keep it. Why?'

'To give it to him. When he came again. To give it back.'

'He never came back.'

'In that car. Dead in that car. That day.'

'Why did you keep it? Something he wished to destroy? Why? Tell me why? What for?'

Irina folded her hands across her belly, turned her head away, sighed. A long, shuddering sigh.

'Why, Countess? What for?'

Irina turned her head, looked up at Mouse, her eyes blazing with pain and fury.

'Money,' she said.

'Money?'

'He had money. I had none.'

'He would have paid you for this?'

'He tried to destroy it. To destroy many of them. I saw, in the furnace, some had not burned entirely. There were fragments. He panicked. He was too frightened. These things do not at once all burn up. Fragments. Obscene. Fragments, perverted things. I raked them to ashes. Raked them to dust.'

'And this remained ... this one?'

Irina's hands plucked at the bedcover.

'Imbecile. Imbecile. The wrong frame! The wrong one. You are a *mad* woman.'

'I am not mad, Countess.'

'Hah! All mad people deny their madness. *You are mad!* You think he came to burn manuscripts? He came to destroy the evidence of his wickedness.' She put out a withered arm. 'Give it to me, give it ... give it here to me.' She took the photograph, slid it beneath the covers. 'Get the money. Bring me my money.'

Mouse took the dollars, scattered them slowly, like dead leaves, across Irina's breast.

'Imbecile! *Mad* creature! Go away, go away.'

For a moment Mouse squinted through tears about the shadowy room, then she picked up the chamber pot and left, closing the door quietly behind her.

Irina scrabbled about feebly, seeking the fallen notes. She collected them together like a hand of cards, counted them, pushed

239

them under the sheets, felt the buckled photograph and drew it up, close to her face.

'What did he do with you? Where do you live? Poor creature. Poor Alice, and Clemency and Hope! But she has a fine new bracelet. I found her that, eh? I found that.' She bent the photograph in two with one hand, crushed it in her palm.

'Poor child. Poor Jupiter,' she said.

The orange Ford swung between the two brick pillars, round a weed-grown central flowerbed, and came to a halt at the steps.

'Sheet!' said the White Rat softly. 'I mean this is weird. I seen some crazy places but this has to be the most. Where's Dracula? I never knew this place existed.'

'It very nearly doesn't,' said Nettles, easing himself out of the car. 'Another torrential rainstorm and it will be quite uninhabitable. It is almost on the edge of the cliff as it is.' He went round to the boot.

'Extraordinary!' said Jonathan. 'A sort of wooden French *manoir*, you know?'

'Built, we are informed, by a very rich industrialist from Louisiana at the turn of the century. So your suggestion is not far off the mark. Definite French influence. Hence the roof, the shutters, the high windows, the little tower. A gothic fantasy – a bastard, in fact. I say ... one of you give me a hand with the junk.'

Together they lifted three cartons from the boot.

'No trees,' said Jonathan. 'Yucca, and dreadful poinsettias gone mad.'

'And ivy. Californian ivy ... that's prolific. There used to be a large cedar tree somewhere, it got blown down in a gale, which is why poor Irina had to string her yellow ribbons of welcome from the poinsettias ... you see? So forlorn. Fluttering in the wind. Snapped streamers after the ship has left ... God!' he said. 'I'm getting prosey. I think the desolation has something to do with it.'

'Yellow ribbons?' said the White Rat. 'For the hostages?'

'Doesn't it all seem a long time ago? Six days? Jonathan, ring the bell, will you?'

Mouse opened the door, looked through the narrow gap made by the holding chain.

240

'Miss Ivanova! Nettles, do you remember? We are rather late with the promised stuff . . . traffic on San Vicente.'

Mouse removed the chain, opened the door. She was drawn and pale, fingers fidgeting at her throat. She wore a hand-knitted cardigan of assorted wools and colours.

'I hope we have not incommoded you?' said Nettles.

She spoke suddenly. 'No, no. Not at all. The Countess is unwell . . . she . . . she can not see anyone today.'

'We'll stay only moments. Just to put these down somewhere, rather heavy.'

'Oh! Of course . . . of course . . . come with me, please excuse the kitchen, it is not as I would wish, but then I am single-handed, you know . . . come in, come in, do.'

She scurried about clearing space on the long kitchen table, pushing papers, pots, untouched trays of congealed food, to one end. 'I did tell you, I recall now. About the Countess. I am so sorry you will not see her today. I am so sorry. But arthritis, you know . . .' She suddenly saw a tin in one of the cartons.

'Tea, is it? English tea?'

'Indian, to be exact,' said Nettles, 'but since it is clearly labelled Jackson's of Piccadilly, I think that we can allow that it is, in fact, English.'

'How excellent! How kind. We quite finished the last of ours yesterday. We had a little tea party. The Countess was seeming to be quite well. We had a guest.'

'Well, now you can have a few more parties.'

'In St Petersburg we had them quite often, tea parties. It was very fashionable.'

'Indeed.'

'And shortbread too.'

'How splendid.'

'Lipton's tea. From Darjeeling. Do you know this perhaps?'

'Ah, yes. Lipton's! Of course. Very famous.'

'It was, of course, many years ago. When I was quite a child.'

'Miss Ivanova,' said Nettles deciding to end the conversation at this moment, in order to avoid the unpacking of the cartons lest Jonathan should discover the two jars of asparagus beneath a pile of books. 'I wonder if we might prevail upon your good nature and

241

ask you if Mr Pool might have a quick look at the big room? He leaves for London very shortly. It would be sad to have come to California and not seen the big room. Might we do so?'

Mouse replaced the tin of tea.

'Oh, of course! Of course! The big room ... it is perhaps not quite as it looked in the happy days, but please come ... follow me.' She put one hand on Jonathan's arm as they walked into the hall. 'It is a little dusty I'm afraid. I am often scolded.'

'Wayne,' said Jonathan as they passed him leaning against the kitchen doorway, 'do you mind waiting a moment or two? We shan't be long.'

'Okey-dokey. I'm easy. Take your time.' He wandered across the hall out into the sunlight.

'Now,' said Mouse. 'Here we are. Of course the shutters are not all opened I am sorry to say, my hands are very ...' She stopped and pushed a chair gently into line. 'Rheumatism, so painful. But I think you can see well enough, and you will not see the dust.'

Jonathan looked about him.

'Such high ceilings!' he said. He found it difficult to make any other comment for the big room oppressed him; bleak, dim. Chairs set about in a wide semicircle, empty, impersonal. A Harley Street waiting-room.

'Yes. High. You don't find them today. Stravinski played this piano. And do you know what he played? So capricious! "Three Blind Mice". You are acquainted with this rhyme? It is English in origin, I believe?'

'Yes, yes ...' said Jonathan. ' "She cut off their tails with a carving knife"? That one?'

'Correct,' said Mouse. 'But can you imagine? Stravinski playing a children's song! It was most amusing. And this chair, you see here, was always for the Countess. She sat here with the tea-table before her. It held the samovar ...'

'And Brecht was here? Feuchtwanger? The Manns . . goodness, what splendour.'

'Oh it was, it was. Of course, all the paintings have gone, alas. To New York. But oh! the conversations in this room, the wondrous things one heard.'

'I can well imagine.'

'All writers and musicians, you see. We *never* had picture people

242

here, you know. Never. I was, I confess, a little sad sometimes. It would have been most amusing to meet Mr Charles Chaplin, I liked him so much. So droll. And Miss Garbo, of course. But they told me she was rather shy.'

Nettles, who had stayed at the door, was aware that she was chattering, not from loneliness, as she did so often, but to conceal some deeper grief. Her hands, he saw, were never still, fluttering, or touching things; she moved her head continuously, nodding and bobbing; and although her voice was light and pitched high, and she spoke of amusement and of a time which she had so much loved, her eyes were dulled, and she did not, at any time, smile.

'Well, Jonathan. There you are. You have set foot in the big room, and I really think that it is time we left before the evening traffic starts ... hellish, you know.'

Mouse followed them out into the hall, closed the doors carefully. 'This district was once a very fashionable place in which to live,' she said. 'Most select and quiet. But things change, I fear, things change.'

'You have been extraordinarily kind, Miss Ivanova,' said Nettles as they reached the top of the steps leading to the garden. 'I really cannot thank you enough.' He stopped as he saw Wayne coming towards them across the gravel below.

'The darnedest thing! Do you believe it? Are you ready?' He held up a hand, extended his index finger, a red plastic bracelet ringing it like a quoit. 'See this? I fixed this thing last night! Right?' He looked up at Jonathan.

'Did you? Something ... I don't recall.'

'Sure I did. At the Arlington place, remember? The girl Hoppy. That her name? Well, she asked me to fix it real good for her. Too big, she said. And goddamn it, now it's right here, in the ivy, right at my feet. I mean that is just amazing, man!'

'Couldn't be the same one, surely,' said Jonathan. 'Or perhaps the Arlington children were here today, were they?' He turned to Mouse who was looking beyond Wayne to a distant place in memory. 'Were they?' he said quietly. 'The Arlington children? Here?'

Mouse turned as if he had touched her with a branding iron. 'Children? Here? No! No! No one was here today! No one in the world came here.'

A thin black arm slid through a fold in the tartan rug: a lifeless hand dangling like a dead flower.

'No one was here,' said Mouse.

'Well. I fixed it just like her daddy did, she said. She insisted. Most particular. Two daisies close together, okay? I took out one ladybug, made it tighter, she got the two daisies right together, same as this, see? Just the very same. That's why I recall it clear. Two daisies close together. It's the damnedest thing.'

'Finders keepers, we say, Wayne. And we really must make a move. The traffic will be fearful, do come along,' Nettles said, and started down the steps.

Wayne tossed the bracelet a couple of times in his cupped hand. 'Kinda old and scratched. Hers was real new and shiny. It isn't the same ...' He dropped it into the ivy at his feet. 'What in the name of goodness would I do with a ladybug bracelet?' He nodded briefly to Mouse and followed Nettles to the car.

'Thank you, most sincerely,' said Jonathan. 'And I hope the tea is useful, that you enjoy it.'

Mouse looked at him without expression. 'We will enjoy it greatly. You were all so kind. But no one was here, you know, today. No one.'

'Goodbye. And thank you again.' Jonathan turned and went to the car. He looked back as he ducked into his seat, Mouse half waved, he waved back, watched as she closed the door behind her.

They drove round the weed-hidden flowerbed, through the iron gates and the two brick pillars onto the street. Yellow ribbons trembling, twisting, in the leggy poinsettias.

'You want the hotel?' said Wayne into the driving mirror.

'No. No. Twentieth Street, Santa Monica,' said Jonathan.

'I'm afraid it was not much of a trip, I'm sorry,' said Nettles. 'Trying to recapture a past like that is quite hopeless. I think if Irina had been well ...'

'I really saw all I wanted to, thanks. I loathed the place if you want to know the truth. Can't tell you why.'

'I didn't ask.'

'No, but ... I don't know. The life has gone. An undertaker's parlour. Strange. I had the most extraordinary feeling of loss, of desolation, of grief. What in the name of God goes on in that house, I wonder?'

'I couldn't tell. One would have to be a second Champollion to do that.'

'What did he do?'

'Deciphered the Rosetta Stone, so now we can all read Ancient Egyptian.'

'Do you want to?'

'Not particularly. But it would take someone like that to decipher the hieroglyphics written all over that house.'

'Extraordinary feeling of evil. How strange.'

'Oh, dear me,' said Nettles. 'You writer-fellows. Far too much imagination.'

'I know what ground beef and aubergines mean,' said Clemency as Alice pushed the supermarket trolley to the car. 'It means awful moussaka. And it should be lamb, not beef.'

'Whatever, it's better'n that soup he makes,' said Hope. 'A long way better.'

'Just stop grumbling, you two, and help put these things away.'

'Peanut oil. One Kleenex. The dreaded aubergines. What's the cauliflower for? It's all wilted.' Clemency dropped it into a basket, brushed her hands on her jeans.

'Tomorrow's lunch, that's what for,' said Alice.

'Yeuch! Cauliflower-awful-cheese.'

'You don't have to eat it. Have crackers instead. With arsenic jam.'

'Arsenic jam! Hey that's great! Do you remember Marmite?' said Hope filling a second basket.

'*I* do,' said Clemency. 'But you couldn't. You're too young.'

'I do too remember! Don't I, Mom? Mother?'

Alice slammed the boot lid, pushed the trolley into a stack of others. 'I don't know. I hardly remember it myself. And if you two so dislike Dubrovnik's cooking, I have good news. You won't be getting it for much longer. When he's gone you'll just have to put up with mine: lump it.'

'Which means,' said Clemency, sliding into her seat beside Alice, 'that we'll have to eat yards and yards and yards of spaghetti in tomato sauce for ever and ever amen. Oh, well . . .'

'I really could brain you two. Ungrateful, spoilt little beasts.' She switched on the ignition. 'I really could, you know.'

Hope leant over from the back seat, put her arms round her mother's neck. 'But you wouldn't, would you, Mommy? Mother. You know that we love you really, don't you. I mean way deep down inside we do. You know that, right?'

'I know that. Yes I suppose that I do,' said Alice. 'Of course I do. But let it show a little more, could you? Sometimes, you know, people can't go on guessing at love. We have to have a few signs. Don't bury all yours "way down deep inside". Let it show, just now and then, could you?'

'All right,' said Clemency unexpectedly.

'She's only saying that because Alan Spinner Junior hasn't looked at her for the last three days. That's why,' said Hope.

'You shut up Miss Know-all, that is *absolutely* not true!'

Alice pulled out into the traffic on Beverly, turned onto Wilshire. Above them the sky was feathering with plumes of saffron, pink, and orange. A desert sky; and setting sun.

Mouse drove her small car tight against the closed iron gates in the last of the light, locked the doors, threw the keys into the ivy. There was almost no twilight here: a moment's hush, then darkness fell. She crossed to the house, closed and bolted the door, slid home the chain, made her way across the darkening hall, lit the table lamp among the dusty china cats on the centre table, carried it up the stairs and sat, leaning against the heavily carved post at the top.

Irina's voice drifted faintly from the closed door of her room down the corridor. '*Mouse! Mouse!* Oh! Bloody Mouse. Where are you? Where are you, Mouse? *Idiot! Mad woman!* Help me! Come and help me, oh come and help me please, please Mouse? Come to me.'

Mouse got to her feet, stood for a moment at the top of the stairs, looked down into the black hall, and with one deliberate swing hurled the oil-lamp into the darkness below: watched it explode in a flower of flame against the curtains which she had earlier drenched with petrol from the can she carried in the back of her car. For emergencies. Saw the great leap of yellow fire; sat down again. Arms folded contentedly across her knees.

By the time anyone saw the blaze, and by the time they had dragged her car from the locked iron gates, there would be nothing very much left to worry about.

246

She looked around her, smiling.

'Mama? Papa!' she called. 'Are you waiting for me? I am very near. Please be patient, I know that I have been a long time. But I am coming now, I am not far away. Not far away, and all is well. All is well.'

Above the crackling of burning wood she heard Irina crying, but she paid no heed; there was nothing that she could, or would, do now, and very soon everything and everyone in the house would be obliterated. Wickedness would crumble to ash, evil would be purified by fire, the havoc brought by the Golden Man would be all burned away. And no one would ever know.

She looked up into the curling smoke, the dancing sparks, heard the growing roar, saw the heavy wings of a great crow tremble high above her in the fiery updraught, and, putting out her hand, she called again into the flickering light, her eyes filled with the joy of release.

'Wait for me! Mama! Papa! Wait for me! I am coming, I am coming. All is well, all is well!'

Jupiter leant over the sagging rail of Etty's porch, idly kicking one heel against the other, hands relaxed, an empty beer can swinging between finger and thumb.

'There's a breeze. A real keen breeze,' she said. 'I sure am glad I kept this old coat. Been meaning to get me a new one, but what the heck. Saved the money.'

'You goin' to catch your death, you hang around there on that old porch,' Etty shouted from the house. 'You come in here, I got a real sweet batch of cookies I baked up.'

'Is God's pure air. I'll catch my death just as soon as the Good Lord is ready for me, and He ain't given me no sign yet He is. So.'

'A mule, Jupiter. You always were and you always is.'

'I reckon. That's how I got through this weary life. Is how I am. A mule,' she said agreeably.

Fire sirens began howling urgently in the distance, came closer, swung away, faded.

'A fire someplace?' called Etty, switching on the porch light.

'I reckon. Or a accident.' Jupiter looked up into the night. 'Oh Lordy, Lordy. There is one beautiful sunset way off there.'

247

'In the dark? You don't get no sunset in the dark.'

'When you get it then?'

'Afore the darkness comes, is when.' Etty came out onto the porch, shrugging into a man's jacket. 'Shit! But this is a cold wind. It is one cold wind...' She looked over the rail. 'Ain't no sunset, that. No way.'

'Is west, all right?'

'One hell of a fire, that's what,' said Etty. 'Ain't no sunset about it; west or not.'

'All aglowin' on the clouds. Ain't that just the prettiest sight you ever did see? That's how the Sweet Lord will come... when the time is ready. All in light.'

'You expecting the Second Coming right in the middle of a scrub fire? You is one dumb critter,' said Etty, folding her arms about her body.

'A scrub fire? Think that's what it is?'

'Santa Monica. Somewheres... all those old eucalyptus burn like torches...'

'That's sad.'

'You come on in now, gal. Ain't nothing to do with you, that old fire. Is a long way away. You come and taste my sweet cookies.'

Jupiter dropped her empty beer can into the bushes, stood looking towards the red glow in the west, wavering, fading, bursting up again in a carmine thrust, curling like a question mark, dying, loitering gently on the low cloud.

'Glory, glory!' she said. 'Ain't nothin' to do with me. Amen, and thank you Sweet Lord.' She began to walk cautiously across the rotten planks of the porch. 'I reckon that's a long, long ways off. Right? West of Sunset someplace, where the nobody-people live. Missis Etty Baker?' she called. 'You got another little can of beer for me? I got a real wicked thirst this evenin'.'